TP 13007967
KJOUR

STOP PRESS
A LIFE IN JOURNALISM

Inam Aziz

STOP PRESS
A LIFE IN JOURNALISM

INAM AZIZ

Translated from Urdu by
Khalid Hasan

OXFORD
UNIVERSITY PRESS

OXFORD

UNIVERSITY PRESS

Great Clarendon Street, Oxford OX2 6DP

Oxford University Press is a department of the University of Oxford.
It furthers the University's objective of excellence in research, scholarship,
and education by publishing worldwide in

Oxford New York

Auckland Cape Town Dar es Salaam Hong Kong Karachi
Kuala Lumpur Madrid Melbourne Mexico City Nairobi
New Delhi Shanghai Taipei Toronto

with offices in

Argentina Austria Brazil Chile Czech Republic France Greece
Guatemala Hungary Italy Japan Poland Portugal Singapore
South Korea Switzerland Turkey Ukraine Vietnam

Oxford is a registered trade mark of Oxford University Press
in the UK and in certain other countries

The Urdu original *Stop Press* by Inam Aziz was published by Nigarshat,
Mian Chambers, 3 Temple Road, Lahore in 1991.

ISBN 978-0-19-547576-0

Second Impression 2009

Typeset in Times
Printed in Pakistan by
Kagzi Printers, Karachi.
Published by
Ameena Saiyid, Oxford University Press
No. 38, Sector 15, Korangi Industrial Area, PO Box 8214
Karachi-74900, Pakistan.

Dedicated to

my late parents
Haji Sheikh Aziz-ul-Haq and *Hamida Begum*

my wife
Zohra Jabeen

and to
Anjum, Fozia, Adeeba, Muniza, Imtiaz, Tariq, Nadeem and
Faheem

Contents

Foreword
By Khalid Hasan   ix

Speaking the Truth
By Inam Aziz   xi

1. Who's Your Leader?   1
2. Meeting the Quaid-i-Azam   11
3. After Pakistan   20
4. Purana Qila   31
5. The Departure   38
6. Working for the Army   44
7. The Oldest Profession   50
8. The Great Khan   59
9. City of Lights   70
10. Colonel Majid Malik   82
11. Ayub's Martial Law   91
12. BBC Days   98
13. Flying Libel Writs   107
14. Ziaul Haq   117
15. Zia Digs In   133
16. How Bangladesh Came to be Born   144
17. Bhutto's Hangman   153
18. Zulfikar Ali Bhutto   159
19. Exile Politics in London   170
20. Benazir Bhutto and I   182

Foreword

Inam Aziz, who passed away when there was still so much left for him to do, remains in my book the ideal journalist. He was bold, upright and the last thing on his mind was his own material or even physical well-being. He was in his teens when Pakistan came into being and he chose the profession of journalism because that was where his heart was and that was where it remained till his dying day. Starting out as an apprentice in an Urdu daily in Lahore, he spent an exciting time in Peshawar in another paper and ultimately moved to Karachi where he rose to become news editor of *Jang,* which hit, during his stewardship, what was then the magic circulation mark of a hundred thousand copies. From print journalism he went into broadcasting in the 1960s. When I first met him in London in 1968, he was working for the BBC Urdu service with his great friend and old *Jang* colleague, Athar Ali.

Inam was one of the most inventive journalists I ever knew. I have never seen anyone write faster and slap better headlines on a story than Inam Aziz. Someone once called him '*Surkhiyoon ka Badshah*' the king of headlines. I think the only other journalist who can be said to come anywhere close to him in that respect is Abbas Athar. During the dark days of Ziaul Haq in Pakistan, there was only one newspaper in the whole world that fought his dictatorship with courage and conviction; it was Inam Aziz's *Millat.* He lost both his money and his health in that lonely fight but he will forever occupy a place of honour in Pakistan's history because of his crusade against military rule and for the establishment of representative government in Pakistan. It is ironic that one of the first acts of the Benazir Bhutto government in 1988 was to have Inam Aziz dismissed from his post as London correspondent of *The Pakistan Times.*

Inam was one of my closest and dearest friends and I was among those who kept urging him to write an account of his life in journalism. I was then living in Vienna, and when he finally did write the book, characteristically completing it in a matter of months where others would have taken years, he also made me promise that I would translate it into English. Years passed. I left Vienna, moved to Pakistan, came to the United States, returned to Pakistan and eventually settled down—if people like us can ever settle down—in the United States. The original Urdu edition remained with me all these years as a valued possession. On and off, I would think of my promise to Inam but something else would come up and so time passed. What induced me this time was a dream of his wife Zohra, who lives in London with her children. Inam came to her one night and said, 'Ask Khalid to translate my book.' And that is what I have done. It has taken me a year because other things kept coming up, including the books that I continue to write.

Saadat Hasan Manto once said that forewords are unnecessary. He compared them to the little boy who rides in front of the bridegroom. I don't want to be that boy.

So over to you, Inam Aziz.

Khalid Hasan

Speaking the Truth

Let me make it clear, as I present this book, that I have neither tried to write a history, nor have I attempted to analyse the restrictions placed on journalism today, or restrictions that may be placed on it tomorrow. The truth is that I have not tried to peep into the future either. What I have produced is a piece of reportage to show what varied and interesting experiences anyone wishing to be associated with the profession of journalism in a developing country has to undergo.

There is no question that in a developing country, the profession of journalism guarantees extraordinary experiences to those who choose it. Thus, I was a witness to the beginnings of the independence movement and how they reached fruition. I observed from close quarters the eruption of military rule in Pakistan and the ensuing struggle for the revival of democracy. The ordinary reader of today many not consider these dramatic events that I have lived through so extraordinary, but at the same time, I do not think he will find them lacking in interest, which is why they may merit his attention.

The imposition of restrictions on independent thinking and the freedom to express an opinion have become the norm. The methodology employed can be broken down into different segments. For instance, wherever there are extreme right or left wing elements in power, it is a given that they will ban independent thinking or free expression. The upheaval in the Soviet Union in the 1980s, especially at the end of 1989 is living proof of my contention.

In November 1988, I went to Pakistan after an absence of eleven and a half years. During my stay, I met my old friend Abdullah Malik several times. I once told him that the direction that political events had taken left little doubt that the era of suppressing free speech was about to come to an end. The Soviet empire, I predicted, would not only end, but it would no longer be possible to maintain the present political shape of Eastern Europe. Abdullah Malik, an eminent journalist and a respected figure among progressive thinkers, was in sharp disagreement with my views. He thought that the rise of Gorbachev was a consequence of the struggle of the people of the Soviet Union and Eastern Europe against Stalinism. During Khruschev's time, protests staged by the people of the Soviet Union and Eastern Europe against the excesses of personalised dictatorial rule had remained low key. Abdullah Malik was of the opinion that Gorbachev's rise to power would strengthen the unity of the left and it was just wishful thinking that the ties that bound the so-called Soviet empire and Eastern Europe would give way.

Abdullah Malik may now rationalise what he said then, but there is no question that the Soviet empire has reached the end of its power and territories annexed and made part of the Soviet empire from the times of the czars to the days of Stalin, will go their own way one by one. Gorbachev and his party are now trying to find relatively painless ways of saving the essential nature of the Russian state through constitutional means. Eastern Europe's political structure is breaking down and the people are desperate to get rid of communism as quickly as they can, something that was unimaginable until recently.

In countries with right-wing or left-wing governments, the ruling class arrogates the right to rule and considers itself superior to all other actors. The rulers become the keepers of the nation's conscience and see themselves as the intellectual leaders and teachers of the people.

They determine what will reach the people and how it will reach them. Conservative societies are much like their counterparts on the left and their members are made to adhere strictly to a set of religious beliefs, ideology and directives. In these societies, it is almost impossible to transgress the limits that have been imposed. However, no matter how stringent the restrictions, voices of protest continue to be raised from time to time.

Let us now turn to societies in which people like us live. Here too, restrictions on thought and expression exist. Although the name of democracy is often evoked because of political and economic backwardness, and the belief of our rulers that they have the innate right to exercise power, every effort is made through existing or new-fangled laws to eliminate the political opposition. It is because of this attitude on the part of our rulers that there have always been restrictions on freedom of speech and opinion. In fact, the state deliberately creates conditions conducive to the adoption of additional restrictive measures. Pakistan, being a developing country, falls into this category.

If we take a look at developed and democratic countries, one finds that some restrictions on freedom of expression exist there as well. However, these restrictions are applied with the greatest discretion, and the ordinary citizen is never even aware of the process. I would like to cite Britain as an example. Freedom of expression can be curbed through laws relating to libel and defamation and by the application of the Official Secrets Act, which is such an all-embracing law that if the government so wishes, it can proceed against any individual or institution. Newspapers are on top of the list when it comes to institutions and there are many examples where action has been initiated against them. Of late, the government has been running up and down trying to ban a book—*Spy Catcher*, published in Australia—by a former officer of MI5, the British intelligence agency. Millions of pounds have been wasted on litigation in British and Australian courts. What Peter Wright put in his book were accounts of events that took place many, many years ago and were no longer even secrets. The government, however, saw the publication of his book as a challenge to its authority. In no way could the book have compromised British security. However, no Australian court sided with the British government. The interesting thing is that when four British newspapers—*The Guardian, The Sunday Times, The Observer* and *The Evening Standard*—tried to serialise the book, British courts fully supported the government. The four newspapers tried for some time to fight the orders, since the book was selling openly anyway, but were unable to have the rulings overturned.

The method employed in Britain by the government to block publication is the D Notice, which is imposed by an official committee established for that express purpose. The concerned newspaper or broadcasting organisation is ordered not to divulge official secrets. Normally the government meets little resistance in such cases. The Official Secrets Act is so stringent that a journalist can be ordered to not even mention in his story that he had a cup of tea with a certain government official. This is why there is a move now to demand that such laws should be revised and replaced by freedom of information legislation.

Then there is the law of defamation the scope of which is so wide that it acts as a blocking wall for journalists out to seek the truth. Even after they have discovered the truth, they are not at liberty to name names or even hint at the identity of wrongdoers. Failure to abide by the restriction can result in heavy penalties. This is a strange way of treating those who only seek to establish facts. While any number of examples can be cited from British case law involving defamation, I would like to mention just one. Lord Aldington, a former army officer, was said to have handed over to the Russians a number of Cossack soldiers who were taken to Russia and killed. The court did not attempt to investigate the charge but imposed a fine of £1.5 million on the man who had made the allegation. It is possible that such heavy fines have something to do with the perceived financial position of the sentenced person; it is also possible that such amounts may increase even further. The paper that has incurred the heaviest fines in defamation cases is the satirical journal *Private Eye*. Because of the punishment it has repeatedly received in libel and defamation suits, it has earned much public respect.

In Western democracies, the right of the journalist to protect his source is one of the pillars on which freedom of expression can be said to rest. However, courts can demand that a journalist divulge the source of his report; if he refuses to do so, he can be sent to jail. In European countries, freedom of expression is included among fundamental human rights. In the United States, this freedom is guaranteed by the Constitution, though this has not always been an easy right to exercise. In 1954, Senator Joseph McCarthy and his 'un-American activities' committee of the Senate launched a ruthless campaign against communism, throwing the net over a whole range of 'offenders', from movie industry figures, to writers, to journalists. The McCarthy interlude was a brief one, but while it lasted it demolished several citadels of free speech in the United States.

It must, however, be stressed that in Europe and the United States, no prior government clearance is required for publishing information. Parliaments or their counterparts in Western societies also provide a platform for the free expression of opinion across the political spectrum. Those elected by popular vote are expected to respect and maintain parliamentary conventions, no matter how bitterly opposed they are to political viewpoints other than their own. In these countries, protest demonstrations, marches and meetings are not the chosen means of making political demands, as governments rule through parliaments. In developing countries, the scant respect shown to parliamentary institutions forces the people to resort to street agitation and protest marches, avenues that the governments in power try their best to block. Because of this widespread lack of tolerance of dissent, the press and the broadcast media often become sycophants.

It is indisputable that whenever restrictions are placed on the press and other avenues of expression, the printed word loses its value and credibility and rumour-mongering is born. I have seen this happen repeatedly in Pakistan. I have also seen that, no matter what steps the government takes, it fails to curb the rumour industry. It is only fair to admit that in Pakistan newspapers do not enjoy the same position as they do in Western countries, especially when it comes to the quality press. I use the term quality press because the popular papers generally tend to practise what is called yellow journalism, aimed at gaining circulation rather than printing the truth. Often, these papers print defamatory articles.

Greed and temptation are to be found in every society, the only question being whether journalists also fall prey to them for a price. In this context, I would like to narrate my own experience. In 1977, the elected government in Pakistan initiated the centennial celebrations of the birth of the great poet and philosopher Allama Dr Mohammad Iqbal. I attended some of the centenary-connected events which continued into 1978. By that time, the military government had managed to sink its roots deeper into the soil. A year later, after Zulfikar Ali Bhutto's hanging, Nazir Ahmed, Education Attaché at the Embassy of Pakistan, London, wrote me a letter, dated 15 October 1979, that recognised my contribution to the centenary celebrations and offered to award a medal to me. I was told that other scholars, prominent citizens, journalists and students had been similarly honoured. My wife and I were invited to a ceremony at the Pakistan Embassy on 9 November 1979, where the medal was to be conferred by Ambassador General Akbar Khan. I found the offer nothing more than an attempt at bribery. I therefore wrote to tell Mr Nazir Ahmed that I rejected the honour, since this was not the Pakistan that Iqbal and Jinnah had dreamt of; they believed in a country where the rule of law would prevail and where the people's elected representatives would rule. It had not been their wish that Pakistan should become a vast military cantonment.

When I began to put together my memories to write this book, looking through old papers and my incomplete diary to check dates, I did not find the going difficult at all because the events of my life are such that I can recall them easily. I have done my best to remain truthful and except that here and there I have not mentioned real names, I would like to say that I did not hesitate to recount past events as they happened. While writing what is really a long piece of reportage, I have remained intensely conscious of two things. First, that although I was editor of *Daily Millat* for seven years, I possess no record of that period because it was lost when, in 1980, we moved from the newspaper's office in the Angel area of London's East End to a new office in King's Cross. The people who were assigned the task of shifting the printing machinery, cameras and furniture to the new premises, got rid of the newspaper's old files while cleaning the basement where they were stored, because they thought that the precious record was just waste paper. There was nothing we could do except curse. When I sat down to write this book, I felt the need to consult my old writings but unfortunately, they had all been lost. I wish I had newspaper clippings that would lend authenticity to several of the points that I make in this book. However, there was nothing I could do to retrieve what was so inadvertently lost. I went to various London libraries but failed to find any back-issues of *Millat*. However, when I approached the British Library's Oriental Collections, I found some of the old files there. While they were by no means complete, their discovery was great news. I chose some clippings from those files in order to highlight the role played by *Millat* during its years in print.

The other mistake I made which cannot be compensated for was the loss of a letter which an old orderly of General Ziaul Haq mailed to me from Quetta in mid-May 1979 containing details of the execution of Zulfikar Ali Bhutto. The sender had simply signed the letter 'A former orderly to General Ziaul Haq'. This priceless piece of evidence stayed with me for a long time but got lost along the way. How I wish I had that letter, whose facsimile I could have included in this book, today. I only hope that its absence in these pages will not affect the credibility of what I have reproduced from memory.

As for the title of this book, it is the first title that came to my mind when I decided to write it. *Stop Press* indicates a story that arrives late, when the newspaper is about to go to press, and all the editor can do is include its important information in the space remaining under the Stop Press heading. But the title has a double meaning because it stands for the attempts made in countries like Pakistan, where political upheaval and military

coups are the norm, to prevent a journalist from expressing his
opinion.

Inam Aziz
London, February 1990

From: Mr. Nazir Ahmad,
Education Attache

EMBASSY OF PAKISTAN,
EDUCATION DIVISION
35, LOWNDES SQUARE,
LONDON, SW1X 9JN
TELEPHONE No: 01-235 2044 EXT. 24

IN REPLY PLEASE QUOTE

NO. 57/EA/78   Dated 5 October, 1979.

SUBJECT:- IQBAL MEDALS - PRESENTATION CEREMONY

My dear Mr Aziz,

    1977 marked the centenary of the birth of
Allama Muhammad Iqbal, the great poet and philosopher.
Numerous functions were held in Pakistan and other
countries during 1977 and 1978 to pay tribute to the
man who conceived the idea of Pakistan and laid the
intellectual foundations of an Islamic polity in
consonance with the demands of modernism in the
contemporary world. As you would recall, a large
number of admirers of Iqbal contributed to the success
of the centenary functions held in the United Kingdom.

    As a token of appreciation of the services
rendered by scholars, dignitaries, journalists, students
and organizers in U.K. (list enclosed), the Government
of Pakistan has decided to award Iqbal centenary
commemorative medals. Inscribed on one side of these
medals is the beautifully-designed centenary emblem
and, on the other side, is Iqbal's image with one of
his appropriate verses super-imposed.

    It is proposed to hold a simple ceremony in
which the medals could be presented to recipients
individually on behalf of the Government of Pakistan.
This ceremony would be held at the premises of the
Embassy on Friday, 9 November, 1979 (which is Iqbal's
birthday) between 3 and 5 p.m. Full details of the
programme would follow. The purpose of this letter is
to ask you, as one of the recipients of the award, to
indicate your convenience and the convenience of your
wife to come to the Embassy on that day. The Ambassador
and his staff would feel greatly honoured by your consent.

    With regards,

                         Yours sincerely,

                         (Nazir Ahmad)

Mr. Inam Aziz,
333 Goswell Road,
London EC1.

Facsimile of the letter sent to Inam Aziz by Mr Nazir Ahmad (Education Attache,
Embassy of Pakistan, London) regarding the presentation ceremony of Iqbal centenary
commemorative medals.

MILLAT

333 Goswell Road
London E C 1

Telephone:
01 837-9267 8

26 October, 1979

Mr Nazir Ahmad
Education Attache
Embassy of Pakistan
39 Lowndes Square
London SW1X 9JN

Dear Mr Ahmad,

I thank you for your letter of 5 October 1979 informing me of the Government of Pakistan's offer to me of the Iqbal Centenary Medal as a "token of appreciation" for services rendered to mark the poet's centenary.

Your letter describes Iqbal as "the man who conceived the idea of Pakistan and laid the intellectual foundations of an Islamic polity in consonance with the demands of modernism in the contemporary world."

This, indeed, is true; however, I must express my inability to accept the honour. The Pakistan of today, groaning under the military jackboots of General Zia ul Haq, is not the Pakistan conceived by Iqbal and established by the Quaid Azam. Pakistan was to be a free, democratic and progressive state, governed by the Rule of Law and the elected representatives of the people. Pakistan was not achieved so that it could become a fiefdom of mercenary Generals.

The Government of General Zia ul Haq is a slur on the fair name of Iqbal and Jinnah. It is one of the most repressive and shameless dictatorships in recent history. Therefore, it has no moral right to try to honour the memory of the man who conceived the idea of Pakistan. Iqbal's Pakistan was to be a land of sunshine and hope, not a vast military cantonement, surrounded by barbed wire. Since I honour Iqbal's ideals and the principles of democratic Islamic social justice that he advocated, I have no hesitation in rejecting the Medal that this illegal and immoral regime has chosen to confer on me.

Yours sincerely

Inam Aziz
Managing Editor

Facsimile of Inam Aziz's reply to Mr Nazir Ahmad.

1 Who's Your Leader?

There are two aspects of the leadership of Quaid-i-Azam Mohammad Ali Jinnah that must be highlighted for an understanding of the man. Between July and October 1946, in line with the Cabinet Mission Plan, tripartite negotiations were taking place between the British government, the All India Muslim League and the Indian National Congress on the formation of an interim Indian government. The Muslim League viewed this interim arrangement as no more than the viceroy's advisory council, in accordance with the requirements of the Government of India Act of 1919. Pandit Jawaharlal Nehru wanted it to become the central government of India. When the Quaid-i-Azam told the viceroy that Congress had not formally accepted the plan and, under the constitution, the viceroy's advisory council could not attain the status of a central government, Lord Wavell had no option but to accept this sound legal argument.

The second problem that arose at the time was the Quaid-i-Azam's insistence that Congress should not nominate a nationalist Muslim to the interim government. When the viceroy tried to bring about a compromise, the Quaid-i-Azam said that if Congress was allowed to nominate a Muslim, he would nominate a representative from the scheduled castes, mostly made up of untouchable Hindus. This was an unexpected development for the Congress leadership, but in the end it agreed. In October 1946, the Quaid-i-Azam, on behalf of the Muslim League, announced five names including that of a non-Muslim; not only that, he also named the portfolios they would hold. The five men were: Nawabzada Liaquat Ali Khan (finance), I.I. Chundrigar (commerce), Sardar Abdul Rab Nishtar (post and telegraph), Raja Ghazanfar Ali Khan (health) and Jogindar Nath Mandal (parliamentary affairs).

When the interim government ministers took the oath of office, the viceroy having formally announced their portfolios, the reaction among Muslims was one of disappointment. The Muslims of Delhi were particularly depressed about the new development because not only was Jawaharlal Nehru the foreign minister, but Sardar Vallabhbhai Patel had been put in charge of information and broadcasting. It also did not go unnoticed that he lost no time in modifying the style and content of All India Radio broadcasts. Congress had also nominated to the cabinet Sardar Baldev Singh, who was deputy to the Akali Dal leader, Master Tara Singh. According to observers, this step had been taken to rule out any cooperation between Muslims and Sikhs, and had effectively sabotaged the efforts the Muslim League had started in 1945 to reach accommodation with Master Tara Singh. Soon the idea began to take root among Muslims that the Muslim League had been politically defeated and the conspiratorial relationship between Congress and the British would prove detrimental to Muslim interests. Consequently, the new interim government became the hottest subject of discussion in both homes and restaurants. No one knew at the time that it was the Quaid-i-Azam himself who had chosen the Muslim League ministries.

I remember every single moment of that day in October 1946 when the Muslims of Delhi gathered on the steps of Jamia Masjid; it soon turned into a protest meeting, though not a very organised one. Some local Muslim League leaders were there along with some professional slogan-raisers whose only job in such situations is to incite the crowd's emotions. As time passed, the size of the crowd grew till it had spread as far as Edward Park. Among those who were now leading this crowd was Rashid Tabassum who worked in the civil supplies department of the Government of India. He was a Muslim League loyalist and was also involved with various hockey and football associations, including the famous Jinnah Gymkhana football team. The basic demand of the crowd that had gathered was that the Muslim League should quit the interim government, and if that was not possible, at least obtain more important portfolios for its ministers. The crowd was being told by some of the orators that if Nehru was to keep foreign affairs, a Muslim League minister should be assigned the department of the interior or information and broadcasting. It was decided, after several speeches, that the crowd should move in the form of a protest procession and demonstrate in front of the offices of the two Muslim League newspapers, *Dawn* and *Manshoor*, which should be asked to publish the people's demands. The two offices were no more than a mile from the Jamia Masjid.

By now, the crowd had taken the form of a proper procession. It began to move towards Darya Ganj and its size grew as people from different neighbourhoods joined in. The first stop was the *Manshoor* office where much sloganeering was witnessed. Some workers of the newspaper also came out to join the march. When the marchers arrived at the *Dawn* office, someone suggested that there was no point in protesting in front of newspaper offices because the proper place for protest was the Quaid-i-Azam's residence. That was where, ran the argument, the demand should be made for the Muslim League to quit the interim government. This new stratagem appeared to give a new energy to the crowd which now agreed that the correct place to make this national demand was the Quaid-i-Azam's residence.

Quaid-i-Azam lived at No. 10 Aurangzeb Road in New Delhi. It was a large residence fronted by a well laid-out garden. Although I had seen the Aurangzeb Road from a distance many times, I had never actually been there, so viewing it as a good opportunity to see what that part of New Delhi was like, I decided to tag along. Soon we were marching towards our destination in a most organised manner. It was not an age of 'security consciousness' and so it was not necessary to obtain police permission for the march. I could not see even a single policeman around as we marched forward, though it was, of course, possible that some of them were among us in plain clothes to keep an eye on things. When the marchers came out of the Delhi Gate, their numbers had swelled to somewhere between 25,000 and 30,000. Some people were carrying the green crescent and star flag of the Muslim League and some had even found time to slap together placards bearing the demand 'Muslim League should quit the interim government'. I was now at the front of the procession, carrying a Muslim League flag and shouting slogans making the same demand. The marchers went past the Feroz Shah Kotla ground and the Khooni Darwaza and wended its way towards Aurangzeb Road.

It took the marchers nearly two hours to get to Aurangzeb Road. At first the people just stood outside the Quaid-i-Azam's residence chanting slogans, but after about ten minutes someone opened the front gate and thousands of noisy demonstrators burst in, trampling flower beds under their feet and causing havoc in the elaborately laid-out garden. However, nobody seemed to be conscious of this as the mood grew more raucous by the minute. Not everybody had been able to get in and hundreds were out on the road making a great deal of noise. The leaders had placed themselves at the head of the demonstration and I had also joined them, still holding my green crescent and star flag. There was absolute silence inside the residence and it seemed that we were being ignored. This only intensified the resolve of the marchers to shout out their demand in even louder voices.

After about ten minutes, the front door of the residence opened and the Quaid-i-Azam's youthful secretary, K.H. Khurshid, stepped out. He took one look at the marchers, surveyed the ruined garden and said, 'The Quaid-i-Azam is willing to receive your delegation, so please choose five from amongst you and I will take you inside.' For a few moments, there was silence and then the sloganeering started again, the prominent cry now being 'Quaid-i-Azam, *zindabad!*' One of the leaders told Khurshid that there was no delegation as such that could go inside to meet the Quaid-i-Azam because this crowd was made up of the Muslims of Delhi who had all come to meet the Quaid-i-Azam. They were not a delegation. Khurshid kept insisting that the Quaid-i-Azam would only meet a delegation, however, when the leaders refused to go along, he walked back into the house looking annoyed. With his disappearance, the chanting was resumed.

There was a balcony on the first floor which the Quaid-i-Azam perhaps used sometimes in the winter months to take the sun and look at his garden. Ten or fifteen minutes passed before we saw the door to the balcony open and the Quaid-i-Azam appeared. As soon as the crowd saw him, it began to scream enthusiastically, 'Quaid-i-Azam, *zindabad*!' 'Quit the interim government,' etc. The Quaid-i-Azam said nothing for a few moments, then raised his hand, asking people to be quiet. He looked furious and asked in an angry voice, 'Who is your leader?' A silence fell over the crowd. He asked his question again and Rashid Tabassum, who had a stammer, replied in a loud but stammering voice, 'Sir, sir, you are our leader.' When the Quaid-i-Azam heard this he said, no longer looking angry, 'Then why are you here? Go back to your homes.' That one simple sentence hit the crowd like a command. The Quaid opened the door that led to the balcony and was gone. The crowd had fallen silent. People began to leave, some of them looking shamefaced, others with a confident bearing. When everyone was out on the road, Rashid Tabassum found himself surrounded. 'You let us down. You led us out of Jamia Masjid and when the time came, you threw in the towel.' Tabassum's response was, 'What could I do. He is the only leader we have, so how could I accept anyone else as leader? Well, if any of you has the guts, then you go and face the old man.' 'That's right,' someone said, 'there is only one leader and if he wanted to know why we were here, he was right, wasn't he? In any case, who can stand up to the Quaid?' Tabassum ended the angry talk by saying, 'The Quaid says it is right for the Muslim League to be in government; that being so, who are we to object to that? We have conveyed our feelings to the Quaid; the decision is his and it is our duty to follow him.'

In small groups, people had begun to walk back towards the Jamia Masjid, but the discussion of the day's event was continuing, some of it rather emotional. Some were saying that the Quaid had been made aware of the people's feelings and

whatever decision he took should be accepted. The interim
government stayed intact and no more demonstrations against it
took place in Delhi because no one could muster the courage to
defy the Quaid-i-Azam.

Although the Quaid-i-Azam was a man who was resolute and
who stuck to his decisions, once taken, he was, at the same time,
sensitive to popular opinion. This can be seen from the historic
3 June 1947 announcement that put the seal of finality on the
partition of India. The last viceroy of India, Lord Mountbatten,
departed for London to report to his government, and the Muslim
League Council was left to decide whom it should appoint as the
governor-general of Pakistan. It is generally believed that the All
India Congress, enemy number 1 of the British, named Lord
Mountbatten the first governor-general of India, hoping that
Pakistan would accept him as well, so that the two dominions
would have a common governor-general. Lord Mountbatten's
press secretary, Campbell Johnson, writes in *Mission with
Mountbatten* that Lord Mountbatten was caught by surprise when
told in London that the Muslim League had refused to accept
him and, in fact, had come up with the proposal that the two
dominions should have separate governors-general or they
should have their own governors-general with Lord Mountbatten
acting as the supreme governor-general. The League's argument
was that if its proposal was accepted, the distribution of assets
and the division of the Indian army would take place smoothly,
with a neutral supreme governor-general at the top. According
to Campbell Johnson, when Mountbatten placed the three
governors-general proposal before Prime Minister Attlee, he
rejected it, arguing that this would create constitutional
difficulties which may be insurmountable. It was also felt by
some at the time that were Mountbatten to be appointed as
supreme governor-general, it would not be right for him to be
based in Delhi and it would be difficult to find a 'neutral' place
for him to stay. After the British decision was known, the Quaid-
i-Azam received a message that said that if the Muslim League
was not prepared to accept Lord Mountbatten as the common

governor-general, it should nominate a person to be Pakistan's governor-general.

On 29 June 1947, the Quaid summoned a session of the All India Muslim League in New Delhi to nominate a governor-general. Held in the Imperial Hotel, the councillors were seated in the main hall, while three enclosures had been set aside for guests. Because of the declared enmity of the Khaksar Tehrik against the Quaid and the League, inside and outside the hotel the Muslim League National Guard volunteers stood to attention and no one could enter without an invitation. Irfan Ali, who was the *Salar* (commander) of the National Guard and who lived in our neighbourhood of Mohalla Machliwalan, had obtained an invitation for me. I reached the hotel quite early and took my seat in the gallery reserved for guests. One section was set aside for journalists, both Indian and the large number of foreign representatives. From where I sat I could see the stage and those sitting on it. I could see the Quaid-i-Azam, Nawabzada Liaquat Ali Khan, Sardar Abdul Rab Nishtar, Nawab Ismail Khan and the Nawab of Bhopal. Before the session began, a rumour began to circulate that the Quaid was going to nominate the Nawab of Bhopal, and after the acceptance of this proposal, the Quaid would announce his retirement from politics. By then, the Quaid's health had deteriorated considerably. He was also said to have been upset by an editorial in *Dawn* which said the people had begun to call the Quaid the *Shahenshah* (king of kings) of Pakistan and eighty million people had agreed that a crown should be placed on his head. The Quaid was not in favour of becoming the prime minister; he did not consider it an office suited to his temperament since he had no wish to work under the common governor-general, Lord Mountbatten.

The Quaid-i-Azam held a unique position in the All India Muslim League: the rest of the League's leadership was no match for the leader in terms of political understanding or the art of negotiation. Not only his supporters, but even those who disagreed with him, agreed on one point: Mohammad Ali Jinnah was the one man who could not be bought. In 1941, when some members of the Muslim League from the provinces had felt tempted to accept office, those from Sindh being in the lead, the party's working committee had been forced to decide that all powers now rested with the Quaid-i-Azam and those delegated to the party's provincial branches had been withdrawn. This had been a delicate time, as talks were in progress between the British Government on the question of transfer of power. When the All Indian Muslim League Council session was summoned in Madras in 1941, the Quaid was given full powers for a period of one year, the only proviso being that he would take no step that would depart from the Council's previous decisions. A year later, in April 1942, when the Muslim League Council met in Allahabad, a similar resolution was moved at which Maulana Hasrat Mohani, the League leader from the United Provinces, rose to declare that he was not prepared to accept Mr Jinnah as a dictator. He was of the view that, since the Cripps Mission proposals were under consideration at the time, there might be fears that Mr Jinnah would move in a direction that could place the prospect of independent dominions in doubt, which would deprive the Muslims of India from gaining their due rights. Mohani was the sole voice of dissent but the Quaid continued to respect him and his opinions.

When the Council met again in New Delhi in June 1947, the Quaid-i-Azam presented a report on his meetings with Lord Mountbatten after the initial speeches and announced that he would not be acceptable as the joint governor-general of the two dominions. He said the party had now to choose Pakistan's first governor-general. This was greeted with loud cheers, but what the Quaid said next changed the gathering's mood to one of disappointment. The Quaid said, 'I have finished my work. I am like a field marshal who is no longer needed after his army has become victorious. His duties are then transferred to other citizens who are expected to take charge.' What the Quaid was asking the League to do was to let him step down and let someone else take on the responsibility of consolidating Pakistan. No one appeared to be ready to accept such an onerous burden because, compared to the man they wanted to crown as the *Shahenshah* of Pakistan, they saw themselves as pygmies.

At this point, Maulana Hasrat Mohani rose and said in a loud voice, 'This is not possible. We reject your decision.' It was the same voice that had been raised at the Allahabad session of the Council in 1942 in opposition to the Quaid. But this time, he was not alone, because the majority of the members were in accord with what he had said. When the auditorium, which had begun to ring with slogans supporting Mohani's 'rejection', was quiet, the Quaid addressed the veteran leader directly and asked him who, in his view, should be the first governor-general of Pakistan. Mohani greeted the question with a smile, then said emotionally, 'Pakistan's governor-general can only be a man who has won Pakistan for the Muslims, and the Muslim League Council can never be prepared to name anyone other than Mohammad Ali Jinnah.' This created a commotion in the auditorium and people began to chant the slogan 'Quaid-i-Azam, *zindabad!*' Those who were sitting next to Mohani began to embrace him, one by one. In the next few minutes, the Council formally approved the proposal.

The first reaction to Quaid-i-Azam's nomination came from Sardar Abdul Rab Nishtar, who said, 'There can be no two opinions as to who the leader of the hundred million Muslims should be. It should be someone who has the complete trust of the people, and the Quaid-i-Azam is the only person who enjoys that trust. He is not only Pakistan's founder and a man who can be entrusted with the responsibility of governing Pakistan, but we are confident that all is going to be right now.'

Nawabzada Liaquat Ali Khan said, 'We began the struggle for independence under the Quaid-i-Azam's leadership and his nomination brings that struggle to completion.' The Quaid's nomination did not please the British, but most upset were the Congressites who felt that their position had been undermined since it was they who had launched the Quit India movement and had now agreed to accept a representative of the British crown as their first governor-general. And this was how the constitutional struggle of the Muslim League and the intrigues of Congress reached their point of completion.

2 Meeting the Quaid-i-Azam

Like the young men of my generation, my political sympathies also lay with the Muslim League. It is another matter that I was the only one in the family who was interested in politics, my father being busy with his job in the railways and my elder brother involved with his government post. I left Zamindar College, Gujrat, without finishing my studies and came to Delhi where I joined the Anglo-Arabic College. I had become fond of reading newspapers when I was in the sixth grade. At that time, my father was posted to the Mandi Bahauddin railway station in the Punjab and through him I was able to read a host of newspapers like *Zamindar*, *Pratap*, *Milap* and *Vir Bharat,* which arrived from Lahore by the morning train. After reading through them, I would return them to the local newsagent. In 1945, when I came to Delhi, the political climate was hot, the Pakistan Resolution having been passed five years earlier. Negotiations between British government ministers and Indian leaders were ongoing. In Delhi, Congress leader Asif Ali and Muslim League leader and owner of *Anjam* daily, Sheikh Mohammad Usman, were preparing to run for the same assembly seat. We were among Sheikh Mohammad Usman's workers. It was at this time that the Quaid-i-Azam came to Delhi to address a public meeting.

The venue of the meeting was Edward Park, which lay between Jamia Masjid and the Red Fort. The park faced our neighbourhood of Machliwalan. (Why it had been given that name, I could never find out because there was no fish shop anywhere in the area, nor did we ever see any anglers setting out for the nearby Jamuna River.) The house where I lived had belonged to the famous Urdu short-story writer, Akbar Haidri, who was already dead when I rented the house. The Edward Park meeting turned out to be big. People had begun gathering for it

from early morning and when I got to the park, the crowd was
so thick that it was almost impossible to get to the raised dais.
I, therefore, found a spot in one of the corners to listen to the
proceedings. When Quaid-i-Azam rose to speak, the applause was
deafening. He began in broken Urdu and after a few minutes
announced that he would continue in English. Next to me stood
an old man with a beard. In order to have some fun with him, I
asked if he understood what the Quaid was saying. His reply was
sharp, 'Look here young man, don't try to be funny. If the Quaid-
i-Azam is speaking, obviously whatever he is saying is right'.
His answer left me with a comforting feeling. It showed that the
Quaid was a unique leader of the Muslims and one they trusted
completely. He rarely wore the traditional Muslim *sherwani* and
shalwar or pyjamas; he preferred western clothes and felt at
home using English. However, the Muslims had complete faith
in him because they knew that he would never sell them down
the river. The British, the Hindus and the Sikhs made many
attempts to shake him but he was resolute and they failed to
deflect him from the path he had chosen.

It was early 1947 when I saw a report in the daily *Manshoor*
that the Quaid-i-Azam would be at a football match between the
famous Kabul team, the Afghan Sporting Club and Jinnah
Gymkhana at the Feroze Shah Kotla ground. This report was also
carried by *Dawn*, and *Al-Jamaiyat*, the organ of nationalist
Muslims. Both *Dawn* and *Manshoor* were Muslim League papers
and I used to visit the Muslim League office near Jamia Masjid
every morning to read them. *Manshoor* was edited by Hasan
Riaz and its staff included Ayub Kirmani, Tufail Ahmed Jamali
and Khaliq Naziri. I was too young to have formed a friendship
with any of them, but when I came to Karachi to work with *Jang*,
we became close and most of my evenings were spent in their
company. Another newspaper that I used to visit off and on was
the evening *Jang*, edited by Syed Muhammad Taqi, who
remained my colleague in Karachi for eighteen years after
Independence. Mir Khalil-ur-Rehman was the newspaper's

owner, its circulation manager, its advertising executive and its cashier. Little did I know at the time that I would spend many years of my life with *Jang*.

But to return to the football match: entry was by ticket priced, I think, at one rupee. I don't know why but I simply saw no point in having to pay to watch a game, so in order to get a gate pass, I set out to look for the Jinnah Club secretary, Rashid Tabassum. He used to drink tea with some of us in Babban's Hotel close to Jamia Masjid. When I ran into him at the Muslim League office and asked him for a gate pass, Tabassum, of whom I saw a great deal in Karachi after Independence, pretended that he did not know me. His response was, 'Look, if you want to watch the match, spend the money; such matches cannot be expected to be freebies.' I felt belittled by his attitude and returned home.

As match day approached, my desire to be there intensified. I did not have any money of my own, I should add, being a student. A day before the match, I asked my elder brother for two rupees, but was refused. A good friend of ours, Sultan Mahmood, who used to live in our house, also proved to be of no help. He was a fine poet and wrote under the pen name Masroor Jullandhari. In money matters, he was a tightwad. When I asked him for two rupees, he replied that when he was paid in the coming month, he would consider my request. For now, he said, he would have to be excused. So, it seemed there was little I could do.

On the day of the match, I took a shower—I was too young to shave—put on a freshly-laundered shirt and pyjama combination, and began to walk the three miles that separated our house from the Feroze Shah Kotla ground. I knew the ground like the back of my hand as I had watched at least a dozen cricket matches there, most of them from a prime spot in the main pavilion, and without buying a ticket. My favourite players of the day were Mushtaq Ali, Vijay Merchant, Col. C.K. Naidu and Lala Amarnath. This was the ground where the famous match between the Australian Services Eleven and the Combined India Eleven was played. The Australian team was captained by

Lindsay Hasset and included Arthur Morris whose performances I had read about in newspapers and whom I was keen to watch in action. But more than those two, I was interested in two Muslim students from Lahore who had scored centuries against the Australians in their home town. They were Abdul Hafiz and Imtiaz Ahmed. Hafiz was later to become even better known as the Pakistan cricket captain A.H. Kardar. There was another young bowler in the home team, Fazal Mahmood, who was said to be Lala Amarnath's protégé. He was to be included in the Indian team that was shortly to leave for a tour of Australia. Fazal Mahmood became a great bowler and it was he who, during Pakistan's first official tour of England, ran through the English side and won Pakistan a memorable victory at the Oval in 1954. England was led by Len Hutton and the team included the great batsman, Dennis Compton, as well as many famous players of the day. Fazal Mahmood's haul in that match was twelve wickets.

Life in the days I am writing about was free of security cordons and body searches, nor were club-wielding policemen ever seen at sports grounds. There was little, if any, violence around, including political violence. When I arrived at the Feroze Shah Kotla ground, I first tried to enter from a point that would have taken me to the main pavilion but I found the entrance closed. There were three or four other points of entry into the ground but I found them all blocked by Jinnah Gymkhana officials and the Muslim League National Guard. A round of the ground's perimeter brought me to the entrance facing the Khooni Darwaza. I found a small crowd gathered there. When I got close, I recognised among the crowd Muslim League leaders Raja Ghazanfar Ali Khan and I.I. Chundrigar. The former became a central minister and Pakistan's ambassador to Iran and India. Chundrigar was to become Pakistan's prime minister, albeit briefly. After a few minutes, a car pulled up, close to the spot where I was standing. When the door opened, out stepped Nawabzada Liaquat Ali Khan, and I noticed that his wife, Begum Liaquat Ali Khan, was not with him. Liaquat was the Quaid's right-hand man and general secretary of the Muslim League. His leadership, like the Quaid's, was accepted unquestioningly. He was to become Pakistan's first prime minister.

With Liaquat's arrival, things came to life. There were several women present and it seemed they were all waiting for the Quaid-i-Azam to arrive. A reception line was being formed, of which I took advantage and joined it close to the end. A few minutes later a young man appeared on the scene and gave everyone in the reception line, including me, a garland of fresh roses. Fate had decided to smile on me: not only was I going to see the Quaid up close, but I would also be able to watch the football match. I did not have a watch, but I think it was around four in the afternoon when a car drove up and the Quaid and his sister Fatima stepped out of it. Although those in the reception line were not chanting slogans, others were. People in our line were standing upright like soldiers receiving a general. The Quaid was dressed in a brown *sherwani* and *shalwar* and wearing the cap that to this day is known as a Jinnah cap. He was a slightly-built man but he had such presence that nobody could fail to be impressed by him. His sister was also slim and extremely graceful.

They were received by Nawabzada Liaquat Ali Khan, who brought him to the reception line where they first met Raja Ghazanfar Ali Khan, I.I. Chundrigar and other Muslim League leaders, along with officials of the Jinnah Gymkhana. The Quaid shook everyone's hand and allowed himself to be garlanded. When he came to me, I found myself trembling with excitement. He shook my hand and said in a very affectionate voice, 'Hello, young man, nice to see you'. Then he put his hand on my shoulder and it was clear that he wanted me to walk with him. Miss Jinnah was behind us, walking next to Nawabzada Liaquat Ali Khan. The Quaid did not remove his hand from my shoulder. I was so nervous that I felt as if I would faint at any moment. The Quaid's presence and personality were overpowering.

There were thousands of people in the ground. A colourful canopy had been set in place with chairs laid out for about two

hundred people, all of which were already taken. The moment
we entered the ground the crowd started shouting 'Quaid-i-
Azam, *zindabad*!', 'Muslim League, *zindabad*!' and 'Pakistan,
zindabad!' Everyone under the canopy stood respectfully to greet
the leader, while joining the crowd in the stirring slogans it was
shouting in praise of the Quaid. The main pavilion of the ground,
I realised, had not been opened for the match. The two teams
were now in the middle of the field, as were the organisers and
referees. The front row under the canopy had sofas reserved for
the Quaid and his sister. On each side of the sofas, ten chairs had
been placed. As the Quaid approached the sofas, he said to
Liaquat Ali Khan, 'This young man will sit with me'. Then he
asked his sister to take her seat. Taking his place in the middle,
he asked me to sit on his left. I was so nervous that I began to
pray to God to kindly forgive my past wrongs.

Once we were all seated, three officials of the Jinnah
Gymkhana, including Rashid Tabassum approached the Quaid
and requested him to walk onto the pitch so that the two teams
could be presented to him. The Quaid smiled and stood up, as
did the others. The crowd came to life again, shouting 'Quaid-i-
Azam, *zindabad*!' The two teams were standing in line, along
with the referees and officials and were all presented to the
Quaid. When the introductions were over, Rashid Tabassum
whispered something to the Quaid, after which he walked up to
the spot where a football had been placed. He kicked it away
gently and the crowd burst into applause. After the match, this
football was kept as a memento by the Jinnah Gymkhana. After
the Quaid returned to his seat, the football was placed in the
middle of the ground once again and the match got underway.

I had quite forgotten that I had come to watch the football
match. Everything appeared to me to be enveloped in a haze.
The Quaid sat down next to me as I desperately tried to take hold
of myself. As soon as he had taken his seat, he asked me, 'Are
you still at school?' 'Sir, I am in a college', I replied respectfully.
'Which college is it?' he wanted to know. I was nervous and I
gave an answer that was not true. I said, 'Sir, I am at St.

Stephen's College'. St. Stephen's was a famous Delhi college and generally only the children of the rich entered that institution. Maybe that was why I had named it. I wanted to impress the Quaid. But the Quaid was not impressed, because he said, 'So sad. Aren't you a Muslim?' This struck me like a bolt of lightning. I had named St. Stephen's in order to impress but I had landed myself in a catastrophic situation. I managed to stutter an answer, 'Sir, sir, I am a Muslim'. The Quaid smiled and said, 'If you are a Muslim, then why not choose a Muslim institution? Here you also have the Anglo-Arabic College'. 'Sir, I shall change my college,' I replied. I was feeling so uneasy that I wanted our conversation to end.

The Quaid did not appear to be much interested in football. He turned to me once again and, speaking in a soft tone, explained to me why Muslim educational institutions were important. He said that if a student went to one of these institutions at a young age, he would come to gain knowledge of his religion, culture, art, history and values. Such an education would stand the youngster in good stead when he grew up. I was not mentally prepared for the sort of lecture he seemed to be in the mood for. I was cursing myself for having placed myself in such an awkward spot. I had left home planning to watch football and here I was sitting next to the Quaid-i-Azam himself and feeling uneasy and self-conscious. Maybe I should have joined the queue with the others at the ticket window. Suddenly, Miss Jinnah interrupted her brother, 'Let's leave, you have another appointment', she said. It was obvious that the Quaid had more important things to do than watch a football match till it ended. As soon as he heard Miss Jinnah, he rose, looked at me and said, as he shook my hand, 'Sorry, I have to leave early.' I stepped aside and as all those under the canopy stood up in respectful farewell, he and Miss Jinnah left. As soon as Miss Jinnah walked past me, I followed behind her. I was no longer interested in the match. I noticed that people were looking at me intently and I felt as if I were ten feet tall. This feeling of euphoria stayed with me for many days.

The Quaid-i-Azam approached his car as I watched him, well out of the ground by now. He got into his car and never looked back. Afterwards, I was hit by a sense of apprehension. What if someone were to ask me what connection I had with the Quaid? I might even be arrested. I began to run towards Delhi Darwaza, but slowed down after a while and walked at a leisurely pace as my self-confidence returned. Sometimes I would raise my right hand in the air and sometimes I would rub my shoulder where the Quaid had placed his affectionate hand. I was talking to myself like a half-mad fellow, as if I were a schizophrenic. 'Come on, what match are you talking about? Who cares? Today, you have touched history and greatness itself which is the privilege of only a few'. Then another voice would rise from within me, 'But you are a liar. Why did you have to lie to the Quaid-i-Azam about St. Stephen's College?' Here the positive voice would take over, 'Well, what of it? Had I spoken the truth, the Quaid would have found me out, so forget it. What is important is that not only did I meet the great man but I also held a conversation with him and came to know his views'. The three-mile walk back to the house seemed to have taken no time at all.

The pages of history turn rapidly. It is forty-three years since that day and I still feel as if I met the Quaid only yesterday. I have seen Pakistan come into being and I have seen blood shed for the sake of this country. I have also met women who were abducted on their way to Pakistan, recovered and brought to a camp near the main Lahore refugee camp in the hope of being reunited with their families. But no one was prepared to come forward and claim them. In the same Pakistan, I have seen governments created and destroyed through political intrigue. I have seen military takeovers and the country at war with India. I have met very many world leaders, from Pakistan's various prime ministers to President Ayub Khan, President Iskandar Mirza, Prime Minister Zulfikar Ali Bhutto, Pandit Jawaharlal Nehru, Prime Minister Zhou En-lai, President Ahmed Sukarno, Prime Minister Benazir Bhutto, Turkey's Prime Minister Adnan

Menderes and several Third World statesmen, but I have no
hesitation in saying that after the Quaid-i-Azam, the man who
impressed me most was Zulfikar Ali Bhutto.

3 After Pakistan

I was still in Delhi when Pakistan came into being. In anticipation of the great day, the Red Fort was suitably bedecked. Quaid-i-Azam Mohammad Ali Jinnah, Nawabzada Liaquat Ali Khan and other Muslim League leaders had already said goodbye to Delhi and gone to Karachi. Pakistan's first constituent assembly had come into existence by common consent and its first session was held on 11 August 1947, presided over by Pakistan's first law minister, Jogindar Nath Mandal, the same man whom the Quaid had nominated as the scheduled caste representative in the Indian interim government. The Quaid was elected president of the assembly when it first met. The historic speech that he made on the occasion is important for a number of reasons.

Addressing the people of a country that had been established on the basis of the two-nation theory, the Quaid said:

> You are free; you are free to go to your temples, you are free to go to your mosques or to any other place of worship in the state of Pakistan. You may belong to any religion, caste or creed—that has nothing to do with the business of the state ... Now, I think we should keep that in front of us as our ideal and you will find that in course of time, Hindus would cease to be Hindus and Muslims would cease to be Muslims, not in the religious sense, because that is the personal faith of each individual, but in the political sense as citizens of the state.

The words of the Quaid are like a milestone in our life as journalists and as a free people. All his life, the Quaid remained a powerful supporter of freedom of speech and civil liberties. When the government of India began to move against the press under the Defence of India Rules, the Quaid was the first to protest. The year was 1915 when, while protesting the action taken against B.J. Horniman, editor of the *Bombay Chronicle*, the Quaid said that all his life he had drunk deep from the fountain of constitutionalism and had always remained aware of the fact that the snatching away of the freedom of the individual, no matter under what law, is an exercise in futility.

Commenting on the Press Act of 1910, he wondered how the government intended to deal with people's complaints. Did it want to strangle critical newspapers through the imposition of a Press Act? It had brought in a law that prohibited any gathering it considered rebellious. The only object of such a law was to deprive people of the right of assembly. Was that how the government wished to rule? Should there be a law that crushed the spirit of the people?

In Delhi, we listened to the Quaid's constituent assembly speech on the radio, in the same way that we had followed the Independence Day celebrations in Karachi. Although the Quaid-i-Azam was head of state, it is important to recall how the newly-formed government of Pakistan reacted to the speech. *Dawn*, the Muslim League's organ, was already being published from Karachi. The other newspaper of the time was the *Sindh Observer*. The prominent Pakistani journalist Zamir Niazi, recalling the Quaid's 11 August speech, says that immediately after it was over, the principal information officer, Colonel Majid Malik, phoned the *Dawn* office and instructed F.E. Brown, the journalist who took the call, that the portion relating to citizens' rights and religious beliefs in the Quaid's speech should be omitted. Brown, much mystified by the call, conveyed the message to M.A. Zuberi and Mohammad Asheer, both members of staff, who informed Altaf Hussain, the editor. Altaf Hussain hit the ceiling when informed. He tried to reach Colonel Majid Malik but was unable to contact him. He then spoke to his deputy, F.D. Douglas, who proved to be of no help. Eventually, Colonel Majid Malik was found. It turned out that the first 'press advice' in the history of Pakistan had come from Chaudhri Mohammad Ali, the government's secretary-general. Enraged Altaf Hussain told Colonel Majid Malik, in no uncertain terms, that if such instructions were issued in future, he would consider taking the matter to the Quaid himself. He also told him that he was not prepared to excise anything from a speech that the Quaid had delivered. Colonel Majid Malik took the message back to Chaudhri Mohammad Ali and called Altaf Hussain back to say that what Chaudhri Mohammad Ali had said was by way of advice; it was not an order. He told Altaf Hussain that nobody would dare censor what the Quaid had said.

The real reason for trying to censor the Quaid's words was to show that he had 'lost his way'. To advocate that Muslims would cease to be Muslims and Hindus would cease to be Hindus was a negation of the two-nation theory on which Pakistan was founded, and according to which, those following faiths other than Islam could not be accorded equal civil rights. Even though so much time has passed, that speech of the Quaid is still wrapped up in controversy.

In his book, *The Press in Chains*, Zamir Niazi, quoting Zulfikar Ali Bhutto writes that General Yahya Khan's information minister General Sher Ali Khan Pataudi was so critical of this particular speech of the Quaid that at one point he issued orders that it should be removed from the official records and burned. Bhutto put this into an affidavit he filed in the Supreme Court. Zamir Niazi also disclosed that in 1981, when an Islamabad newspaper wanted to publish this passage from the Quaid's speech, it was forbidden to do so by government censors. This was during Ziaul Haq's absolutist rule.

But to return to Delhi and Independence Day. From where I lived, we had a good view of the Red Fort wall that overlooked Edward Park. Nehru was preparing the speech he was to deliver at midnight on 14 August. The British had decided that Pakistan would be free at midnight on 13 August, and India a day later; one ceremony was to take place in Karachi, the other in Delhi. On 13 August, Lord Mountbatten and Lady Mountbatten arrived in Karachi to attend the ceremony that was held in front of Sindh High Court.

Lord Mountbatten and Pakistan's first governor-general, Quaid-i-Azam Mohammad Ali Jinnah, were brought to the ceremony in a procession. On the stage, Mountbatten sat to the right of the Quaid. Mountbatten read out a message from King George VI welcoming the birth of Pakistan as a new dominion of the British Commonwealth. The King said that if the new country was run on democratic lines, there would be no diminution in the support to be extended to it by the British government. The King also paid tribute to the leadership that had brought the gift of independence to its people.

In his address to the Pakistan constituent assembly, Lord Mountbatten said that although he was speaking as Viceroy, the next day the government would be in the assembly's hands, while he would become the constitutional head of the government of neighbouring India. He said the two nations shared a long and proud history and their leaders were men of great eminence who were known and respected the world over. He said the poets, philosophers and scientists produced by the two nations had left their indelible mark on history. These two states were now ready to carry forward the mission of world peace and amity. He paid warm tribute to the Quaid and said that it was because of him and other Muslim leaders that the discussions leading to independence had been conducted in a peaceful and civilised manner. He regretted the fact that there had been widespread killings across India but due to the efforts of Mr Jinnah and Mahatma Gandhi, the situation was improving. He also made a reference to Emperor Akbar the Great and the religious harmony that had prevailed during his reign. He hoped that what had happened was only a parting of friends, and any remaining differences, would be resolved amicably.

The Quaid, who was greatly perturbed by the blood letting in the country, spoke only briefly. He said,

I thank you for the expression of goodwill and good wishes for the future of Pakistan. It will be our constant endeavour to work for the welfare and well-being of all the communities in Pakistan, and I hope that everyone will be inspired by the idea of public service,

and will be imbued with the spirit of cooperation and will excel in
their political and civic virtues which go to make a great nation and
help to advance greatness ... The tolerance and goodwill that the
great Emperor Akbar showed to all the non-Muslims is not of recent
origin. It dates back thirteen centuries when our Prophet [peace be
upon him], not only by words but by deeds, treated the Jews and
Christians, after he had conquered them, with the utmost tolerance
and regard and respect for their faith and beliefs. The whole history
of Muslims, wherever they ruled, is replete with those humane and
great principles which should be followed and practised. Finally, I
thank you for your good wishes for Pakistan, and I assure you that
we shall not be wanting in friendly spirit with our neighbours and
with all nations of the world.

Before this, as the Quaid was departing from Delhi for Karachi
on 7 August, in a farewell message, he said that he was bidding
goodbye to a city which was full of his friends. He appealed to
them to live together in peace and amity and bury the past. He
invited them to begin anew now that there were two independent
countries, Pakistan and India. For the people of India, he added,
he had nothing but goodwill and he wished them well.

Another important day in history was 22 July 1947 when,
under the 3 June agreement, the Partition Council was
established. The first session was devoted to all matters
pertaining to the transfer of power. The session was presided
over by Lord Mountbatten, with Sardar Patel and Dr Rajendra
Prasad representing the Hindus, Sardar Baldev Singh the Sikhs,
and the Quaid and Liaquat Ali Khan the Muslims. The joint
communiqué issued by the council began,

Now that the decision to set up two independent Dominions from
15 August has been finally taken, the Members of the Partition
Council, on behalf of the future Governments, declare that they are
determined to establish peaceful conditions in which the processes
of partition may be completed and the many urgent tasks of
administration and economic reconstruction taken in hand.

Both Congress and the Muslim League had given assurances of fair and equitable treatment of minorities after transfer of power. The two future governments reaffirmed these assurances, asserting that it was their intention to safeguard the legitimate interests of all citizens irrespective of religion, caste or sex. In the exercise of their normal civic rights, all citizens were to be regarded as equal and both governments became committed to assure to all people within their territories the exercise of liberties such as freedom of speech, the right to form associations, the right to worship in their own way and the protection of their languages and culture. Both governments further undertook that there should be no discrimination against those who, before 15 August, may have been their political opponents.

The guarantee of protection which both governments gave to the citizens of their respective countries implied that in no circumstances would violence be tolerated in any form in either territory. They wished to emphasise that they were united in this determination. To safeguard the peace in the Punjab during the period of changeover, both governments agreed to set up a special military command from 1 August 1947 covering the civil districts of Sialkot, Gujranwala, Sheikhupura, Lyallpur, Montgomery, Lahore, Amritsar, Gurdaspur, Hoshiarpur, Jullundur, Ferozepore and Ludhiana. With their concurrence, Major General T.W. Rees was nominated as military commander for this purpose and Brigadier Digamber Singh (India) and Colonel Ayub Khan (Pakistan) were attached to Rees in an advisory capacity. After 15 August, Major General Rees was to control operationally the forces of both new states in those areas and be responsible, through the supreme commander and the joint defence council, to the two governments who were not to hesitate in setting up a similar organisation in Bengal, should it be considered necessary. Both governments also pledged themselves to accept the decisions of the Boundary Commission, whatever these may be. The Boundary Commission was already in session; if it was to discharge its duties satisfactorily, it was essential that it should not be hampered by public speeches or

writings threatening boycott or direct action, or otherwise be
hampered in its work. Both governments were also to take
appropriate steps to secure this end and, as soon as the awards
were announced, were obliged to enforce them impartially, and
at once.

The communiqué issued on 24 July did not say on what basis
military stores were to be apportioned between the two countries,
but records that came to light later show that according to the
ministry of finance, the British Indian government held a cash
balance of four billion rupees. Congress was willing to discuss
the distribution of this asset, but unwilling to settle the question
of the distribution of state investments already made and the
profits that had accrued from them. Extensive discussions took
place on this issue in the Partition Council, as a result of which
Congress agreed to transfer only Rs750 million to Pakistan. The
Muslim League leaders were not willing to get into a fracas over
this issue, at least not at that time. The British Indian government
which, in fact, was by now a Congress government, decided that
it would transfer Rs200 million to Pakistan by way of the first
instalment. The balance was to be delivered in the weeks to
follow. So, when Pakistan was born, that was all the money it
had. The new government had no offices, nowhere for the civil
servants to sit, no furniture, no pens and not even any paper
clips. Half the civil service that was to come to Pakistan was still
in India and those who were in Pakistan were practically on the
road. There were no old government records either. The first
instalment of Rs200 million came through but the next instalment
was not paid until 15 January 1948.

The Partition Council had decided that one-third of military
stores would go to Pakistan, an arrangement that was to be
supervised by the supreme commander of the two armies, Field
Marshal Sir Claude Auchinleck. The question of military stores
could not be disassociated from the fact, that barring a couple of
ordnance factories and arms depots, the rest were located in areas
that were now part of India. When Auchinleck began to take
steps to have Pakistan's share transferred, Congress leaders, with

the full backing of Mountbatten, created such a rumpus that Auchinleck handed in his resignation and left the country. Pakistan never received its share. In accordance with the decision of the Partition Council, such records as related to Pakistan's geophysical aspects were put on trains bound for Pakistan, all of which were looted in transit, with the result that none of these papers ever reached Pakistan.

While Delhi was preparing for its independence celebrations, the Muslims of the city had their eyes fixed on Karachi where preparations for the great day were also in progress. On the night of 13–14 August, at 11:50 p.m., the Karachi station of All India Radio was taken off the air, an exercise that was replicated in Dhaka and Lahore. The stations remained off air only for a few minutes, then began their transmissions. Lahore opened with a national anthem hurriedly composed by the celebrated music director Khurshid Anwar. Half a minute before midnight, Zahur Azar announced in English, 'At midnight the independent and autonomous state of Pakistan will be born.' These words were repeated in Urdu by Mustafa Ali Hamdani. On the stroke of midnight, Zahur Azar came on the air again, 'This is the Pakistan Broadcasting Service.' He was followed by Mustafa Ali Hamdani in Urdu, after which Maulana Zahir-ul-Qasimi recited verses from the Quran that convey good tidings of victory to Muslims.

On 15 August, Pakistan Radio began its transmission with a recitation of verses from the Quranic Sura of Al-Imran. The same day, Chief Justice Abdul Rashid administered the oath of the office of governor-general to the Quaid. After the ceremony, the first head of state of Pakistan was given a twenty-one gun salute. The Quaid then went on air to address the nation. He said he was thinking of those courageous men who were willing to offer the supreme sacrifice of life for the establishment of Pakistan. Addressing the forty million Muslims of India, he said that although they had become a religious minority in India, Pakistan would never forget or ignore them. He recognised that it was the Muslims from the minority provinces who had begun the struggle for Pakistan. Under the changed conditions, they would have to make difficult adjustments. They were hated by the Hindus, he added, because they had supported the demand for Pakistan. The same day, Liaquat Ali Khan was sworn in as the first prime minister of Pakistan. His cabinet was made up of Sardar Abdul Rab Nishtar, Raja Ghazanfar Ali Khan, Fazlul Rehman, I.I. Chundrigar, Ghulam Mohammad and Jogindar Nath Mandal.

The four governors appointed were Sir Fredrick Bourne (East Bengal), Sir Francis Mudie (West Punjab), Sir Ghulam Hussain Hidayatullah (Sindh) and Sir George Cunningham (North West Frontier Province). All three service chiefs chosen were British. The demarcation of the country's borders was of crucial importance and my research has shown that the Quaid and the Muslim League leadership were under no illusion about Lord Mountbatten, being fully aware of the soft spot he had for Nehru. It was clear to them, therefore, that Pakistan would feel the rough end of the stick and no protest against such discrimination would be effective. Mountbatten, after consultations with Indian leaders, had decided that the transfer of power would not take place in June 1948, but in August 1947. There is no doubt that Sir Cyril Radcliffe had been instructed by Mountbatten that he alone would draw up the dividing line in the Punjab and Bengal and that the other members of the Boundary Commission would have little input in this decision. Justice Mohammad Munir later recalled that when the Boundary Commission held its first meeting in Lahore, Radcliffe made it clear that he would not necessarily associate his members with hearings featuring representatives of the parties involved. He also stated that the final report of the commission would be his and it would be up to him to include or exclude the views of members of the commission.

Justice Munir later wrote that after this, the four judges who sat on the commission became ciphers. At best, they could be said to be representatives of the four parties involved—Hindus, Muslims, Sikhs and Other Minorities—and not in any way responsible for, or even associated with, the commission's

awards. Munir said that seeing the situation, both he and Justice
Din Muhammad, the two Muslim members, decided to resign
from the commission, but when the Muslim League learnt of
this, it advised them to continue to remain part of it, although
by now there was no doubt as to how the dice were loaded
against its interests.

During a visit by Radcliffe to Simla, Justice Din Mohammad
called on him and was shocked to discover that the entire district
of Gurdaspur was to be handed over to India. He had no idea
that such a plan to make it easier for India to grab Kashmir was
being hatched. Justice Munir recalled that at the time he even
feared that Lahore was going to be made over to India. It was
being said that most of the industry and landed property in
Lahore was owned by Hindus and the number of Hindu
university graduates was much higher than that of Muslims. It
was only after Justice Munir had argued against it forcefully
before Radcliffe that he thought better of the idea of gifting
Lahore to India. Ferozpur, Zira and Fazilka, that were to become
part of Pakistan, did not do so.

On 17 August, three days after the establishment of Pakistan,
Mountbatten announced the awards of the Boundary Commission.
According to Justice Munir, the award was delayed for three
days because of a conspiracy. Radcliffe had signed the award on
12 August and the changes that were made—and they could only
have been made by Mountbatten—were made between that date
and 17 August. On 17 August, Radcliffe invited members of the
commission to lunch at the Simla Services Club. During the
meal, Justice Mehr Chand Mahajan, the Hindu member, asked
Radcliffe whether, since he had heard all the parties and
examined the record, he would like to tell the members where
the dividing line in the Punjab was going to be. Radcliffe
regretted his inability to disclose this information because,
before making the announcement, he wanted to ascertain the
views of Governor-General Mountbatten. Justice Munir
suggested that, under the circumstances, would it not be

reasonable to assume that the governor-general advised Radcliffe to modify the award?

Justice Munir also referred to two statements by Sir Zafrulla Khan. According to him, Chaudhri Mohammad Ali, later Pakistan's prime minister, but then a senior civil servant, walked into the room of the viceroy's private secretary, Lord Ismay, one day and found a map nailed to the wall which showed the dividing line across the Punjab exactly as it later turned out to be in the Radcliffe Award. When Muhammad Ali asked Ismay about the map, the latter became cagey and finally said that somebody had probably played a joke. Zafrulla also disclosed that Radcliffe had wanted to fly over certain areas of the Punjab but the plane could not take off because of bad weather. However, Zafrulla happened to take a look at the map given to the pilot and discovered that the flight path was to be exactly where the dividing line was later placed. Mountbatten wished to punish the Muslims and the award was his way of inflicting that punishment. He had told the Quaid during their discussions once that all he would get would be a moth-eaten Pakistan. The Quaid had replied, 'What will be, will be'. The relationship between the two men remained bitter, as did their exchanges.

From the beginning, Mountbatten had created difficulties regarding the demand for Pakistan. At the time, the expert opinion was that the moth-eaten Pakistan being given to Jinnah would not last long. The dividing line in the Punjab was placed at a point where not only would India be able to gobble up Kashmir, but a dispute would be created that would keep both countries at loggerheads for all times to come. Former NWFP Governor Sir George Cunningham wrote that Jinnah knew for certain that Mountbatten was aware of the Boundary Commission Award before 17 August. He had been holding on to it, so that it could be announced after Pakistan had come into being so that no dispute could arise on that point. The Quaid knew this and never forgave Mountbatten for this treachery; nor did the people of Pakistan.

4 Purana Qila

Pakistan had come into being but Masroor Jullandhri (who used to live in our house and whom I have mentioned earlier in the book) and I were still in Delhi. My elder brother had gone to Pakistan. On the afternoon of 16 or 17 August, I was sitting in Masroor's office when a British army officer walked in to announce that bloody rioting had begun in Delhi and a curfew would come into effect at 5 p.m., in both Old and New Delhi. All government offices had been closed and people were being advised to return to their homes. Within minutes people had left. I realised that it was already a quarter to five and there was no way I could get to the Jamia Masjid area. When I mentioned this to Masroor, he said if we hurried, we might be able to make it to Hague Square in New Delhi where his father lived. The two of us therefore rushed out and began to walk briskly towards our destination. We saw police and soldiers on the way but nobody tried to stop us; they just told us to hurry home. By around 5.30 p.m. we were in Hague Square.

From then on the curfew became a permanent feature of our lives, lifted now and then, but only for short intervals. On the first night, there was a great deal of bloodshed in Qarol Bagh, which was not too far from Hague Square. We could not only hear gunfire but could also see homes and stores that had been set ablaze. In the morning, we realised that a virtual line had been drawn across Hague Square, separating Muslims and non-Muslims. Close to Masroor's home lived a Hindu civil servant of mature years, who dropped in to tell us that it would be better for us to vacate Hague Square because once Hindu–Muslim rioting broke out, nobody would be able to escape. This warning was chilling for Masroor's family. There were three or four Muslim families living in Hague Square. I advised them all that the best thing would be for them to remain together in one place.

It was not easy to convince everyone to follow this advice because some were not prepared to abandon their homes. The older people were unwilling to listen to a raw young man like me, but by about 10 p.m., when slogans of '*Jai Hind!*' began to rent the night air, every family had sought refuge in Masroor's home, bringing their valuables with them.

The Masroor home had three bedrooms on the first floor, which, it was decided, should be given to the women; the men had to make do with what space there was on the ground floor. The heat was stifling and everyone was restless. No one slept even a wink on the first night. In the morning, the only question on everyone's lips was: where do we seek refuge? All were government employees and were sure that the new government of Pakistan would take steps to ensure their safety. The problem was: where did one go to seek such help? Once again, I came up with a workable idea, which was that we should all go to the Jamia Masjid area where our house was large enough for everyone. I told them that they could stay there for a few days and it would be much easier to make contact with some key government official from there. Masroor approved of my plan, saying that if there was one area in the entire city of Delhi that was safe for Muslims, it was the Masjid area. There were two large rooms in our house, each fifteen by thirty feet, which could sleep four to five families. Of course, under those circumstances, there could be no privacy. After everyone agreed, we began our move to Jamia Masjid.

The curfew had been lifted for a couple of hours and it was decided that some tongas should be hurriedly engaged. We managed to get hold of three. The fare they demanded was exorbitant but expense was the least of our considerations at the time. Each family packed its personal and household effects and locked up what, until then, had been its home. When it came to getting into the tongas, the women wanted to all get into one with the children and have sheets slung across by way of curtains so that they could remain in purdah. Attempts to reason with them were unsuccessful. Even the men were for it in the end.

Finally, six or seven women with children got into these curtained tonga, while the men took the other two. The women's tonga was led by one of the men's tongas, while the third brought up the rear. We had hardly gone half way when some Hindu youths carrying long sticks tried to attack us. The curtained tonga had betrayed the fact that we were Muslim. Since all three tonga drivers were Muslims, they whipped their horses and we sped away, out of the reach of our attackers. The sheets that had curtained the women's tonga were removed by the driver because it invited attention and trouble. The nearest route to Jamia Masjid was through Turkeman Gate, which is the one we took, going through narrow streets till we reached our house.

We used to eat at Babban's Hotel, a wayside eatery, opposite the great mosque. The man who ran it knew that we lived alone, so when he saw us with all those women and children, he knew that they had come to this area in order to be safe. In the evening, when we went to him to pick up food for the rest of the party, there was a discussion about the situation that now existed in the city. Babban, the eatery's owner, named various city localities, not one of which had escaped Hindu–Muslim rioting. Curfew hours in the Jamia Masjid area were much more relaxed than in the rest of the city. The families to whom we had given shelter stayed with us for three days, during which time they managed, through the Muslim League office, to establish contact with their respective offices. One day a military truck came to take the men to Hague Square, but they found it utterly destroyed. They came back disappointed and decided that it would be best to move in with their relatives, wherever they were. Before long our house became a virtual transit camp. No day passed without fifteen or twenty refugees coming to us from riot-affected neighbourhoods in search of shelter. Once, after a lot of bloodshed in the Sabzi Mandi area, so many people came to our house that Masroor and I had to leave to make space for them. We moved next door to a famous Muslim hockey player's home.

By the first week of September 1947, the rioting had come even to the Jamia Masjid area. While there was peace during the day, at night the air would be rent with violent slogans and homes and shops would be set on fire. Not only in our neighbourhood, but in all Muslim areas of the city, makeshift security systems had been set up by the residents. In our area, the tallest building had been chosen to build a lookout. We wired up to it two powerful lamps, one red, one white. If there was danger, the red lamp would be lit to warn the people; if things were normal, we would switch on the white one. There was a heavy steel gate at the entrance to the street that led into our neighbourhood. This gate was kept shut at night and the two small watch towers that had been built on either side were kept manned all night.

The truth was that Delhi was now a riot-torn city. In the beginning, when refugees began to seek shelter in our house, our landlady, Malika Hyderi, Sir Akbar Hyderi's daughter, took strong exception to it, but when she saw that things were going from bad to worse in the city, she relented. Malika Hyderi observed strict purdah and when we went to pay our monthly rent, we were required to remain mindful of her modesty. Years later, when we met her in Karachi at the house of one of her relatives, she was no longer in purdah but we recognised her because we knew her voice. Perhaps, she recognised us as her erstwhile tenants in Delhi.

One day we ran into Anis Hashmi in front of the Muslim League office. He was an office-bearer of the party. He told us that the governments of India and Pakistan had set up a refugee camp in the Purana Qila and anyone who wanted to join it was free to do so. This camp was to be protected by Pakistani troops so that the life and property of the Muslims who sought refuge there would be safe. Masroor and I thought over the situation we were in and decided that there was no better way of getting to Pakistan. We had been told that special trains were to be run for those in the camp, so that the people could reach Pakistan in safety. It was not clear how long we would have to wait for one of those trains. Some time earlier, Masroor had managed to send some of our baggage to Pakistan. All we had between the two

of us now was a small briefcase. Thus one day, we talked a
tongawala into taking us to Purana Qila in return for fifty rupees.
Between the two of us we had five hundred rupees, so we felt
quite secure financially.

We were familiar with Purana Qila, having often been there
on picnics, but when we saw it this time, it was full of thousands
of refugees and looked very different. Some of the refugees had
a roof over their heads; others camped under the open sky. There
was no settlement within miles of the Qila in those days. There
were sentries posted at the main gate who permitted no one to
leave the camp. The flow of refugees seemed endless. Some had
brought food and provisions with them, but there were others
who had nothing to eat. The Pakistan army had set up a small
store, but all it sold was condensed milk, with each person
allowed to buy just one tin. The two of us, however, managed
to befriend the man who ran the store and talked him into selling
us four tins for a rupee. Condensed milk thus became our
breakfast, lunch and dinner. Our nights were spent sprawled on
the floor, fighting flies and mosquitoes. Our bodies bore evidence
of the mosquito attacks that we suffered all night, but there were
hundreds of others in the same condition. We had never lived
like this, but there was no alternative. We once spotted some
relations of ours in the camp but were reluctant to ask them for
help.

One day word went around the fort that chickpeas were being
distributed among the residents. We ran to the distribution centre
and were given a day's ration, but had nothing in which to cook
them. The condensed milk tins were too tiny. Finally, we
mustered the courage to approach a relative by the name of
Abdul Wahid who was married to my first cousin and worked at
army headquarters. He lent us a small saucepan. Next we
gathered some dry twigs, and found a few bricks which we used
to build a makeshift hearth. Masroor went with the saucepan to
get some water from the fort's main outlet. This was at 10
o'clock, but three to four hours later he had not returned. After
requesting a person camped next to us to keep an eye on our

things, I went looking for Masroor. I found him standing in a
line about half a mile long. There were about fifty persons ahead
of him and there was just one tap in the entire fort and it did not
always run. It took another hour before Masroor's turn came,
because many people had brought with them not one, but several
pots to fill. He filled his little saucepan so quickly that several
of those waiting in line burst into cheers. When we returned to
our spot, all we found there were the hearth and the twigs we
had gathered. Our briefcase and the milk tins were gone. The
man whom we had asked to keep an eye on our things was not
there but his stuff was. When he returned after a while, he told
us that when he had left the place five minutes earlier, both the
briefcase and the milk tins had been there. We asked some other
people nearby if they knew anything about our loss but nobody
seemed to know anything. All we had now were the hearth and
the twigs. Our only clothes were the ones we were wearing, but
our money was still ours, secure in our pockets in two-rupee
bills.

We started a fire and emptied the bag of chickpeas into the
saucepan; God knows what happened to make the saucepan tilt
over and spill its content into our poor little hearth. This
happened just as the water came to the boil. It was like an
earthquake. Someone should have seen our faces at that time.
We made vain efforts to retrieve some of the chickpeas from the
ashes but it was no good. We considered getting more water but
gave up the idea when we thought of the long queue in which
we would have to stand. Finally we sat down on the bare ground,
content with the thought that it was not in our stars to eat any
solid food that day. We did make a trip to the army store however
but were told that we had already been issued with our day's
ration. That night was hard on us.

Some days later there was suddenly great commotion in the
camp because Gandhiji was going to visit us. He arrived, walking
slowly with his hands resting on the shoulders of two young
girls. Everyone was firing questions at him, some telling him that
there was no food to eat and no water to drink. Nobody was

supposed to leave the Qila and if anyone did manage to do so, there was no certainty as to what might befall him. There were a couple of army officers with Gandhiji, who also listened to our tales of woe. People wanted more water and food. All one could hear Gandhiji say was, 'What can I do?' Someone shouted from the crowd, 'All this has been done by your government.' Gandhiji replied, 'I am not even a member of Congress, but I will ask the government to come to your aid.' There certainly were changes as a result of Gandhiji's visit, as three additional taps were installed in the fort which gave us generous quantities of water. A food and provisions store was also set up.

As for us, we were so sick of eating chickpeas every day that we no longer even wished to go to the ration shop to get more of the same staple. One day there was an uproar in the fort, the news being that food supplies had arrived from Pakistan. It was said that a special plane was bringing *parathas* and *pulao* prepared by Pakistani women in Karachi and Lahore for us. This turned out to be true because it was timed with Liaquat Ali Khan's visit to Delhi to meet Jawaharlal Nehru. The two signed an agreement which expressed their mutual desire to cooperate. We all gathered to wait for the trucks that would bring the food flown all the way from Pakistan. Some of the residents who had emerged as camp leaders made everyone stand in line to ensure orderly distribution. Masroor and I also found a place in one of the lines. At noon, when an army truck driven by a Pakistani army *jawan*, drove in and came to a stop in the middle of the Qila, those waiting in line rushed pell-mell towards it, pulled down the rear hatch and began to grab what they could. Rice and *parathas* now littered the ground. Some people tried to pick them up but found them coated with sand. Masroor and I just stood aside, watching the unruly scene. It did not take long for the truck to be emptied of all it had brought. We were back to living on condensed milk.

5 The Departure

On 23 September 1947, it was announced that arrangements had been made to transport to Pakistan by train those who had sought refuge in Purana Qila. Lists would be drawn up to determine exact numbers with all necessary particulars. The majority was made up of civil servants whose names were the first to be put on the list. The first train was to leave on 24 September, the second on the evening of the 26th. Masroor and I were going to be on the second train. Before departure, we called on the manager of the food canteen that had been set up and persuaded him to part with six tins of condensed milk. That was all we had; no other preparation was necessary.

Those who were to take the second train were trucked to the Palam railway station, which, despite our long stay in Delhi, we had never seen. We had thought all along that all Palam had was an airport. Some of the civil servants were trying to get to Pakistan on special Dakota flights to Karachi. However, it was of no interest to us since we had been approved to go by train. The railway station was a picture of despair and sadness. No railway staff were to be seen. The soldiers who had brought us to the station belonged to the Baluch Regiment, but their primary duty was at Purana Qila and their stay at the station was short. The refugees were confined to one side of the station and no one was allowed to leave that area. At about three or four in the afternoon, some soldiers, who appeared to be South Indians, arrived. They, it turned out, would be guarding the train that would take us to Pakistan. Shortly after that, our special train arrived and we were told to board it. There were so many refugees that there was hardly any space for most of them even to sit. Many had brought a lot of baggage which they placed on the upper berths. A good deal of it was placed on the floor. So confined were we that it was simply impossible to move from the spot we had found. Masroor and I were mainly concerned with protecting our tins of condensed milk. Although we had all been living together in the same camp for two weeks, everyone behaved quite selfishly, treating this extraordinary journey as yet another train trip. People seemed to have little inkling of the dangers we faced.

The train moved out in the evening and at an impressive speed. I had travelled several times between Delhi and Lahore and it was my estimate that if we continued to maintain our speed, we would be in Lahore by the morning. The Toofan Mail used to take seven to eight hours between the two cities. For the first two hours the train did not stop anywhere but around ten, when we arrived at Saharanpur, we found a warm welcome awaiting us from dozens of local Muslims. We were not allowed to get off the train, those being the strict orders of the soldiers escorting us. The people who had come to receive us had brought with them roasted chickpeas, soft drinks and large containers of water. With permission from the soldiers, they went into every carriage to serve those inside. We had nothing out of which we could drink but someone handed us two clay cups which we used to quench our enormous thirst. As the train began to move out of the station, our hosts chanted 'Pakistan *zindabad*!' with great warmth and enthusiasm, making us feel that we were not alone and there were people who cared about us.

The journey from Saharanpur on, however, was quite different from the first leg of the trip, as the train stopped every now and then, at times for hours on end. We did not know whom to ask what was happening. Every time the train stopped, soldiers would jump out to stand guard in front of every carriage. They would not let anyone get out. People had plenty of chickpeas to munch but because of the heat, they were all thirsty. Roasted chickpeas are also known to cause thirst. I noted that every station we passed had its name covered with a piece of cloth. Not only that, but every water outlet appeared to have been sealed. There was only one conclusion to be drawn: by the passengers: no water for the Muslims. It took us two days and two nights to get to Jullandhur, which should give the reader some idea of how slowly the train was moving. By now, people were suffering from both hunger and thirst. We had managed to conserve some of our milk. Since we were talking little, our thirst was not so bad. At one point, I saw one infant crying inconsolably in its mother's arms. The child was obviously very thirsty. On an impulse, I handed over the two tins of milk that I had to the woman because I could not bear to hear that child cry. We really had not eaten much for the last seventeen days but I just could not resist doing what I did. Masroor gave me a dirty look when he saw what I had done, but could do nothing.

As our train came into Amritsar, a train full of Hindus and Sikhs steamed in from Pakistan. The moment those people saw us, they began to shout hostile slogans. We were so terrified that nobody made even the slightest movement. To our good fortune, the soldiers who were guarding us under the command of a British major trained their guns on those people and the major made it clear that if any attempt was made to attack our train, he would order his troops to open fire. His words relieved the tension which had gripped us. The occupants of the train from Pakistan were being offered food and plenty of water to drink but as for us, there was not even a drop. The heat was intense. We sighed with relief as our train left the Amritsar station, only to come to a stop at a place where we could see no sign of life. It was about eight in the evening. The troops guarding us kept marching up and down alongside the carriages. We were still there when day broke. At about nine or ten, a hundred to two hundred young Sikhs, armed with swords, lances and daggers began to move towards us. Had our soldiers ignored this, even briefly, few of us would have survived.

Although we were on a train and had no means of contact with the outside world, a rumour began to go around the carriages that the train that had left Delhi on 24 September had been waylaid and only a few had survived to reach Pakistan. A bearded man who was sitting next to me was the one who whispered this bit of news in my ear. I asked him, 'Sir, you have

been on this train for several days with no contact with anyone
or anything from the world outside, so how do you know that
the first train was attacked?' He looked first left, then right and
replied, 'I heard this right in this very carriage. And who says
that what I have heard is not correct? Just look at those Sikhs
who, were they to attack our train, would leave nobody alive.'

However, that did not come to pass as our guards ordered the
armed men to disperse. But still the train did not move. At about
two, with the sun beating down without mercy on our stationary
train, we noticed a dirty pool of water about twenty yards from
where we were. It was the kind of stagnant pool buffaloes use
to cool themselves. I do not know what came over me but I
requested the soldier who was standing in front of our carriage
to permit me to get down and get some water from the pool. I
told him how desperately thirsty people were. I promised to
complete my to-and-fro run quickly. I do not know why he
showed me the sympathy that he did, but he said that if I did not
complete my run in 25 seconds, he would not let me reboard. I
was leaning out of the window, while he stood below. I asked
someone to give me a jug and then, jug in hand, opened the
carriage door and jumped out. The soldier said that he was going
to start his count. The people on the train were watching me as
if I were about to start a hundred metre run in the Olympics. I
ran to the pool, filled my jug and when I was climbing back into
my carriage, the soldier had only counted up to twenty. I really
felt as if I had won Olympic gold!

I was out of breath when I returned to the carriage, but I could
now quench my thirst. However, when I looked in my jug, I felt
sick because the water was so dirty. I thought of cleaning it up
by using my shirt as a filter, but then I remembered that I had
been wearing that shirt for the last seventeen days and it looked
dirtier than the water I had collected. I looked at Masroor but
his clothes were as dirty as mine. In fact, all we had on our
bodies now were rags, which was also true of others on that
train. There was nothing more I could do. I offered my jug to
Masroor and then to others, but nobody was able to muster the

courage to drink that foul water. We felt so helpless. I peeped out of the window and asked the guard on duty if he would please move aside so that I could empty my jug. He asked me if the water had been drunk. I told him that no one would dare drink that filthy water and it was better to stay thirsty. The soldier told me that our train was without an engine and would only move after the arrival of an engine from Pakistan. He also said that the platoon protecting the train would end its duty and return to its base the moment the engine from Pakistan arrived.

At around five in the evening, we felt a jolt and we knew that the engine from Pakistan had arrived. Two or three military trucks and a jeep had also driven up to the stationary train and were now parked beside it. The men of the platoon guarding us, picked up their baggage from the carriages, loaded it into the trucks and before they left, the major commanding the platoon raised his arm and waved goodbye. After some time, our train also began to move. Every window on that train was now open and people were looking at the horizon, dying to know where India would end and Pakistan begin. Suddenly, one man with a very impressive appearance shouted in an emotional voice, 'Pakistan *zindabad*!' We all continued to crane our necks to be the first to catch a glimpse of Pakistan as we approached it. The train was now moving full steam ahead and the emotions of the passengers were such that it is impossible for me to put them into words. We had all begun to shout—including me and Masroor—'Pakistan *zindabad*!' like mad men. It was then that I felt what power and magic the boundaries of your own country hold and how much love and security they provide. It was like a festival.

As the train slunk into Wagha, we jumped out as if just set free from prison. There were hundreds of people waiting on the platform to receive us and we were embracing one another as if we had met after years. We were all Pakistanis. All distinctions of age and rank had been transcended. Huge *degs* of food had been put out and there were dozens of stalls serving ice-cold drinks. Masroor and I had not really eaten for the last seventeen days but, strangely enough, we felt neither thirst nor hunger. People were offering us plates of food and glasses of cold sweet drinks but we just did not feel like eating or drinking. Our arrival in Pakistan had fulfilled all our needs. Never again in my life have I felt such a sense of security and never have I been showered with so much love.

We arrived at the Lahore railway station at ten at night. I asked a railway official if the address to which I used to mail letters to my father was close to the station, and was told that it was. When Masroor and I arrived at the house, my father was home. He looked at us as if we had risen from the dead and told us that riots had broken out in many places in Pakistan and special trains containing Hindus and Sikhs were leaving for India. We had suffered hunger and thirst for seventeen days and survived a punishing three-day train journey, but we had no ill feelings towards anyone, no matter to what religion he belonged. We wanted those who were going to India to do so in peace and safety. My father confirmed the rumour we had heard on the train, namely, that the train that had left before ours had been attacked and dozens killed or injured. I have never been able to solve the mystery of how that story reached our train.

My father took Masroor and me to a tailor's shop next door where we picked up a change of clothes. We showered to our hearts' content but were too excited to sleep and talked all night. This was our first night—and what a wonderful night it was—in Pakistan. After a couple of days in Lahore, Masroor and I left for Rawalpindi, where we were soon able to find jobs at the Pakistan Army General Headquarters, though we did not keep them for very long.

6 Working for the Army

I worked at the Pakistan Army GHQ's Military Secretary branch for no more than a few months. Abrar Siddiqi, who was to become a lifelong friend, and who had been working for the department of defence in Delhi for over two years, was now at GHQ, Rawalpindi. He told me that he had been fond of writing and reading even as a child. When he started college, he began to write for the magazine it published. His family came from Rohailkhand, he told me. There were two factions of the family. His father's side was staunchly anti-British, having fought in the 1857 uprising. After it was over, the family suffered reprisals and several of its members were blown from cannon or hanged. So deep was the family's anti-imperialism that its members had vowed neither to learn nor speak English. They had also committed themselves never to seek employment under the British. The mother's side of the family was more pragmatic and greatly impressed with the Aligarh Movement of Sir Syed Ahmed Khan, which urged Muslims to acquire a modern education. Abrar's grandfather considered it no crime to learn English and work under the British. Abrar was raised by his mother's side of the family, but when he reached employment age, his uncle created a family crisis by insisting that, although the boy had read English, it did not mean that he should accept the slavery of the British and break with family tradition.

Abrar told me that from his boyhood it was M.N. Roy's leftist movement that had impressed him. With some of his friends he even brought out an Urdu weekly newspaper but it did not survive beyond a couple of issues. His father knew the owner of a Rohailkhand newspaper and asked him to hire young Abrar as a translator. This was not really work because it was practically unpaid. The family opposition to working for the British continued, so it was decided to approach the famous Indian

National Congress leader Rafi Ahmed Kidwai, who found Abrar a job on *The Pioneer,* Lucknow. This newspaper was owned by the UP aristocrat and millionaire, Sir Jwala Prashad Srivastava. Abrar was taken on probation and might have continued except that he fell ill and had to leave. After he recovered, he rejoined college and completed his master's degree. He moved to Delhi at the suggestion of some friends and found a job, thanks to Prof. Muhammad Mujeeb, in the Jamia Millia's publications section. But it did not last long.

His next venture was to produce an Urdu weekly called *Imroze* in partnership with some friends. This too was short lived. His friend, Attique Siddiqi, told him not to waste his time chasing shadows but to try to earn a proper living. He advised Abrar to join a business school in Delhi, which would help him obtain work. Abrar took his advice, while also working on a voluntary basis for *Dawn*, Delhi, as well as for another paper called *National Call.* The money he earned was so meagre that he decided to seek a job with the department of defence, which was where he stayed for the next two and a half years, and in 1947 he moved to Pakistan.

But to return to Rawalpindi. Masroor and I decided to bring out a literary journal. Masroor, who had worked for a magazine called *Phulvari* in Delhi, was to be the editor. In Rawalpindi, we had befriended Ahmed Zafar and Muhammad Sharif Ahmed. Zafar was a fine poet and Sharif a good short story writer. It was Zafar who introduced us to the poet Qateel Shifai. The four of us got together to bring out the magazine Masroor and I had been planning. Everyone was to contribute to the initial capital. Ahmed Zafar and I took a trip to Lahore to gather material because all the established writers lived there. Qateel suggested that the first person to approach should be Saadat Hasan Manto. We met him through his brother-in-law who was a co-owner of the city's Plaza Cinema. Manto told us that he would write a story for us which he would call *Khali Botlain Khali Dibbay* (empty bottles, empty boxes). We paid him the money forthwith and were promised the story once we arrived in Rawalpindi.

Qateel was furious with us for having paid Manto far too much. He told us that he received no more than a hundred rupees for his movie lyrics. The result of his lecture was that we decided not to pay anyone in advance. However, Zaheer Kaashmiri and A. Hamid were as good as their word. Manto never sent us the promised story. Later, when he published a book with the same title, all we could do was remember with regret the hundred rupees we had paid him.

We produced an issue or two of the magazine. We also became regulars at the weekly meetings of the Anjuman-e-Tarraqi Pasand Mussanfeen and the Halqa Arbab-e-Zauq, where members would read their poems and stories, which would be followed by a discussion session. Masroor and I were disillusioned with government service and after several trips to Lahore, the garrison town of Rawalpindi held no attraction for us. One day we decided to move to Lahore to make our names in the literary world. We had Rs250 when we landed in Lahore after quitting our jobs, a sum of money that did not last beyond a month.

We had begun to hang out at Paradise Restaurant where the city's writers and poets often gathered. Some of them would take one look at us and whisper, 'They appear to be freshly-ensnared fools'. They would join us on our table, drink our tea, lecture us on art and literature and leave. We must have hosted Ahmed Rahi, Zaheer Kaashmiri and Abdullah Malik scores of times in that restaurant. Abdullah Malik was a leading light of the communist party. He also owned a bookshop where party literature was sold. He had been living in Bombay, working for the party with Hamid Akhtar, Sibte Hasan and Ali Sardar Jafri. The party sent him to Karachi on an assignment but for some reason he did not return to Bombay. He was not involved with journalism in those days but was active in Lahore's literary and journalist circles. Despite being a member of the communist party, he was a diehard follower of the Ahl-e-Hadith sect.

In 1949, we came to befriend Ibne Insha. We were as poor as church mice but Ibne Insha was not among those who look for people they can cadge a meal or a drink from. After some running around, Masroor finally found a job at railway headquarters, which ensured two square meals a day for the two of us. I was without work, the main reason being that I was against taking a government job; I wanted to work for a newspaper or a magazine. However, none of the people I had met were willing to help. One day, when Ibne Insha and I were chatting not far from the office of daily *Imroze*, we saw Abrar Siddiqi walking by. After greeting us warmly, he asked when I had arrived from Rawalpindi, where he thought I was still working. I told him that I had chucked my GHQ job. Abrar, it turned out, had also resigned from GHQ and joined *Imroze* where a sub-editor was paid Rs210 a month, a princely sum of money in those days. Other newspapers paid not even one-third of this figure. Abrar offered us tea and lectured us against becoming journalists. 'Take my advice. Stay away from this profession because once it bites you, you are enslaved for life. Whatever you earn, you will spend and you will also pick up certain evil habits which you will never be able to get rid of.' However, his words had no effect on us and we asked him to suggest a newspaper which would hire us. When we told him that we were practically on the street, he promised to make inquiries and get back to us.

Next day, we dropped in at *Imroze* to see Abrar, who told us that two newspapers were looking for translators. One was Waqar Ambalvi's *Safeena* and the other Malik Ehsan Ilahi's *Ehsan*. It was his opinion that we would not be able to get along with Waqar Ambalvi because of his temper and his reputation of not being very nice to his staff. As for *Ehsan*, it was edited by Abu Saeed Bazmi, but he did not know him well enough to put in a word for us. He suggested that we should go and see him on our own. 'After all, if you have talent,' he said consolingly, 'getting a job should be no problem'.

A couple of days after this meeting, I was in Rawalpindi on a brief visit. I was sound asleep when someone pulled me out of the bed and announced that Quaid-i-Azam Mohammad Ali Jinnah was dead. I must have gone into shock because my entire

body felt paralysed. The man whose personality and politics had
had such a profound effect on my life was gone. I remembered
that memorable meeting with him in Delhi when I had shaken
hands with him and he had put his hand affectionately on my
shoulder and led me into the Feroz Shah Kotla ground. I recalled
the loving questions he had put to me and that dramatic encounter
when thousands of us had marched to his Aurangzeb Road
residence demanding that the Muslim League should quit the
interim government. I remembered him appearing on the balcony
and asking angrily who our leader was. When the overawed
crowd had answered that he was the leader, the Quaid had said,
'Then why are you here? Go back to your homes'. Within
minutes the large, emotional crowd had dispersed.

I also thought of the speech in which he had said that Muslims
no longer needed titles conferred on them by the British and they
should return them because the last battle with British
imperialism had begun. The Muslims of India had obeyed his
call. I remembered his 3 June 1947 speech which he had ended
by saying 'Pakistan *zindabad*!', infusing new determination in
the Muslims of India to carry the struggle for freedom to its final
victory. I had seen the Quaid-i-Azam at close quarters and
although he was physically frail, no other leader could match the
forceful personality God had given him. He was a complete
leader, who single-handedly led the Muslims of India to the final
goal of freedom and won them a state of their own. How could
I forget yet another speech of his, the one he had delivered days
after the establishment of Pakistan on Eid day? I was still in
Delhi and I had heard some people saying that the Quaid was
responsible for the killing of Muslims. Some people who had
decided to stay on in India had also objected to his strategy. I,
along with others, had argued that the Quaid-i-Azam had led the
legal and constitutional fight for Pakistan against the full might
of the British and the Hindus but without allowing a single drop
of Muslim blood to be shed. It was another matter that the
underhand politics of the British and the Hindus had led to the
massacres at Partition.

These thoughts were running through my head when suddenly I broke down like a little child. My tears just would not stop. As far as I can remember, I have never again cried like that. Attempts to console me had no effect on me. I simply could not stop crying. The Quaid's distant funeral prayers which I joined were offered at Company Park, off Murree Road, Rawalpindi but even during the prayers my tears kept welling up. In the evening, my friends and I continued to talk about the Quaid. I told them how I had met the great man and with what affection he had treated me.

7 The Oldest Profession

I took up Abrar Siddiqi's suggestion to try my luck at *Ehsan,* a newspaper I had only glanced at once or perhaps twice. Normally I would look through *Imroze, Zamindar or Inqilab*, and sometimes *Nawa-i-Waqt*. Among all the Urdu newspapers, the one that stood out was *Imroze*, both editorially and in terms of layout. But it was to *Ehsan* that I made my way. Maulana Abu Saeed Bazmi was the editor and his room was on the first floor. His two assistant editors were Ahmed Bashir and A. Hamid. It was the first time I had entered a newspaper office. Not only did I need a job but I was dying to fulfil my boyhood ambition of becoming a journalist. I walked up to the first floor and asked the first person I came across where the editor's room was. He pointed to a door, 'That's where you will find him.' I later learnt that the kind, short man who had guided me was Malik Noor Elahi, the newspaper's owner. His elder son was the Punjab advocate-general at the time.

I knocked at the door. 'Please come in,' said a voice from the other side. I stepped in. 'And what brings you here?' Abu Saeed Bazmi asked. I replied, 'Maulana, I have heard that your newspaper needs a translator, so that's what brings me here.' He asked me to take a seat. I had hardly done so when he told me that there was a sub-editor's vacancy in the paper, so it was good that I had turned up. 'We need an experienced journalist; obviously, you have worked for a newspaper before?' he added. 'I have no such experience,' I replied. 'That is bad news. What we need is an experienced journalist, so it is going to be difficult to proceed any further,' he said. 'Maybe I can come up to your expectations, but you'll have to first give me a chance,' I suggested. 'That seems difficult,' he replied.

Maulana Bazmi had been editor of the famous nationalist newspaper *Madina* and was well-known in Lahore's journalistic

world because of his editorials. I was disappointed by his reply
but what could I do? I had no experience of journalism and now
the possibility of getting a job had slipped by. I rose from my
chair, turned and was about to walk through the door when I had
a brainwave. I turned, only to find Maulana Bazmi absorbed in
some papers on his desk. I said, 'Maulana, if you will forgive
me, may I ask you a question?' 'By all means,' he replied.
Without hesitation, I asked, 'There must have been a first time
for you in a newspaper?' 'Yes, indeed,' he answered. 'You could
not have acquired journalistic experience while still in your
mother's womb,' I said in a very low voice, without any attempt
to hide my disappointment. The Maulana began to laugh. So loud
was his laughter that it felt as if the entire room would rise a few
feet in the air. Then he said, 'You most certainly have a point. I
think you deserve a chance.' He picked up that day's *The
Pakistan Times*, shuffled through its pages, pointed to the
editorial, gave me a pad and pencil and asked me to translate it
into Urdu.

I had hardly finished the first paragraph when he said to me,
'Let's see your handiwork. 'He took one look at what I had done
and said, 'Very good.' Then he marked a couple of news reports
in the paper and told me to go to the next room, translate the
stories and bring them back to him, complete with headlines. It
took me ten minutes to translate those fairly long stories, place
headlines on them and bring them back. He smiled and said,
'Have you translated those two stories completely or did you
take a shortcut?' I replied that I had translated them in full and
he could take a look. He glanced through them and said, 'Your
Urdu is polished and you translate well. I am prepared to give
you a chance. Tomorrow will be your first day and we will pay
you Rs70 a month.' I was beside myself with joy. Had I not
asked him that rude question, he would never have hired me.
Bazmi said, 'Now that I have settled your salary, let me introduce
you to Ahmed Bashir and A. Hamid.' He led me to the next room
where I met the two men. 'Very interesting young man this here,'
he told them. 'From tomorrow, he will be working the day shift,'

he added. The two shook hands with me but did not appear to be too interested in a new recruit like me. They were probably busy writing an editorial or an editorial note. Maulana Bazmi also took me to meet other members of the editorial staff, which made me realise what a gentleman he was, taking me around as if I were someone important or an experienced journalist.

Masroor and I were now on top of the world. The next day, we hired a room in a section of Macleod Road which was home to Lahore's movie people. We vacated the servant's quarters attached to a large house in Railway Road we were living in after paying the rent, picked up our baggage and moved to our new place. Most of the people who lived here were connected in one way or another with the movie industry. Some actors and actresses also lived here and various film companies had set up their offices in the area. I worked diligently on my first day at *Ehsan*. When I looked at the newspaper the next day, I was pleased to see that all the stories I had translated had made the paper. I clipped them out, pasted them on a sheet of paper and put it safely in my suitcase. I gradually formed a friendship with one of the reporters named Fazil. In those days, Mian Mohammad Shafi was the city's most celebrated reporter. From the *Civil and Military Gazette*, he had moved to *The Pakistan Times* as chief reporter. I would meet him often, but to him I was just a boy of eighteen or nineteen starting out.

Some days later, I met Sher Mohammad Akhtar, editor of the weekly *Qandeel*. At one point, the conversation turned to *Nawa-i-Waqt*. 'Working there is tough going,' he said. When I asked why, he replied that those who work the morning shift remain sitting at their desks waiting for that day's *The Pakistan Times, Civil and Military Gazette* and even the *Nawa-i-Waqt* to come back from Hamid Nizami's residence, after having been read. What happened was that the morning papers were delivered to the Nizami residence, where he went over them and then pointed out mistakes in translation and other shortcomings he had noticed in his own newspaper that day. The editorial staff could not leave until it had seen and made note of the mistakes identified by Nizami. If someone had translated from English inaccurately, he was either sacked or given a serious warning. The night shift fared no differently.

In those days, Zahoor Alam Shaheed was news editor at *Nawa-i-Waqt*. He and Nizami had been at college together and although they were close to each other, as far as the newspaper was concerned, his opinion received no special consideration. There can be no doubt that Zahoor Alam Shaheed was a seasoned and extremely polite gentleman. It was by a quirk of fate that he had formed an association with a man who was adamant in his views and always wanted things to be done his way. He could not tolerate his decisions being questioned. Nizami was a man of strong loyalties when it came to his province of Punjab and that remained the focal point of his newspaper. Shaheed's association with Nizami was a long one but eventually there came a point when the two parted company, both professionally and in personal terms.

For the first few months, my position at *Ehsan* remained that of a translator, but as time passed, I began to take part in the editing and layout of the paper. We would sometimes get a number of London newspapers in our office. I would study them carefully, look at the display of stories, try to understand what factors determined a story's display and what constituted noteworthy items. When I began to share with my colleagues what I was learning through my study of British newspapers, it did not take me long to notice that they were often in agreement with me as to what story should receive what kind of display. I had been with *Ehsan* barely two months, when Bazmi sent for me one day and said, 'You have been hiding your light under a bushel, so I have decided that you will move to the second storey so that you can work the night shift. You will have to work harder and you will have to take decisions. The front and back pages are put to bed by the night shift, which is work of great responsibility.' He also ordered a raise in my monthly salary of Rs30 which made my monthly take-home Rs100.

In 1949, the annual session of the Progressive Writers' Association was due to take place in Lahore and expected to be attended by the leading poets and writers of the day. Faiz Ahmed Faiz, editor of *The Pakistan Times,* it was announced, would preside over the session. It was *Nawa-i-Waqt* that launched a big movement against the gathering, calling the Progressive Writers '*Surkhas*', a derogatory description that sounds much worse in Urdu than its English equivalent of 'Reds'. Although *Ehsan* too was quietly in on the side of the Progressive movement's detractors, it was far more reticent. Muzaffar Ehsani, who used to write a humorous column for us, being on the staff, was known as one of Hamid Nizami's intellectual allies. His column was always critical of the Progressives and, at times, his choice of words was objectionable. As for Ahmed Bashir and A. Hamid, they were supportive of the Progressive movement but would not ask the staff to write in its favour nor against it.

The annual session took place in the Simla Pahari neighbourhood. I was on night shift and under strict instructions that the final copy should be in no later than 12.30 a.m. No one was authorised to countermand those instructions. There were two reasons for this deadline: one being that the newspaper was printed on litho and all copy was calligraphed on special yellow paper in special ink. Once the copy had been pasted, the pages were placed on a plate in the press and a heavy stone was run over the plate for half an hour or so, till the writing on litho left a clear impression in reverse on the plate. Certain chemicals were then used to make that impression indelible. This plate was fed into a printing machine to begin printing. The press was so slow that no more than 2,500 pages could be printed in time for the next day's issue. The rest of the pages had been printed earlier in the morning. The entire newspaper was collated manually. If the final copy was late, then the newspaper could not be dispatched to other cities and towns by train. If the paper missed the last train, there was no other means of getting it to the agents in outlying areas.

I recall the day of the Progressive Writers' meeting distinctly. A colleague and I had sent in the final copy and were drinking tea and chatting when Muzaffar Ehsani, accompanied by a number of men, burst into the office and said, in an authoritative voice, 'Here you are drinking tea. Where is the final copy?' 'The final copy has gone,' I replied with a smile. 'The copy can't go; get it back.' Ehsani was a big man with a deep voice and he sounded like someone who was about to smash my head. He only wrote a column for us, sometimes in the office and at other times from his home, when he would bring it in. He had little idea how a newspaper was printed and what difficulties we ran into every day. He was in a temper, but I decided to keep mine under control and told him calmly that the final copy had gone and there were strict instructions from the administration about the deadline. I told him that if the final copy was delayed, it would mean that the paper would not be printed in time. However, that was something he could not understand. 'Recall the final copy otherwise we will miss a sensational story,' he screamed.

Then he began to explain. According to him, there had been pandemonium at the meeting of the *Surkhas* which Faiz Ahmed Faiz was presiding over. Chairs had been thrown and various people had had suffered injuries. The story, he said, had to appear in *Ehsan* in order to expose 'these communists'. In fact, if *Ehsan* did not carry the story, it too would begin to be counted among communist newspapers. Then he asked me why I was reluctant to recall the final copy. Was I also a communist? I replied that what he had brought in was a story and it should appear as one. I asked him what its appearance or non-appearance had to do with my being or not being a communist. Finally, I agreed to talk to the printing press, which was the Ilmi Printing Press, not very far from our office, and suggested to Ehsani that he should go there right away and dictate a one-line story to the printer, who would inscribe it in inverted letters directly onto the plate and it would appear in the morning. I also warned him that it was not going to be easy.

Ehsani was not happy to hear what I had told him. His face had gone red and he was breathing heavily. What he did next was to pick up the phone and call the *Nawa-i-Waqt* newsroom, where the final copy was being hurriedly completed with a colourful report of the disturbance at the meeting. Ehsani told whoever he was speaking to that something had gone wrong at *Ehsan* with a new sub-editor who looked like a *Surkha*, which was perhaps why he was being uncooperative. Then he moved to the next room muttering under his breath. He and his buddies stayed there for quite some time, but my colleagues and I called it a day and went home. We were not bothered that our reporter had missed the story; in fact, we were sure that we had done the right thing by refusing to revise the final copy. As for *Nawa-i-Waqt*, the whole fracas at the meeting was said to have been engineered by Hamid Nizami. *Nawa-i-Waqt* had its own press and could put the paper to bed much later than we could since we did not have a press of our own.

Next day, when I arrived at the office at about four in the evening, I found Malik Noor Elahi, our owner, waiting for me by the steps on the first floor. He asked me to go to see Abu Saeed Bazmi straight away and attend to my work later, adding, 'if necessary'. My surprise must have been apparent from my face, but I did not ask for any details and walked into the editor's office. He took one look at me, burst out laughing and asked, 'And how is the founder of the Red Revolution?' 'Red Revolution!' I shot back, 'What have I got to do with that?' I then told him what had happened the night before and how angry Muzaffar Ehsani had been. I told him that I had tried my best to explain to Ehsani why it was difficult to do what he wanted but he had not been willing to listen or to understand. Bazmi heard me out, then assuming a more sober tone, told me that Malik Noor Elahi had been assured that I was a member of the communist party, which was why I had prevented the report of the fracas at the Progressive Writers' meeting from appearing in *Ehsan*. It had therefore been decided, he informed me, that I should be fired. He asked me to go and sit with Ahmed Bashir, while he conferred with Malik Noor Elahi.

Ahmed Bashir and I had become good friends by then. Some time earlier, when the government of Hasni Al-Zaeem had been overthrown in Syria, he had asked me to write an article, which I had done after reading the history of the country and analysing its politics. Ahmed Bashir had liked my article and he had published it prominently on the editorial page. When I entered the room, Ahmed Bashir welcomed me by calling me a *Surkha*. Then he laughed and complimented me on dealing with Ehsani the way he should have been dealt with. When I asked him to tell me more, he informed me that Ehsani was a scheming guttersnipe, who worked for our paper but sang Hamid Nizami's praises all day. He had been kicking up hell about me since the morning and the decision now lay with Bazmi. 'Let's see what he decides. We will determine our strategy after that, but worry not: all will be well,' he assured me.

Ahmed Bashir spent a lifetime in journalism. In between, he went into filmmaking and the one movie that he directed was a flop. It had no continuity; in the same scene, the actors made various changes of costume. Years after it was made, I saw it with my friend Athar Ali in Karachi. The showing had been arranged by Ahmed Bashir and there were just the three of us in the screening room. We managed to sit through the entire thing and when it ended and Ahmed Bashir asked for our opinions, Athar Ali asked if the movie had already been released or whether a date had still to be determined. Ahmed Bashir replied that it would be released the following Friday. Athar Ali's advice was that the release should be held back and the cinema owners should be told to insure their furniture because it was in great danger of being smashed. Ahmed Bashir smiled and said that while that was good advice, a great deal of his own money had gone into the making of the movie, *Neela Parbat*, and it deserved to run for at least one day to bring in some revenue.

But to return to my situation at the office. Abu Saeed Bazmi returned after conferring with Malik Noor Elahi and informed me that a decision had been taken. Because of Muzaffar Ehsani's mischievous campaign against me, it was not advisable for me to stay in Lahore, but if I would like to move to Peshawar to work for another of Malik Noor Elahi's newspapers, *Shahbaz*, there was a job for me there. My salary, he added, would be raised to Rs150 a month. I would also be the paper's news editor, although my letter of appointment would not say that. When I asked for time to think the offer over, Bazmi left the room. Ahmed Bashir was the one who spoke. He told me that in journalism such things were the norm rather than the exception and if I wanted to stay in the profession, I would have to get used to them. 'Your salary has gone up and you are well on your way to becoming news editor. So what is the problem?' he asked. He advised me to go into Bazmi's room and tell him that I accepted the offer before Muzaffar Ehsani made Malik Noor Elahi change his mind.

The offer had one attraction for me. My father was in Nowshehra, which was close to Peshawar. If I took the job, I would be able to see my family frequently; so I walked into Bazmi's office and told him that I accepted his offer. He laughed loudly, which was his style, and assured me that he would issue my letter of appointment immediately, asking me to report at Peshawar in a week's time. He was sure that would give me enough time to pack up and leave. I left his room and went back to Ahmed Bashir. My letter of appointment arrived half an hour later. I had been appointed assistant news editor at a salary of Rs150. Ahmed Bashir was thrilled. 'Instead of being dismissed, you have been promoted. This calls for a celebration.' I said goodbye to Ahmed Bashir and Abu Saeed Bazmi, took an advance of Rs100 from the cashier and went home. I told Masroor what had happened and that I was going to Peshawar to work for *Shahbaz*. I showed him my letter of appointment. The flat in MacLeod Road that we had jointly rented, I added, would now be entirely his. He was a sport. 'Peshawar is not that far; we will continue to meet,' he said.

8 The Great Khan

After Lahore's lively literary and political life, it did not take me long after landing in Peshawar to realise that I was in Khan Abdul Qayyum Khan's country. The local politicians seemed to lack the enthusiasm and commitment that one associated with politicians from the Punjab. Barring the daily *Shahbaz* and a weekly or two, there was no newspaper in the entire province. In other words, what press existed was under the control of Qayyum Khan, which was perhaps why he had come to be known as the Iron Man of the Frontier. Politically, the province seemed to be separate and isolated from the rest of Pakistan. During the 1945 elections, the Red Shirt Movement had been in full swing in the province, with its leadership in the hands of Khan Abdul Ghaffar Khan, the Frontier Gandhi, who had carried his party to a decisive victory. His brother, Dr Khan Sahib, had been made chief minister of the province. So total was the hold of the Red Shirts on everything that other political parties were not even able to hold public meetings. Even if a party dared call a meeting, it failed to take place because of a lack of public interest. However, the people of the province were well aware of political developments in the rest of the country. Before independence, Khan Abdul Qayyum Khan had been elected to the Central Assembly of India on a Red Shirt ticket. The All India Muslim League had few supporters in the province, the most prominent being Sardar Abdul Rab Nishtar, who was a key figure in the League's high command. He had taken part in the 1945 elections, but lost. Despite that, the Quaid-i-Azam had had great faith in Nishtar's abilities, which was why Nishtar was considered the principal representative of Frontier Muslims in the League.

Given the big political changes that had begun to take place in the rest of India, the situation in the Frontier province had also begun to change. Red Shirt leaders were beginning to abandon Khan Abdul Ghaffar Khan. Among them were such men as Arbab Abdul Ghafoor Khan, who had been known as the right hand man of the Frontier Gandhi. Others who had left the Red Shirts to join the Muslim League were Khan Sameen Khan, Khan Ghulam Mohammad Khan of Lundkhor and Khan Bakht Jamal Khan. These men had played leading roles in the civil disobedience movement in 1930. They had remained steadfast in their support for Abdul Ghaffar Khan and they had all spent time in jail. But now they were in the Muslim League, where they were soon joined by Khan Abdul Qayyum Khan. Some said that he had defected because Ghaffar Khan had told him in no uncertain terms that he would not be given a party ticket in the next elections. Qayyum Khan belonged to Kashmir and before announcing his departure from the Red Shirt Movement, he had paid a brief visit to Kashmir where he had held meetings with Sheikh Muhammad Abdullah. One of Khan Qayyum Khan's brothers, Sardar Abdul Hamid Khan later became the prime minister of Azad Kashmir.

When the Muslim League first began to gather support in the Frontier province, it was under the control of Pir Sahib of Manki Sharif, who became Qayyum Khan's main political rival. It is true that while Manki Sharif was the one who popularised the League in the province, it was Qayyum Khan who broke the Red Shirt Movement. His brand of partisan, hard-hitting politics also led to a break between Qayyum Khan and men like Arbab Abdul Ghafoor Khan and Khan Ghulam Mohammad Khan of Lundkhor. Qayyum Khan successfully convinced the central leadership of the League that he wielded the greatest influence in his province. His principal support was believed to come from Nawabzada Liaquat Ali Khan, the League's secretary general and the Quaid-i-Azam's first lieutenant.

The acid test of Muslim League's popularity came with the referendum when the people of the province sided overwhelmingly with the League and cast the Red Shirts aside. It was only natural therefore that Khan Abdul Qayyum Khan should have emerged

as the leading political force in the province. He was an effective
orator and he had an efficient political machine backing him.
Ironically, even after Pakistan's establishment, Dr Khan Sahib
continued to remain the chief minister of the province which had
voted against his party.

On 14 August 1947, the Red Shirt Movement committed a
mistake that proved fatal. Those close to the Governor House
said that Red Shirt leaders were undecided over what they should
do when the Pakistan flag was raised for the first time in the
province. Should they be present at the ceremony and salute the
new flag of a country they had opposed or should they stay
away? Dr Khan sought advice from Sir George Cunningham, the
new British governor, who told him that the people of the
province were seething with anger because of the hostile role of
the Red Shirts during the independence struggle and the presence
of its leaders at that solemn ceremony could cause that anger to
burst forth. The crowd might lynch them if things got out of
hand. It is said that Dr Khan Sahib decided, after speaking to the
governor, to stay away. No other leader of the Red Shirts came
to the flag-raising ceremony either. Those who defend the Red
Shirt leaders' decision to sit out the ceremony would find it hard
to explain why Ghaffar Khan and his companions had coined the
slogan of Pakhtunistan—the separate Pakhtun homeland—during
the referendum. Not once in his long life did Ghaffar Khan
accept the establishment of Pakistan. He remained ideologically
tethered to undivided India. In his will he wrote that he should
be buried in the Afghan city of Jalalabad, and that was where he
lies. He did not want to rest in the earth of the province which
was once his stronghold but which had later abandoned him and
his political philosophy.

The boycott of the birth of Pakistan event led to the dismissal
of the Dr Khan Sahib ministry by the central government. And
thus it came to pass that Khan Abdul Qayyum Khan, who had
already enticed away quite a few of the Red Shirts, was able to
form a government. Muslim League leaders at the time were of
the view that along with the dismissal of the Frontier government,

the Frontier assembly should also have been sent home and fresh elections held. Some leaders were of the opinion that if that happened, Qayyum Khan could not have captured power through the backdoor, as it were.

My father, who worked for the railways, was posted to Nowshehra. He advised me to work in Peshawar and live in Nowshehra. At the end of my day, he said, I could easily return home by train. The Khyber Mail left Peshawar at one in the morning and reached its first stop, Nowshehra, in no more than half an hour. I liked the arrangement and being, a railwayman's son, I travelled free. The *Shahbaz* office was located in the Qissa Khwani Bazaar, the heart of the city which was always full of life and activity. There were three teashops in front of our place and from the first floor, where we were, we only had to open a window and shout for tea. If it was three teas that we wanted, one of us would raise three fingers. This sign language ensured perfect communication. The way tea was served in Peshawar was quite different from what we were used to. The cups were small and came without saucers, while the tea was served in a small teapot. The brew was always strong and piping hot. It was instant tea, milk already added. When I went to China, a certain type of tea that I drank there reminded me of Peshawar.

I was happy to have run into an old Lahore acquaintance by the name of Tanvir at *Shahbaz*. He briefed me on how the place was run. He told me that although there was an APP teleprinter in the newsroom, it functioned only occasionally, being generally out of order. Even when it was working, not much copy flowed out of it. The APP office in the city was headed by Salim Alvi, who was both manager and reporter. Then there was Shahbaz Khan who only came in the evening and whose sole duty was to monitor radio news. He understood many languages, including Afghan Persian, Iranian Persian, Arabic and even Russian. He had a chart listing radio news bulletin timings from various countries. He would listen to all those bulletins, take notes, write out his stories and leave. We never talked to him and he never talked to us. He was like a machine, writing his copy in a spare hand and always leaving us with a pile of material which went into the next day's paper. Tanvir was about twenty-five and *Shahbaz* was his second newspaper after *Ehsan*. A month or two after my arrival, he went on leave to Lahore where he died tragically in a traffic accident.

Shahbaz Khan, who was in his middle years, appeared unwilling to share anything with a raw, inexperienced youngster like me. Once I asked him where he might be reached in case something had to be checked with him. He replied irritably, 'Whatever I hear on the radio, I transcribe. If you like it, use it; if you don't like it, throw it away. I have no phone so you can't start chasing me.' I told this to Tanvir, who told me that he had only one friend, Latif, the general manager of both *Ehsan* in Lahore and *Shahbaz* in Peshawar, who came from Lahore at least once or twice a month. When I tried to dig out some more information about Shahbaz, I learnt that he worked in a government office and had once been in the army. He had learnt the various languages he spoke and understood during his time abroad, though he was not very educated. His Urdu was far from perfect and he made many mistakes in writing.

One day, as was his wont, Shahbaz Khan put a pile of his stories on my table and left. I began to go through them, making corrections here and there, while on the lookout for one that could make the lead the next day. The APP teleprinter had been out of commission the entire day and we really needed a good lead story. When I phoned Alvi at APP, he told me that the Karachi–Peshawar teleprinter line had been dead since morning. He promised that if Karachi phoned in a good story, he would have it sent over. The 8 p.m. Radio Pakistan news bulletin had also failed to report anything of interest. As we approached our deadline, my nervousness increased. Just then in walked Tanvir and I shared my dilemma with him. 'Not to worry,' he said, 'if the news famine is that grave, by the time you order some nice hot tea, I will have brought you the lead story of your dreams.' The tea arrived because all I had had to do was open my window and indicate with my fingers how many cups I needed. Leisurely,

Tanvir poured himself a cup and disappeared into the adjoining room, emerging half an hour later holding six or seven handwritten pages. 'Here is your lead story. All it needs is a headline,' he declared.

My heart missed a beat when I realised that what I was reading was an exclusive interview with the Iron Man of the Frontier, Khan Abdul Qayyum Khan. The Khan had declared his resolve to liberate Kashmir, set Afghanistan right and all but plant the green and white Pakistan flag on the Red Fort in New Delhi. The interview had everything that a headline writer could ask for. The only question was: when and where had the interview been conducted? When I asked Tanvir, he told me, 'You needed a lead story; you have got it, so what more do you want?' I replied, 'Lead story I indeed needed, but how can I print something that will cost me my job and probably result in the newspaper's closure? You know I had to leave *Ehsan* because of a story that I didn't carry. Now I will have to leave *Shahbaz* because of a story that I did carry.' Tanvir told me to relax. 'Have no fear,' he added. I asked him to at least tell me when and where the reporter had met and interviewed Qayyum Khan. Tanvir replied that the meeting with Qayyum Khan had taken place earlier in the day and that was what the story was based on. Then he added, 'I have never seen a more chicken-hearted person than you. You will not do well in the politics of this Frontier province. You have to show guts, even when you decide what letters from readers to print. If they come to the conclusion that you are a coward, it won't take them long to put a gun in your face.'

Tanvir took back the six or seven sheets of paper that he had handed me and announced that he would now choose the headlines and if any questions were asked the next day, he would accept responsibility. He came back after a few minutes with a blazing headline about Kashmir's imminent liberation. I pasted the copy myself (In Lahore and Karachi, the copy-pasting was done by the calligraphist with the sub-editor instructing him as to what copy to place under what headline.) We got the pages ready and sent them in for printing. In the litho printing system,

there was no provision for printing pictures, otherwise we would
have splashed a big picture of Khan Abdul Qayyum Khan on the
front page.

We sent for more tea. It was midnight and my train was still
an hour away. Tanvir winked at me and said, 'Whenever you are
in need of a lead story, all you have to do is let me know.' 'What
do you mean?' I asked nervously. Tanvir said, 'Khan Abdul
Qayyum Khan is a fine fellow and deserves support in national
politics. There is no shortage of his enemies in the province.
They are the kind who can burst into this office, pull out a gun
and demand that the story they have brought should be printed.'
My worst fears had come true. 'Look, it seems our big story is
utterly baseless and imaginary.' Tanvir smiled, 'My friend, drink
your tea and be at peace. This interview is as much of a fact as
Khan Qayyum's being the chief minister of the Frontier. Have
no fear. The Khan will say nothing.'

But I was a very worried man. In Lahore, I had been dubbed
a *Surkha* and sacked and here I was about to be felled by the
Man of Iron. My mind went back to Maulana Abu Saeed Bazmi.
Had he accepted my explanation, I would have been happily
living and working in Lahore. What I had let Tanvir get me to
do was wrong and I was going to be made the scapegoat once
again. Tanvir got up and left but I was so nervous that it felt as
if somebody had chained me to the chair I was sitting in. I
looked at my watch. It was ten to one, which meant that there
was no time to catch the Frontier Mail. I would have to spend
the night in the office and prepare to go to jail. The chief minister
would see his interview first thing in the morning and order my
arrest. Well, what was to be was to be, I consoled myself. Going
to jail, in any case, would be a new experience.

I removed everything that lay on one of the large office tables,
turned a couple of books into a makeshift pillow and lay down,
but I could not sleep. Once or twice I did doze off and dreamt
of doing hard labour in jail and being made to walk around in
circles in a prison yard. In one dream, I was working like a
yoked ox at an oil-grinder. I even had a vision of myself

sweeping the floor of a dark and stinking prison cell. In the early
hours of the morning I slept and was woken up by Abdul Latif
from the head office, who had just arrived from Lahore. It was
about ten in the morning. 'Did you miss your train last night?'
he asked. I told him that was exactly what had happened. 'Well,
never mind, why don't you freshen up and we can have some
breakfast.' There was a guest room in the office with a bed and
articles of daily use, which was where he always stayed. When
I emerged from the bathroom, a nice breakfast of bread, kebabs
and hot tea was waiting for me. Latif said, 'I can see you haven't
slept because you look tired. If you are not feeling well, why not
take a day's leave and go home. Come back when you are
yourself.' I thanked him and replied that I was feeling fine now
and a walk in Qissa Khwani Bazaar would perk me up. Latif
went to his room and I began to leaf through the day's paper,
trying my best to ignore the lead story.

The morning shift arrived and while others began to talk about
our big lead story, I sat quietly in a corner. The general opinion
was that the chief minister had 'let 'em have it.' At about one
o'clock, I peeped out of the window and saw a large limousine
with Government House number plates nosing its way towards
our office. I was now sure that I would soon be under arrest. But
it should have been the police. Why was it a Government House
limo? The vehicle came to a stop in front of our office and a
uniformed man emerged from it carrying a notebook. The
staircase was spiral so it was possible to watch the person
coming up. I stood at the top of the stairs waiting for this
mysterious visitor. He turned out to be a Government House
junior official with a receipt book, and with a sealed envelope.
He opened the book and indicated where I should sign for the
letter that he handed to me. The letter was addressed to the
editor. I signed for it quickly and was happy to see the back of
him.

I took the letter to my room but could not muster the courage
to open it. I knew it must be about the interview, but was I being
asked for an explanation, I wondered? Was I being asked who

had conducted the interview and where it had taken place? What was I going to say? The letter might even state that the publication of the fictional interview was a grave insult to the chief minister and the editor should immediately explain what had made him to do such a thing. The letter might also state that if a satisfactory reply was not provided, action would be taken against both the newspaper and its editor. In my mind, it was now a certainty that not only would I go to jail, but *Shahbaz* would be shut down. It was obvious that journalism and I were not cut out for each other.

While I was lost in these thoughts, Latif came into the room and asked about the Government House limo. Had I been invited to dinner? He took one look at me and noticed that I was on the verge of tears. 'You look worried. Is there something I can do to help? Is it something in the letter you are holding?' he asked. He took the letter from my hand and noticed that it had not even been opened. 'You should at least open it,' he said. Then he tore it open and began to laugh as soon as he had finished reading it, 'You are now in the good books of Government House. I am going to place this letter in your official record.' The letter that he passed to me said: 'The Chief Minister's House, Peshawar. The Editor, Daily *Shahbaz*, Peshawar. Dear Mr Editor, Thank you very much. Signed Mr Shamsul Haq, Private Secretary to the Chief Minister.' While I now felt a great sense of relief, it also gave me my first inkling of the intellectual level and values of our political leaders. But my worst fears had proved false and jail was one place I was not going. I asked Latif to order some fresh tea for me as I felt fully recovered from the previous night's loss of sleep.

Tanvir came at his usual hour in the evening and Latif showed him the Government House letter and the appreciation earned by the newspaper from the chief minister. Tanvir laughed and then motioned me to come into the other room. He said, 'Why were you scared? Are you happy now? They have sent you a thank you letter.' There was nothing I could say, but I thought of a recent incident involving Chaudhry Mohammad Ali, secretary

general to the government who had tried to censor one of the
Quaid-i-Azam's historic speeches about all citizens of the state
of Pakistan being equal under the constitution, regardless of their
religion, caste or creed. I found it sad that the chief minister and
his staff should be happy over an interview that they knew to be
fake. Tanvir left me on a triumphant note, offering similar 'help'
in future if I needed it. The road Tanvir had set me on was
tempting and in the next couple of weeks, we ran two more such
'interviews', one of which was broadcast by Radio Pakistan after
the 8 p.m. national news bulletin. While the newspaper's name
was not mentioned, it was said that the chief minister had made
certain statements in a press interview. Every time we carried
such 'interviews,' Mr Shamsul Haq wrote us a thank you letter.
He was Khan Qayyum Khan's special hand-picked man. When
in 1951, Khan Qayyum rigged the provincial elections, Shamsul
Haq was elected a member of the assembly and made minister
of food. When in 1953, Qayyum Khan was asked to move to the
federal cabinet, he insisted that his place should be taken by
Shamsul Haq. However, nobody, either at the centre, or in the
Frontier province, was prepared to tolerate such nepotism. Khan
Qayyum then nominated the inspector general of police of the
Frontier as his successor, which the central government agreed
to on condition that Shamsul Haq was removed from the
provincial cabinet. That was done on 9 November 1953, and
Sardar Abdul Rashid took over as chief minister.

Sardar Rashid, though from the ranks, was a man of principle
and opposed the formation of the One Unit, which abolished the
Western provinces and clubbed them together into West Pakistan.
He resigned soon after, having rejected an offer to join the
central government. Thus neither of Khan Qayyum's two hand-
picked men lasted very long. I had barely been two months at
Shahbaz when Latif told me that Malik Noor Elahi was planning
to bring out *Ehsan* from Karachi and office space had already
been secured. Negotiations were in progress with a printing press
as well. The moment he said that, I knew that Peshawar was not
for me. I would not come to much working in a place where you

were complimented by the highest for publishing fake interviews. Next time I went to Nowshehra I did not return to Peshawar. A few days later, I began to make preparations to move to Karachi. My plan was to approach Malik Noor Elahi for a job once the Karachi edition of *Ehsan* looked like appearing. I had no interest in *Shahbaz* or how it was to be run nor whether Khan Qayyum Khan's 'interviews' would continue to appear in its pages. I was ready to move to the city in which the prime minister of Pakistan lived.

9 City of Lights

I have no hesitation in saying that journalism as such is what I learnt after moving to Karachi. I can never forget the debt I owe my late friend Yusuf Siddiqi, whom I consider one of my teachers. It was from him that I learnt the art of picking out newsworthy stories, translating their relevant portions and putting a headline on the final copy. He was a past master of all three. His headlines were always memorable and they brought out the true gist of the story. They made the point in such a way that nobody could miss it. In all modesty, I may also have added a few flourishes to the art of headline writing myself, but that is something for my readers to decide.

I joined *Jang*, Karachi a few days after Prime Minister Liaquat Ali Khan's murder in Rawalpindi at a public meeting he had just begun to address. My time with the Karachi edition of *Ehsan* was brief since the Muslim League failed to hand over the money the owner was hoping it would part with. The Karachi edition lasted about six months. I also did brief stints with *Anjam* (Karachi) and a short-lived English daily called *Comment*. My colleagues at *Jang* were Majid Lahori, Syed Mohammad Taqi, Ibrahim Jalees, Athar Ali, Nazish Siddiqi, Raees Amrohi, Shafi Aqeel, Shaukat Thanvi and Abdul Waheed Khan. All these men were masters of their own realms of journalism and writing. Majid Lahori gave a new direction to the art of the light column and the witty turn of phrase. Syed Mohammad Taqi was a philosopher whose editorials bore his very own stamp. When they were critical, a less than careful reading could well induce the reader to think that they were adulatory and when they appeared to be adulatory, a closer reading would show them to be critical. I could never quite decide what was what and which was which. Ibrahim Jalees was a man with a style all of his own, but since he came from the

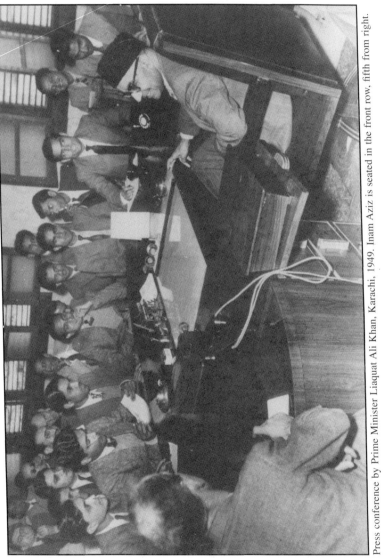

Press conference by Prime Minister Liaquat Ali Khan, Karachi, 1949. Inam Aziz is seated in the front row, fifth from right.

Rumi's mausoleum, Konya, Turkey, 1954 (R to L): Hamid Nizami (2nd), Ghani Eirabie (3rd), and Inam Aziz (4th).

Rumi's mausoleum, Konya, Turkey, 1954 (L to R): Hamid Nizami (1st), Inam Aziz (4th).

Gen. Ayub Khan in Turkey, 1954. Back row (L to R): Sultan Mohammad Khan (2nd), Inam Aziz (3rd), Hamid Nizami (2nd from right).

Iskander Mirza followed by Gen. Ayub Khan leaving Ataturk's tomb, Ankara, Turkey, 1954. Inam Aziz is on the right of the photograph holding a notebook.

Shaking hands with Zhou En-lai.

princely state of Hyderabad in India, there was a touch of the court in what he wrote. Athar Ali could ferret out news as no one else could, which he would write out with amazing speed. Nazish Siddiqi was a fine poet but he had no nose for news. As for Raees Amrohi, I do not think he had an equal when it came to the political quatrain, which was one of *Jang*'s daily features. Shaukat Thanvi was a delightful man and years earlier had won for himself a place of distinction in literature for his popular book *Swadeshi Rail*. However, as a columnist of light humour, he was never quite able to make his mark. Few know that his column was always word perfect, without revisions or overwriting or second thoughts. This came to my notice after his death when a calligraphist told me that Shaukat Thanvi's first draft was fair and final. Every word that he wrote in his neat hand was printed in the paper just as it was. The man was a perfectionist. As for the *Jang* philosophy, it could be summed up in one line: Don't take on the government of the day.

The first action taken against a newspaper in the new state of Pakistan was on 13 May 1949. The newspaper was the *Civil and Military Gazette*, which had carried a story from its New Delhi correspondent reporting that it had been decided at the Delhi meeting of the prime ministers of India and Pakistan, to divide the state of Jammu and Kashmir between the two countries. The two governments were further reported to have agreed to ditch a referendum as the means of ascertaining the will of the people of the disputed state. The report appeared on 5 May. The newspaper was shut down for a period of three months. The report had created quite a rumpus in the country and action had been demanded against the newspaper in a signed statement by leading editors, including Faiz Ahmed Faiz of *The Pakistan Times* and Maulana Chiragh Hasan Hasrat of *Imroze*. This first action proved to be the forerunner of a never-ending process against the press in Pakistan. The system of 'press advice' started, I think, when Khawaja Shahabuddin became minister of information. However, it was conducted discreetly and only the editors were approached by the government. Their staff remained unaware of the practice.

As for political vendettas, they really began with Governor-General Ghulam Mohammad, whose elevation to that office was the result of a joint operation by the army and the civil bureaucracy. It is said that even during Liaquat Ali Khan's time, and while the Quaid-i-Azam was still alive, Ghulam Mohammad, the finance minister, was conspiring to ease out a couple of ministers with the aid of Chaudhry Mohammad Ali. There was also said to be tension between the Quaid and Liaquat and the close working and personal relationship they had had before independence was no longer in evidence. It is not untrue that Ghulam Mohammad was behind the posters plastered all over Karachi, which declared that the real ruler of Pakistan was Liaquat Ali Khan and the Quaid-i-Azam's position as the constitutional head of state was purely ceremonial. These posters also extolled Liaquat's abilities through slogans. Ghulam Mohammad was believed to have taken one of these posters with him to Ziarat in Balochistan, where the Quaid lay seriously ill to prove that Liaquat was becoming an autocratic ruler. Although he was unable to meet the Quaid, he did show the poster to Miss Fatima Jinnah and must have succeeded in prejudicing her further against Liaquat, whom she did not in any case like, nor his wife, for that matter.

After the death of the Quaid-i-Azam, there was much tension in the central cabinet. It was said that Liaquat Ali Khan's murder in the Company Bagh public meeting in Rawalpindi was the result of a conspiracy by four men, and though their names have never come to light through a public inquiry, everyone believed them to have been Ghulam Mohammad, Chaudhry Mohammad Ali, Iskander Mirza and Nawab Mushtaq Ahmed Gurmani. That might explain why, after Liaquat's death, Khawaja Nazimuddin was moved from the post of governor-general and made prime minister, with Ghulam Mohammad taking his place. At that time, this clever move did not raise many eyebrows because it looked like a political balancing act between East and West Pakistan.

The national assembly, which was a leftover from the days of the Raj, was made up mostly of turncoats and enjoyed little public confidence. The Nazimuddin government had the assembly pass a deficit national budget by an overwhelming majority.

Things looked calm on the surface, but it was an illusion. I recall walking out of a cinema after viewing an English language movie and running into Mohammad Ali, a Bengali, who had just returned from England and who spoke superb English. I had first met him in the studio of a designer artist. The first thing he said when he saw me was, 'Imagine you loafing around on the streets, while such major changes are about to take place in the country!' 'What changes?' I asked. Mohammad Ali replied, 'Khawaja Nazimuddin is being eased out and his place is going to be taken by my cousin Mohammad Ali!' (He came to be known as Mohammad Ali Bogra.) I could not believe my ears. 'Who is this Mohammad Ali and what does he do?' I asked. 'He is the Pakistan ambassador in Washington,' he answered laughing, 'and he is arriving from Washington tonight. By tomorrow night, the Khawaja Nazimuddin ministry will be toast.' When I reached the *Jang* office a little later for my shift, I told Yusuf Siddiqi and a few others who were of the opinion that my 'source' must have had more than a few drinks. Nobody took what I had told them seriously.

Nothing happened until the evening of the next day. At about 11 p.m. Yusuf Siddiqi received a phone call from Colonel Majid Malik, the principal information officer, who told him to hold the final copy because he was going to issue an important statement in half an hour's time. Yusuf Siddiqi came to my desk and asked me to drop what I was doing, which was translating news into Urdu. I was the one and only sub-editor/translator in *Jang*. Then I thought of what Mohammad Ali had told me the day before and said that it seemed that Nazimuddin had been sent home. 'Don't concoct stories; your source could not be so reliable,' he admonished me. Yusuf Siddiqi then went to Colonel Malik's office and when he returned at midnight he had with him an official announcement saying exactly what Mohammad Ali had told me. It also said that the Pakistan Army chief, General Mohammad Ayub Khan, would be joining the central cabinet as minister of defence.

The same night, Khawaja Nazimuddin summoned the British high commissioner to his residence and told him that his government had dismissed Ghulam Mohammad and the decision should be conveyed to the queen (who was still the sovereign). The high commissioner was reluctant to do so and suggested that this task would be better performed by the Pakistan high commissioner in London. That was something Khawaja Nazimuddin was unable to organise because by then he was confined to the four walls of his house. In the end he accepted his dismissal without protest. Not only had Ghulam Mohammad dismissed the prime minister, he had later dissolved the constituent assembly, reducing Pakistan to how it had been under the 1935 Act. There was no martial law in the country but pre-censorship was imposed on the press. The next day, the *Jang* editor and owner, Mir Khalilur Rehman, was summoned to the governor-general's house, where he met the chief justice of the federal court, Mohammad Munir who in 1953, had presided over the court of inquiry into the anti-Qadiani riots that had rocked the Punjab. Justice Munir was in the governor-general's house because the speaker of the constituent assembly, Maulvi Tamizuddin Khan, was going to challenge the dissolution of the assembly in court.

We decided to report Justice Munir's presence in the governor-general's house in a brief item, but when it was shown to the chief censor, Commander M.H. Askari of the Pakistan Navy, who was well known to us, he came down on us like a ton of bricks. We had no idea that we were running an explosive story which could create a national upheaval. Askari held back our copy and kept asking for the source of our story. Since we were approaching our deadline, we offered to drop the story but we were not willing to tell him the source. It took half an hour of back and forth exchanges before he let us go. We also learnt that if you wanted to publish a newspaper in this country, it was not advisable to take on the censorship authorities. Like puppet journalists, we too could not be interested in what the people of the land wanted or what the future of the country should be or why the rulers were bent on committing political wrongdoing. We must only be interested in keeping our jobs and helping our owners protect their political and financial assets. The nation itself was adept at conferring high-sounding titles on its leaders. Someone would be given the title of Defender of the Ummah, while another would be named Defender of Islam. It seemed to me that our people were temperamentally attracted to kingship and royal court culture. Madame Noor Jehan indeed was a great singer, but she was given the title Queen of Melody. Mehdi Hasan was given the title Emperor of Ghazal, while a lesser singer came to be known as Prince of Song. Even stunt actors were called Stunt Kings.

The same thing happened to Ghulam Mohammad when some industrialists named him *Muhafiz-e-Millat* (Protector of the Nation). Ironically, few people in the country knew that the man had suffered a stroke and when he spoke his words were unintelligible. The only person who could understand him was his Swedish nurse, Miss Borel. She would lift him from his bed, put him in his wheelchair and push him around the lawn to get some fresh air. Ghulam Mohammad often uttered abuse, which she had learnt to decipher in order to get at the intended message. When Ghulam Mohammad was given the title of *Muhafaz-e-Millat*, the Karachi Corporation arranged a gala event with colourful tents adorning the left front of the building. I also happened to be there. The governor-general arrived wearing a black *sherwani* and a Jinnah cap, accompanied by his army, navy and air force ADCs. The army ADC was the most visible of the three because he was standing next to the governor-general holding a handkerchief. When he rose to speak, the naval ADC stepped forward to stand on the other side. When he started to speak, we who were holding our notebooks were left agog because there was not a single word that we could follow. All we heard were sounds like 'Thoo Thoo, Khoo Khoo' with the two ADCs wiping his *sherwani* because he was dribbling. And this was the man who had been declared the Protector of the Nation. None of us took any notes, because we could not. Some who went up to the stage after it was over were told that the text of the speech would be delivered to their offices. The next day, the story appeared under big headlines in all newspapers. Pakistan had begun its journey towards the dark abyss into which it would eventually fall.

During my days at *Jang* I had the opportunity to travel to several countries, the first being Turkey where I went to cover Governor-General Iskandar Mirza's visit. I met both President Celal Bayar and Prime Minister Adnan Menderes. General Ayub Khan was also on that trip, where a conversation with him left me in no doubt that he was planning to play a major role in national affairs. He had a poor opinion of the country's journalists. On this trip, some of us, including Hamid Nizami of *Nawa-i-Waqt*, paid a visit to Konya because we were not going to leave Turkey without paying our respects to Rumi who is buried there. We also offered prayers at the grand mosque. We realised for the first time that the Turkish people bore great love for Pakistan and despite government disapproval, they liked to offer regular prayers.

I also toured Lebanon, Iraq and Iran and in 1964 I had the opportunity to travel to Bandung in Indonesia where I met President Sukarno and Foreign Minister Subandrio, as well as the secretary general of the communist party. I was also in the group of journalists that went to Hong Kong and China. In China, we met Prime Minister Zhou En-Lai twice. I came back with little doubt in my mind that the Chinese leadership was clearing the path that would eventually lead to better relations with the West and the United States. Addressing one hundred delegates to the Afro-Asian Journalists Conference in the Great Hall of the People, Zhou En-Lai announced that China had no objection to Pakistan's membership of SEATO and Pakistan was welcome to remain an American ally. It was quite clear that

SEATO was essentially against China. I also went to Singapore and Bangkok, followed by a visit to Western Europe and England, which was when I established contact with the BBC and decided to move from print journalism to broadcasting, for a while at least.

In 1964, when Ayub Khan decided to run for the presidency under the constitution that he had himself devised, a number of people jumped into the field to oppose him, including General Azam Khan, who was one of Ayub's coup makers. Pakistan's first martial law was imposed by him during the time of Khawaja Nazimuddin in 1953, but he was now in the opposition camp. The opposition parties that came together under the umbrella of the Combined Opposition Parties (COP) chose Miss Fatima Jinnah as their candidate against Ayub. She was a symbol of democracy, an enemy of military rule and a supporter of the people's fundamental rights. What was more, she was the Quaid-i-Azam's sister and she was above controversy. While the opposition was united, it was widely believed that Maulana Bhashani and one of his followers, Masihur Rehman, had been given a bribe of half a million rupees to betray Miss Jinnah. I am a witness to the fact that millions were spent by Ayub Khan on this election and there was simply no limit to the amount of money his party was prepared to spend. Party fund collection was the responsibility of Finance Minister Mohammad Shoaib. Every member of the electoral college had a price. Their number was 80,000 and they were known as Basic Democrats (BD). The price fixed was said to be between Rs3,000 and Rs5,000. I saw many BD members taking an oath on the Quran to vote for Ayub and accepting envelopes containing cash. Shoaib ran this show as he ran his finance ministry. We had come to call these BD members *Bakra Patri* because they used to gather in a couple of tea houses located at the place known as *Bakra Patri* where they would haggle over their price with Ayub's agents. There was no difference between them and the sheep sold a block away. Both were on sale to the highest bidder.

By 1964, I was news editor of *Jang* and fully authorised to decide what would go into the paper, keeping within the policy limits prescribed by the owner, Mir Khalilur Rehman, who was exercising extreme care because he had applied for an import licence for two printing presses and he wanted to keep on the right side of the government. He had been told in no uncertain terms by Federal Information Secretary Altaf Gauhar that if the newspaper played ball with Ayub Khan during the election, the licences would come through. Mir Khalilur Rehman, therefore, was taking no chances. I recall a number of interesting incidents from those days. In December 1964, Mir Khalilur Rehman's younger brother, Mir Habibur Rehman, came to my office at around 10:30 at night and invited me to meet one of his friends, a dancer who lived and worked in the women's quarter of the city on Napier Road. When we entered her room, where she performed for her admirers, I just could not take my eyes off a large picture of the Quaid-i-Azam that hung on the wall. I asked her if I could buy it. 'Not for a million rupees,' she replied. I said jokingly, '*Baiji*, your price is far higher than a BD member's. Come on, bring it down some.' I even asked Habib to intercede, but she was adamant. However, she agreed that for Rs200, she was prepared to lend it to me for one hour. I borrowed the money from Habib and gave it to her. Then I rushed with the Quaid's picture to our office where I asked our staff photographer to take a picture, which he did. By the time, I returned to the bazaar to give back the picture, it was closed—there were fixed hours during which it opened—and the police were all over the place, blowing whistles. A policeman who stopped me was flabbergasted when I told him why I was there and what I was holding in my hand, a portrait of the founder of the nation. He let me return the picture to its proud, rightful owner.

This photograph of the Quaid had been taken when he had held a 'darbar' at Quetta for tribal elders. To me, that picture had a symbolic value as it showed the Quaid sitting in the chair of honour with rose petals lying at his feet. The rose was Ayub Khan's election symbol and Miss Jinnah's symbol was the lantern. I instructed the *Jang* artist the next day to put the picture on the cover for our issue of 25 December, which was the Quaid's birthday. When the newspaper's special edition hit the streets, it was an instant hit. Wherever decorative gates had been erected by the people to celebrate the day, our picture was given pride of place. People were heard saying, 'Look at it, Ayub Khan running against the Quaid's sister and there he lies at his feet.' We had touched a responsive chord. I also did some work in the campaign to oust Ayub Khan. Whenever I found an occasion to talk to BD members, I would advise them to take the government's money if they so wished, but vote for Miss Jinnah. I was sure Ayub Khan would not be able to carry Karachi and I began to say so openly. News from other parts of the country too was encouraging.

One day, Mir Khalilur Rehamn received word from Lahore that the governor, Nawab Amir Mohammad Khan of Kalabagh, wanted to see him. Though in appearance he was a most impressive looking man, the Nawab was one of the ugliest figures in the politics of Pakistan; he behaved like a master gangster or a godfather. Everyone was in awe of him, from politicians to civil servants. His entry into politics had been violent and in the end he was murdered by his own son. But let me relate what happened at that meeting in Mir Khalilur Rehman's words.

He told us, 'When I was shown into Kalabagh's presence, he received me with the utmost politeness, but when the conversation turned to elections, he twirled his moustache and said, 'Mir Sahib, it's Ayub who will win.' I immediately agreed, but Kalabagh added, 'Don't you try to fool me. There is a man who works at your newspaper who keeps yapping that Ayub is not going to win.' I began to perspire when he said that, but quickly assured him that there was no person who would dare say such a thing. I was glad when I left the governor.' Then Mir Khalilur Rehman said to me, 'This thing has now come to the Nawab's personal notice and you are in danger.' But as far as I was concerned, I was proud of the fact that my views had reached

the very top echelon of state power. The next thing Mir did was
to announce that 'censorship' would come into effect at *Jang* and
he would personally look at all stories and headlines before they
were passed on to calligraphers. He also ordered that from now
on all speeches by Ayub Khan would be published under a six-
column headline. For Miss Jinnah, the headline should be no
more than three-columns. This policy remained in effect till the
elections were over. Ayub Khan won but he suffered a humiliating
defeat in Karachi. The ruling party extracted revenge by going
on a rampage in the city's Lalukhet and Nazimabad areas.
However, the election, despite Ayub's victory, left no doubt in
our minds that his downfall had begun.

After Ayub's election, corruption became the order of the day.
BD members were now like the stock exchange, their rate
fluctuating every day as people ran for various electoral posts
that had been created under Ayub's constitutional dispensation.
There were hard-fought campaigns with dozens of hopefuls
running for local and other councils. Every vote was for sale and
went to the highest bidder. Pakistan's biggest industrialist, Seth
Ahmed Dawood, was very much a part of this political carnival
because his younger brother, Siddiq Dawood, was running for
Karachi's Ward No. 8. Seth Dawood was close to the regime and
had helped establish the National Press Trust, which was taken
over by the government. The Trust had taken over Progressive
Papers Ltd., the independent, left wing chain of newspapers from
Lahore established by Mian Iftikharuddin. *The Pakistan Times*,
the group's flagship paper, had been founded by the Quaid-i-
Azam himself. Seth Dawood's industrialist friends had
contributed millions to the ruling party's coffers. Siddiq Dawood
was pitched against the general secretary of the Karachi Muslim
League, a small-time lawyer who did not have the money to buy
votes. What I did was to place a small item in a single-column
box on the eve of the election, that said, 'When the market
closed last night, the price for a vote in Ward No. 8 was
Rs20,000, as against Rs5,000 in other wards.' The story did not
say who the candidates in Ward No. 8 were.

When the paper appeared next morning, it caused a commotion. The BD members of Ward No. 8 all marched into Seth Dawood's residence with a copy of the day's *Jang* shouting, 'Seth, the rate is Rs20,000 so pay us the going price.' Seth Dawood was furious and got on the phone to Mir Khalilur Rehman, giving him hell. He also announced that he was an honest man and he was not going to pay a penny to anyone. The election, he declared, was an honest exercise. He also asked Mir Khalilur Rehman to bring out a special supplement contradicting the story. When I arrived at the office at noon, I was summoned by Mir Sahib. There was a smile on his face and he looked amused. 'You killed Seth Dawood,' he told me, then added, 'since morning he has been swearing at me. He must have called me twenty or twenty-five times.' When the result was announced in the evening, Siddiq Dawood had lost. Only his friends and relations had voted for him. He became a senator in the handpicked house under the military regime of General Ziaul Haq.

10 Colonel Majid Malik

There was unrest in the country after the military revolution of General Ayub Khan and Iskander Mirza. A few months later, there was a military coup in Iraq during which King Faisal and Prime Minister Nuri al Saeed were killed, along with several of their companions. The Iraqi revolution was a violent reaction to the backing by the United States and Britain of the old regime. In Pakistan, the changeover was peaceful with not a drop of blood shed. It is true that some arrests were made on the night of 8 October 1958 but there was no violence nor was there any resistance.

I recall that on the evening of 7 October, a man walked into my office after delivering a letter he wanted published in the 'letters to the editor' column. 'Sir, something is up in the country. Can you guess what is on the cards?' he asked, taking a chair. I told him, 'I don't think anything is up. The Awami League ministers have resigned from Prime Minister Malik Feroze Khan Noon's cabinet, so we can expect a certain amount of political jousting.' He did not agree. According to him, the army was going to intervene and take over. My reaction, the recent Iraqi revolution notwithstanding, was that such a turn of events seemed unlikely in Pakistan. I had said that because I believed that by training and temperament, the Pakistan army was disinterested in politics and would not want to intervene in such a direct way. I had lost sight of the fact that General Ayub Khan had been a player in national politics for so long and after the 'constitutional revolution' of Ghulam Mohammad, he had earned the office of minister of defence. My visitor said, 'You are a journalist and perhaps your estimate is correct, but in two or three places in Karachi I have seen things that lead me to believe what I have told you. Were you to see them too, I am sure you would come to the same conclusion.' He told me that there were military details posted in front of the main telegraph office and Radio Pakistan.

I was startled by his report but before I could say anything, he offered to drive me to the two places so that I could see for myself. It sounded like a good scoop, if what he was saying was true, and so I accepted his offer. We went first to Radio Pakistan and found a heavy military presence there. The soldiers were making a bunker with sand bags. When I tried to enter through the main gate to get to the reception, I was stopped by an army officer who told me that the reception was not open and that I should come another time. I knew that the Radio Pakistan reception office remained open at all hours, so its closure was significant. From Radio Pakistan we drove to the telegraph office, where we found hundreds of soldiers erecting bunkers. Introducing myself as a journalist, I tried to go in but was blocked by the men on duty. My visitor was right; something was very seriously wrong.

A few days earlier, I had been at a dinner Mir Khalilur Rehman had held at his residence for former prime minister Huseyn Shaheed Suhrawardy, Sheikh Mujibur Rahman and some other Awami League leaders. It occurred to me now that if the army was really planning to move in, the Awami League leaders must have known. But they had not appeared to. Suhrawardy had set out on a tour of the country in preparation for the expected national elections, but Sheikh Mujibur Rahman and his friends were still at the MNA House. So with that gentleman in tow, I arrived at the MNA House where I found Sheikh Mujibur Rahman and Mahmoodul Haq Usmani, general secretary of Maulana Bhashani's party, engaged in a lively discussion on a coming bye-election in East Pakistan. Sheikh Mujib was predicting that the Awami League would not only win, but do so with a margin big enough to have the Bhashani party rival lose his deposit. They were even prepared to place wagers on the outcome.

I greeted Sheikh Mujib and asked him to spare a few minutes for me to discuss a private matter. He was not amused. 'Look,

here we are ready to place our bets on the outcome of the bye-
election and you barge in wanting to know God knows what.'
But he did get up and come out with me onto the veranda. I
asked him if he anticipated army intervention in the country. He
laughed and said, 'Let it happen, we don't care.' Then he added
after a pause, 'Where does this army thing come from?' I told
him about the army contingents at Radio Pakistan and the
telegraph office. 'Don't go,' he said, 'let me check with a
minister. This fellow Iskander Mirza has been trying to frighten
us with the bugbear of the army for the last few days. Maybe he
has done something.' He first phoned a central minister and
found the line disconnected. Then he phoned the prime minister's
residence, where the phone was picked up by a man who
sounded like an army officer. He told Mujib that the prime
minister could not take the call at this time. After he put the
phone down, he told me that I was probably right. Then he asked
me to leave because he wanted to get in touch with his leader
Suhrawardy so that they could plan for the future.

As we drove out of the MNA House, I asked my companion
to go towards the president's house but we were unable to get
through as army trucks were busy disgorging soldiers who were
cordoning off the president's residence. I estimated their number
at between four and five hundred. In the end we were able to
drive past the president's house, but we were not permitted to
stop. I returned to the office and put a halt to all ongoing work
as I wanted to be ready to put the big story in when it broke.
Some copy, however, I handed over to my colleague Nazish
Hyderi, asking him to translate it into Urdu. I next set out for
the Press Information Department (PID) because it was obvious
that if something was happening, the principal information
officer (PIO), Colonel Majid Malik, would know. He was a quiet,
dignified gentleman and a close friend of Faiz Ahmed Faiz, both
of them having served in the war publicity department of the
Government of India during the Second World War and become
colonels; while Faiz had got rid of his title, it remained a part of
his friend's name. I knocked at his door and entered. There he

was with a cup of tea in one hand and the telephone in the other. When he saw me, he put the cup down, placed his hand on the phone to block the sound and said, 'Shut the door securely and take a seat.' Then he began to listen to whoever was on the other side, while he took notes on a pad.

After he put the phone down, he gave me a most unpleasant look and asked, 'What brings you here at this hour?' I looked at the clock on his wall. It said 11 o'clock. I told him that I was passing by and had dropped in to say hello. I also felt that an important announcement was in the offing, so maybe I could pick it up. 'What important announcement?' he asked. 'The one that is going to be issued from the Presidency,' I replied with a smile. 'Who told you?' he asked me. 'It is you who should tell me something, but if nothing is up, I will be on my way,' I answered. This brought a smile to his lips and he rang for the peon and asked him to get me a cup of tea. Then he turned to me, 'It is a long announcement and it is being typed. You will get a copy.' I asked if it related to army intervention. He wanted to know where I had picked that up. I told him, 'I did not hear it; I saw it.' He told me that until the complete announcement was ready, I should stay right where I was. He added, 'But what has happened is not good. It is now in the hands of God.' Then he said, 'Which cigarette do you smoke? You can give me one.' I pulled out a packet from my pocket and commented, 'But you have quit, why do you want one?' He said, 'Say no more. I quit six weeks ago but one cigarette can do no harm. I can stop smoking whenever I want to.'

So I sat there waiting, trying to finish my tea. His secretary quietly entered from a side door and told his boss that copies of the announcement were ready and asked if he should bring them in. The Colonel looked at me and said, 'Yes, get me ten or twelve copies.' Then he began to phone newspaper offices, starting with *Dawn*. When the copies arrived he slipped me one. It was five minutes past midnight. He said, 'It seems reporters from other newspapers are busy gambling in the press club. If I can't get any of them, I will call the editors. But you should go back to work.' I rushed out of his room and was lucky to find a rickshaw. By the time I arrived at the office, I knew (thanks to overhead streetlights) the gist of the announcement, which was that Iskander Mirza had imposed martial law and the assemblies were abolished.

Mir Khalilur Rehman was there, having come in after learning that I was not on duty. 'Where were you today?' he asked. I replied, 'Mir Sahib, I can't waste time talking. Do you know martial law has been declared in the country? I have work to do. I have already alerted the calligraphers.' Then I got down to translating the martial law announcement. Iskander Mirza had dismissed the central and provincial governments and disbanded the assemblies. The 1956 constitution had also been suspended, the same constitution under which he had been made president. General Ayub Khan had been appointed chief martial law administrator, which meant that he was now the most powerful man in Pakistan. And strangely, since there was no constitution, Mirza was still the president. Censorship had been reimposed all over Pakistan.

This was the second of Pakistan's political tragedies, the first being Ghulam Mohammad's dismissal of Khawaja Nazimuddin. Both men had acted in pursuit of their personal ambitions. I got the edition ready and it was just how I wanted it. What space there was left after the big lead story was taken up by reaction stories, both local and non-local. After the paper was put to bed, Mir Khalilur Rehman and I began to chat. He was of the view that since censorship was now in operation, we would have to be very careful.

The next two weeks were eventful. General Ayub addressed large meetings in Lahore and Dhaka and then returned to Karachi. Iskander Mirza restored some articles of the constitution. A new cabinet was being chosen and a story was circulated by the Associated Press of Pakistan that Ayub would be the new prime minister. The oath-taking ceremony was set for 8 p.m. that evening, the story said. The initial announcement did not contain any names. I decided to go to Colonel Majid Malik's office because I also wanted pictures of the new ministers, which I was sure he would have.

I had barely entered his room, when he said to me, 'I am sure the rickshaw that brought you here is gone. Well, what you have come for, you will in any case get. Meanwhile, I suggest you come with me to the prime minister's house. I will drop you at your office on my way back.' We got into his car and I asked him if he had the list of the new ministers with him. He said I could have it when we returned, but they were mostly army people with a smattering of civilians, including a young man by the name of Zulfikar Ali Bhutto, son of the famous Sindhi landlord, Sir Shah Nawaz Khan Bhutto. He also promised to give me the new ministers' photographs. When our car reached the front gate of the prime minister house, we found it guarded by armed soldiers. After the colonel introduced himself and told them that he had been summoned by the prime minister, the gates were opened. As the car came to a stop under the porch, it was ringed by soldiers. We stepped out and walked into a waiting room, while a soldier jumped in, next to our driver. Soldiers of different ranks were going in and out of the house, their shoes click-clacking on the polished floor.

My mind went back to a press conference I had attended here, held by Khawaja Nazimuddin after the assembly's approval of the national budget. Speaking about the food shortage in the country, he had said that the US government had agreed to supply wheat to Pakistan. His government was overthrown a few days later by Ghulam Mohammad. But here we were, the principal information officer of the government of Pakistan and I, just sitting there waiting. Two hours passed. I was desperate to get back to the office and rose from my sofa, but was stopped by an army brigadier who told me to sit down. Colonel Majid Malik told the officer that he was the principal information officer and I was a journalist, who was keen to return to his office. The brigadier replied that he did not want to get into a discussion, but the two of us should remain sitting where we had been asked to sit. He added that tea had been ordered for us. It was now 11 p.m. I asked the brigadier to let me call my office so that I could tell them I was going to be late. For some reason, he agreed. He told me that while I could make the call, I could only tell my office that I was going to be late. On no account, should I say where I was calling from.

There was a phone in the corridor. I gave the brigadier my office number and he had me connected. I told the senior sub-editor, Nasir Mahmood, that I was going to be late and the final copy should be held back. I was told—and I had expected it—that Mir sahib was waiting for me in my room. The next thing I knew, the phone had been snatched from my hand. I returned to my sofa and when I was about to whisper something to Colonel Majid Malik, the brigadier stopped me. 'Keep quiet. You are not permitted to talk to one another.' Colonel Majid Malik asked if he was under arrest. 'For the time being, that is what you should think,' answered the brigadier. By then tea had arrived with some sandwiches. A small table was placed next to our sofa by a colonel upon which the tray was placed.

At 12:45, an officer, probably Captain Abdul Rahman Siddiqi, came out of the big lounge, saluted Colonel Majid Malik and told him that the chief wanted to see him. I was sure that by now there was a riot at the *Jang* office. I could only hope that they were waiting for the final copy and had not started printing the paper. It was clear that something big was in the offing. Colonel Majid Malik returned after fifteen minutes and indicated to me with his finger that it was time to go. We stepped out and a few minutes later our car arrived to take us away. I asked to be dropped first, to which he said, 'Are you not interested in another coup story?' 'And what is it this time?' I asked, rather shocked. 'Wait till we get to my office, but alert your people to remain prepared for a big story,' he replied.

Once in his office, he handed over to his secretary a sheet of paper he had brought with him, while I called my office and was told that the final copy was about to go in and the paper was being put to bed. I had a word with Mir Khalilur Rehman and told him to wait for me because something really big had happened. 'I am on my way to you,' he said. By the time he arrived, I had learnt that Iskander Mirza had been overthrown and flown out of the country. All power now rested in General Ayub Khan's hands. A formal press note was soon placed in our hands and we rushed back to the office and put the big story in under large headlines. We were still in the newsroom when Mir Khalilur Rehman's driver, Bashir, ran in, saying that Colonel Majid Malik was waiting outside in his car for both of us. It was 2 a.m. when we came out. He was indeed waiting in his car and proposed that we drive to Clifton because he wanted to relieve his mental tension. That sounded like a good idea and we got into his car. We learnt that after the cabinet had been sworn in, the military command council had met and decided that Iskander Mirza was to be exiled since he was trying to cause divisions in the cabinet. The army, it had been decided, should take direct control of the country.

Ayub Khan was not present in that session because, after being sworn in, he had stayed back at the presidency. He learnt of what had happened after he arrived at the prime minister's house. He was considered a Mirza loyalist but power knows no kinship. He agreed with the generals and three of them—K.M. Sheikh, Azam Khan, and W.A. Burki—were sent to inform Mirza of the decision. He was ordered to pack and go with them. When he tried to resist, General Azam Khan pulled out his service revolver and warned him that if he tried any delaying tactics, his revolver would not remain silent much longer. When Begum Naheed Mirza learnt of the situation, she screamed a good deal but then picked up her jewels and gold ornaments and said she was ready to go. On her last birthday, she had been presented with a diamond necklace by a Karachi businessman, which she could not find in the rush of events. The couple were put on a small aircraft and flown to Quetta. Another plane flew the two to Iran, from where they were taken to London. Colonel Majid Malik told us that before we put anything based on what he had told us in the paper, we should check it with him. He added that he had only shared things with us because we, like him, had had a pretty rough evening. I can still see the three of us sitting on a bench not far from the beach with a pleasant cool breeze blowing in our faces.

Colonel Majid Malik, who never wore his colonel's uniform after the establishment of Pakistan, was a quiet and dignified man, who became a good friend of mine. Our friendship lasted for years. Once, when there were warrants out for the arrest of Faiz Ahmed Faiz and nobody quite knew where he was, he was at Colonel Majid Malik's home. He told me that he had asked Faiz several times to offer himself up for arrest, to which his answer was always, 'But let me rest my feet for a few days.' After the Rawalpindi Conspiracy Case, for which Faiz suffered several years' imprisonment, whenever fresh warrants were issued for his arrest, the police did not try very hard to pick him up; they did just the bare minimum. Faiz was one of the 'usual suspects', along with other left-wingers and communists. My friend Anis Hashmi was once a member of the Communist Party of Pakistan but even after he had given up politics and taken a job with a printing firm, whenever a round of arrests got underway, he was invariably taken in. He would spend a few days in jail and then be released on orders from a higher authority. He once told us that in every police station a permanent list of 'suspects' is maintained and whenever orders are issued to make arrests, those listed, from Karachi to Quetta to Landi Kotal, are promptly picked up and taken in.

11 Ayub's Martial Law

My direct brush with martial law took place in November 1958. I arrived home from work at about 3 a.m., and had hardly laid myself down, when my wife shook me awake and said, 'Get up, there are soldiers at the door and they want to see you.' My reply was, 'I am terribly sleepy; tell them to come another time.' Little suspecting why they were there, she went to the door and told them that her husband had just come home from work, was already sound asleep and would they please come at a more convenient time. The reply came in the form of a sharp military directive, 'Wake him up quickly. We are from martial law headquarters and we have come to take him.' Nervously, she ran back to me and implored, 'For God's sake, get up and find out what calamity is going to befall us.' I got up, feeling drowsy, and opened the door. An army jamadar told me that I was under arrest and I had been summoned to martial law headquarters by his major. I was in my night clothes and asked him if he would wait a little, while I washed my face and changed. 'You'll have to come with us as you are,' I was told. 'Fine,' I replied, 'I'll go as I am but show me my arrest warrant first.' 'Don't you know the country is under martial law and we need no warrants?' the captain leading the party said sharply. I told him to wait while I washed and changed and banged the door shut.

By this time everybody in the house had woken up, including my mother and my sister-in-law, who looked very nervous. While I was in the bathroom, they whispered to one another, wondering what I had done to be summoned at that hour. My brother was saying that being a journalist these days was crime enough, but who could say what I might have done? When I was about to step out of the house, they all asked me what crime I had committed to be taken in by the army like this. Had I known what I had done, I would have told them, so all I said was, 'Rest

easy, I will deal with it, whatever it is.' Then I told my wife that
if I did not return home by the evening, she should inform
Jang.

When I opened the door to go with my visitors, their anger
was apparent. One of them, a non-commissioned officer, swore
at me and said that had I not come out in another few minutes,
they would have smashed down the door. I paid no attention to
what he said but told him, 'Look, you people are here to take
me to your martial law headquarters, so here I am. I hope we
can all remain calm and civilised.' We lived in an apartment in
the Empress Market area of the city. When we came out onto the
road, I looked up and saw my entire family looking down at us
from the balcony. There were four or five jeeps parked outside
our building with soldiers brandishing automatic weapons and
standing guard as if the entire neighbourhood was under siege.
I could not help but think that I must have done something pretty
awful, which was why I was being taken from my residence
under such heavy protection at this ungodly hour.

I was put in the back seat of one of the jeeps, with one soldier
to my left and another to my right. The few local people who
were up at that hour were standing well back, watching what to
them was a show. There were a couple of men on their cycles,
their lunch boxes slung over their handle-bars, on their way to
start the early morning shift. A cigarette vendor's shop was also
open with a couple of men hanging around in front of it,
watching my departure in military custody. I could not get my
brother's words out of my head. 'You must have done something
to be picked up by the army like this.' I felt humiliated and kept
wondering what the people watching me being taken away were
thinking.

The jeep came to a stop at martial law headquarters. The non-
commissioned officer asked me brusquely to get down and come
with him, which I did. I was taken to a room where a major was
sitting behind a desk. 'I am Major Sharif, please sit in that chair
to my left, while I deal with these people whom you can see
sitting in front of me,' he said to me. When I tried to protest at

the manner in which I had been taken from my house and brought there, he stopped me short. 'I will listen to that later, let me first finish my work.' The desk behind which he sat was huge, perhaps removed from a school headmaster's office by his minions. His room was large and there was a door facing him that opened into an even larger room.

At least a hundred watches were lying on Major Sharif's desk. The man who sat facing him appeared to have been brought in for smuggling watches. He was trying to tell the major that he ran a watch shop and all those watches were his personal property. He just could not understand why he was being accused of being a smuggler. Major Sharif was not convinced because his men had found no documents at the shop that could prove that the watches had been legitimately purchased. 'We are even prepared to give you time to get that documentation, but we know that you are working with a gang of smugglers, so the best thing for you would be to cooperate with martial law authorities and provide us with the full particulars of the smugglers. You know very well how wide our powers are,' Major Sharif said to the poor watch seller. He also told him that not only would all his watches be confiscated but his house would be raided and whatever of value was found there, would be confiscated as well. With every new threat, the man's face lost more colour and in the end it seemed as if had no more blood left in his body. He would sometimes look at Major Sharif, sometimes at me. I wondered who he thought I was. Perhaps another smuggler that the martial law authorities had nabbed. This back and forth exchange of accusation and denial continued until one in the afternoon. All this while, I remained sitting in my chair smoking Gold Flake cigarettes. The watch seller kept repeating the same thing over and over again, namely that he was innocent and he should be let off, but this had no effect on Major Sharif.

A soldier now entered the room, removed all the watches from the table, put them in a small box and ceremoniously laid out Major Sharif's lunch before him, consisting of chicken curry, *shami kebabs*, *tikkas* and freshly-baked bread. The man being accused of smuggling watches was shunted out to another room, while I sat there, by now feeling totally exhausted and still wondering what I had done and why I had been brought here. Major Sharif being the rude, arrogant and selfish man he was, ate his hearty meal with relish without the least care in the world. Of course, he did not ask me to join him. I consoled myself with the thought that I was, after all, an accused and I should not expect to be invited to lunch by the man who was going to decide my fate. The major ate like an animal. He polished off everything in front of him, as if he had never eaten such food before and was not going to have another opportunity in future. There was ice water in a jug on the table. I was parched and asked for a glass of cold water. Major Sharif shouted for his orderly and when the man appeared, asked him to get a glass of water for 'the editor sahib'. The water I was brought was so warm that it was hard for me to swallow it. It could have been used to make tea. I put the glass down without drinking and looked at the jug lying in front of me with its ice-cold water and the tiny drops that had formed on the outside.

Major Sharif finished his lunch, smiled and asked me to take the chair in front of him for 'a little conversation'. When I tried to protest at my treatment at the hands of his men, he ignored me. He then pulled out the day's issue of *Jang* from one of his desk drawers. I noticed that a red circle had been drawn around one story. 'So that's it,' I said to myself, feeling relieved now that I knew what my 'crime' was. 'Are you objecting to one of our stories?' I asked. 'It is not merely the story I am objecting to; a martial law regulation has been violated,' he replied. 'Let me take a look. I want to see what it is that you find objectionable,' I told him. The story circled in red had been filed by our Mirpur Khas correspondent with his by-line. It was I who, a few months earlier, had started giving our correspondents by-lines to credit them with the stories they had dug out, as well as to distinguish our own correspondents' reports from the news agency material that we printed. Our correspondent had attended a reception the evening before where the local martial law administrator had declared bluntly that investigations were in progress into the past deeds of politicians and those found involved in corruption or other crimes would be arrested. He had also said that special martial law courts were going to be set up to deal with such people.

I felt relieved because I was not being accused of smuggling or of a moral offence. When I tried to ask the major a question, he called for his havaldar. When the man appeared, he said to him, 'Read out to this editor sahib the martial law regulation that applies to him so that I can begin my questioning.' The man, who had emerged from an adjoining room where Major Sharif's staff obviously sat, began to read out the regulation that I was supposed to have violated. It said that anyone who knowingly or unknowingly mis-states a fact before a martial law official or tries to mis-state a fact in an attempt to mislead him or to block an ongoing investigation would be liable to life imprisonment and even death. Once the havaldar was done, I said to the major, 'You are welcome to hang me but at least let me know what my crime is and please do so in some detail.' Major Sharif replied, 'You seem to be a man with a temper. You first have to answer my questions and only then can matters proceed any further.'

This is how our conversation proceeded:

Major Sharif: Where did you get this story?
Inam Aziz: Read the story, it says it was filed from Mirpur Khas.
Major Sharif: Who sent you this story?
Inam Aziz: The story answers that too. It bears the name of the correspondent.
Major Sharif: How does this correspondent send you his stories?
Inam Aziz: By telegram, sometimes by phone.
Major Sharif: How did you receive this one?
Inam Aziz: By telegram.
Major Sharif: How did your correspondent come upon this story?

Inam Aziz: The story makes that clear as well; from the local
martial law administrator.
Major Sharif: Why did he meet the administrator?
Inam Aziz: The administrator invited him to tea to impress him
with all the work he is doing.
Major Sharif: Do you have any other details related to this
story?
Inam Aziz: Not so far, but if by the end of the day the chief
martial law administrator, General Ayub Khan, makes a fresh
announcement, you will find it carried in tomorrow's newspaper.
And if you really are a *Jang* reader, do not forget to follow our
Tarzan serial.

The last bit was intended to highlight his ignorance, but it had
no effect on him. 'Fine,' he said. 'Write down your statement.'
Since my 'crime' had already been made clear to me, I asked for
pen and paper. The major gave me both, then added, 'I will
dictate your statement; you will merely sign it.' I tried to argue
with him, but in vain. 'All right,' I said, 'dictate.' My statement
began with my name, my father's name, my place of residence
etc. I wrote down what he dictated, signed it and gave it to him.
After reading it, he said, 'You can go; your job is done.' But I
was not going to go that easily. I went into a harangue about the
way I had been abducted from my house and then made to wait
for hours without food or drink. If all they wanted was this
information, someone could easily have dropped in at our office
and got what he needed in no more than a minute. Major Sharif
made no answer. 'Look, you forcibly lifted me from my house,
now at least have me dropped there,' I said. Major Sharif smiled,
'Don't try to be smart; we have no transport arrangements.'
Angrily, I stormed out of martial law headquarters, hailed a
rickshaw and returned home to the great joy and relief of
everybody.

Major Sharif was also head of a military court where several
student leaders, including Fatehyab Ali Khan, were tried for
defying the government. I had run stories about these trials that

showed how stupid and superficial our new rulers were. Running these stories also gave me the opportunity to get even with those who had humiliated me. It was our custom that after knocking off work, three or four of us would drop into an all-night Iranian café in Karachi Saddar for a cup of tea. One night, as a friend and I came to the Saddar area, I suggested that we should go to a better place instead of the same Iranian café, which we did. When our tea arrived, I felt that a person sitting across the table from us had been staring at me, as if trying to recall who I was. I could not place him. Then he walked across to our table and told me that he had seen me somewhere before. When I looked at him more carefully, I realised that it was Major Sharif. He shook hands with me with much warmth and insisted that we be his guests. When I asked him what he was doing, he replied that he had left the army and was now running a factory. He said he was going to be frank. He had only been assigned to martial law court duties for twenty-two days and in those three weeks and a day, he had made so much money that he did not wish to serve in the army any more. He asked me to pray for the success of his factory.

12 BBC Days

I left *Jang* to join the BBC in London, where I spent five eventful years. When I look back on the circumstances that took me away from my homeland, certain events spring up in my memory, among them my two close brushes with death.

The first incident happened in 1964. I was on a plane I had boarded in Jakarta on my way to Hong Kong. I had been in Indonesia to attend an Afro-Asian journalists' conference that President Ahmed Sukarno had inaugurated. Four of us, all Pakistani journalists, were busy playing cards, which was one way of whiling away time on that long flight, when fifteen minutes into the flight, I noticed from my window seat that one of the engines was on fire. While my friends were telling me to take my turn, I was trying to work out the mystery of the flaming engine. Finally, I pressed the call button to summon a stewardess. There were three of them on duty in our cabin and they were running around nervously. When one of them answered my call, I pointed at the flaming engine and asked her if she knew what was going on. She put her finger to her lips and asked me to keep quiet and all would be well. My three friends, who had not noticed that the engine was on fire, had, however noticed the girl putting her finger on her lips. 'What was she saying?' they asked. I directed their attention to the burning engine and said, 'That's why she wants us to be quiet.'

Their faces turned white with fear as soon as they saw what was happening. The cards were set aside and they all began to pray. The plane kept flying as if nothing was wrong. After about fifteen minutes, the captain announced that because of a minor technical malfunction, we were returning to Jakarta and we should all listen carefully to the crew's instructions and follow them strictly. No one should try to leave his seat. When the plane landed at Jakarta, many fire trucks and ambulances were waiting

Interviewing former chief justice of the Sindh High Court, Z.H. Lari, for the BBC.

Interviewing a RAF Harrier pilot for the BBC.

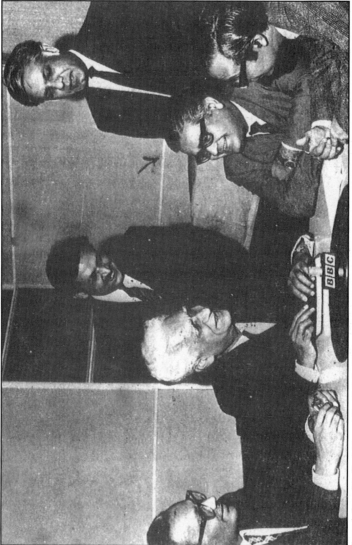

Seated (L to R): Taqi Ahmed Syed, Z.A. Bokhari, Inam Aziz.
Standing (L to R): Rashid Ashraf, Athar Ali.

Interviewing Tariq Aziz, captain of the Pakistan hockey team sent to the Olympics, for the BBC.

Interviewing Pakistani wrestlers, Bholu and Akram, at Heathrow airport, London for the BBC.

Interviewing noted jurist and litterateur, Ijaz Batalvi for the BBC.

for it on the runway. We disembarked as instructed by the crew and the fire was put out with foam. When we entered the passenger lounge, dozens of Indonesians who had come to see us off were still there, some of whom embraced us, saying that they had not been sure that any of us would survive. One journalist told us that he had been driving back home when he heard on the radio about the fire on the plane and had turned back because he was sure it must be the one we had boarded. The plane had emptied its tanks over the sea before it had landed. After a few hours, we were put on another aircraft, though some people, including a couple of my companions, were reluctant to travel by an Indonesian airline, proposing that we should take a later KLM flight. I took the flight that was offered, assuring myself that if my death was ordained, it would not matter whether the plane I had taken was Indonesian or Dutch.

The second time I escaped death was a year later. PIA announced its inaugural flight to Cairo. I was among the journalists who had been invited to join it. I began making preparations for the trip. Some time earlier I had sent off my application for a contract with the BBC because I had been told by some sources that my name had been placed on a 'black list' by the government, since I was viewed as an 'enemy' of the Ayub regime. I was even told that I could be arrested at any time on some trumped up charge. If that turned out to be true and I was jailed, once I came out, there would be no job waiting for me. Under the circumstances, I had felt the best thing for me would be to go abroad. I should mention that I was president of the Karachi Union of Journalists.

Two days before the departure for Cairo, as I sat working at my desk, a young man walked in, introducing himself as head of the press section at the German embassy. He told me that he had come with an invitation from the president of the West German journalists' union inviting me, in my capacity as president of the Karachi Union of Journalists, to pay a three-week visit to Bundesrepublik Deutschland (the Federal Republic of Germany). He told me that the invitation was being given to

me direct and not through the government so that there could be
no possibility of any impediments being placed in my way. Had
the invitation been sent through the government, it might have
preferred someone else or it might have led to other difficulties.
Since the German government was keen that I should accept the
invitation, I was told it was now up to me when to leave. The
German diplomat asked me to give the embassy some notice so
that arrangements could be put in place.

I was not sure whether I should go to Cairo. If I kept travelling
at this rate, it would most certainly affect my work at the
newspaper. After all, I was the news editor, a key position in any
daily publication. I phoned our owner and chief editor, Mir
Khalilur Rehman, asking him to go to Cairo in my place, but he
replied that he was not interested and I could pick out anyone
from the newsroom to go instead; when the fellow returned from
Cairo, I could go to Germany. The only person I could think of
from among the newsroom staff was Nasir Mahmood. He was
busy translating a story when I sent for him. 'Would you like to
go to Cairo?' I asked. 'What do you mean?' he said, 'I thought
you were going to Cairo.' I told him there had been a change of
plan and if he was interested, he could go in my place. He told
me he did not even have a passport, but when I assured him that
it was a detail that could be taken care of, he said he would go.
All we had was one day.

Next morning, we arrived at the office of the principal
information officer, Mr Douglas, to get a no objection certificate.
Nasir Mahmood was about thirty, tall and slim, a good translator
with a keen eye for news. He was good at thinking up headlines
which were always short and pithy. His weakness was *paan*
(betel), one of which would always be in his mouth. He had
married the previous year and lived in his father's house in Laloo
Khet, and had just become the father of a baby girl. He had never
been out of Pakistan and the sudden intimation that he was going
abroad had made him so nervous that he could not concentrate
on his work. I told him to take the rest of the day off, go home
and pack. I also phoned Salahuddin Siddiqui, the PIA public

relations officer, informing him of the change. He sounded
disappointed because he did not know Nasir Mahmood well. He
had drawn up sightseeing plans in Cairo and he would have
preferred it if those on the trip were people he knew. He was, of
course, going to be on the flight himself. When I inquired from
Mr Douglas if the no objection certificate that every journalist
needed to go abroad was ready, he replied that it had to be issued
from Islamabad. When I protested that this made no sense
because all we had was one day and the certificate would not
arrive for at least a week, he phoned Islamabad, obtained the
required clearance and also gave us a letter in the name of the
passport officer asking him to give Nasir Mahmood a passport
that very day. He also countersigned the passport application,
being the nice and helpful officer he was. I should add that he
was a great nationalist and a patriot.

By four in the afternoon, we had the passport. It took quite
some time to obtain foreign exchange authorisation from the
State Bank. The only difficulty now was how and where to get
travellers' cheques because all the banks were closed. When we
asked around, we were told that a branch of the Habib Bank was
open around nine in the evening at the PIA office, from where
we could pick up the cheques with our State Bank authorisation.
In those days, the government maintained strict control over
foreign exchange. In the end, it all worked out and after sending
Nasir home with his new passport and travellers' cheques, I
returned to the office a very tired man. I would never forget the
next day because at around three in the afternoon, news came
that the PIA Cairo-bound flight had crashed on landing. There
were said to be some survivors, but who they were we did not
know. All that we could do was to pray that Nasir Mahmood
would be one of them. That was not to be. The list of passengers
who had perished included his name.

There were five or six survivors, including my friend
Salahuddin Siddiqi, PIA public relations officer in Karachi. He
later moved to London and settled there. A close friend, Tufail
Ahmed Jamali was also meant to be on that ill-fated plane. When

he arrived at Karachi airport, PIA checked him in but when he went to the immigration counter, the officer on duty found that his passport had expired. He was told to get it renewed or have a new one issued. Very disappointed, he returned home. Had his passport been valid, he would have died in that crash, along with his wife, whose passport apparently was in order.

A month later, when I was ready to set out for West Germany, the British embassy press counsellor, Nicholas Leadbeater, came to call on me at the office and asked if I would like to visit London at the end of my German visit. If I was willing to go, the British Central Office of Information would like to host me for a fortnight during which I would be shown around the country. He left an air ticket with me. I would have gone to London anyway because my parents and two of my brothers were already living there.

After a very interesting trip to West Germany, I arrived in London from Frankfurt and one of my early ports of call was the BBC, where I met Mark A. Dodd of the Eastern Service. My application had already landed on his desk. The first thing he asked me was, 'When can you start?' This question was quite unexpected but when I realised that I was indeed being offered a job, I replied that I would be ready to come after all necessary formalities had been completed by the BBC. I was still in London when news of border clashes between India and Pakistan began to pour in. I was certain that a war was in the offing and, therefore, I cut short my stay and flew back to Karachi. I had hardly landed when fighting broke out in Kashmir.

On 6 September 1965, India invaded Pakistan across the international border in a bid to overrun Lahore. The coverage of the war in our newspaper remains a matter of pride for all those who were involved in the effort. The war between the two countries was not only being fought on land, sea and air, but also between the media. *Jang's* contribution to the war effort was exemplary. Ironically, a war in which the entire nation stood as one, ultimately led to the separation of East Pakistan, which felt utterly unprotected for the seventeen days during which the war raged. The war lent strength and encouragement to disruptive forces that wished Pakistan ill. The military rulers of the day did not feel the need to counter those forces effectively.

In January 1966, I received a letter from Leadbeater, who had since left Karachi to become programme organiser of the BBC Urdu service. He wrote to say that my appointment had come through and a letter to that effect was on its way. Leadbeater and I had got to know each other well in Karachi. He understood Urdu and knew a great deal of Persian. Sometimes, he would slip a Persian couplet by Iqbal into his conversation. At the end of his Karachi assignment he had applied for the BBC post and got it. It was good of him to have remembered me. I ended my long association with *Jang* in March 1966 and arrived in London.

The BBC external service is autonomous but receives its funding from the British Foreign Office and acts as a spokesman for British foreign policy. Its English programmes, when I joined, used to go out virtually round the clock, and it broadcast in eighty foreign languages; the Arabic service was the largest. Despite what BBC officials or government spokesmen might say, all external broadcasts were closely supervised and reflected British policy. News bulletins and commentaries were prepared by a central unit and used by all services. I came to the conclusion, not long after I joined, that the newsroom people did not have a soft spot for Pakistan. When India attacked Lahore, the BBC broadcast that the Indian army had taken Lahore. It will be recalled that the Indian commander, General J.N. Chaudhuri, had expressed a desire to have a *chota* peg at the Lahore Gymkhana. The false story about the fall of Lahore shocked everyone, especially Pakistanis living abroad. When I came to London, I asked many people how an utterly baseless story had been put out by the BBC. All I could learn was that it was a news agency report that the BBC newsroom had decided to use, assuming it to be authentic. I also learnt that it had since been decided that no story from a non-BBC source would be used unless independent confirmation of it was available from reliable

outside sources. That may have been so, but I never thought that
the BBC felt much sympathy for Pakistan. It was always my
feeling that the Indian government and the Indian embassy in
London had good contacts in the BBC.

I recall an interesting incident involving a journalist friend of
mine, Mukhtar Zaman, who joined the BBC on a three-year
contract from the Associated Press of Pakistan. His contract was
nearing its end when two Kashmiri youth hijacked an Indian
airliner to Lahore. He was asked to translate the day's news,
prepared by the central news unit, for the Urdu bulletin. He
described the hijackers as 'Kashmiri freedom fighters', which
was how he would have referred to them in Pakistan. When the
story was broadcast, all hell broke loose at the BBC and Zaman's
explanation was called for. So disgusted was he by the reaction
of his superiors that he handed in his notice and left. Leadbeater
did not stay long with us but returned to the Foreign Office. He
and I always got along very well. He entrusted me with the task
of producing the popular BBC progamme, *Newsreel*. I was also
given the responsibility of producing a programme called
Sub-Rus, which covered the arts, including music, and carried
interviews with visitors of interest from Pakistan. I conducted
dozens of interviews for this programme, including those with
such personalities as the legendary broadcaster Z.A. Bokhari. I
even organised poetry-reading sessions for this slot.

I stayed at the BBC for a memorable five years. Among the
people I interviewed for *Newsreel* was a former chief justice of
the Sindh High Court, Z.H. Lari. I wanted to speak to him about
the changes President Ayub Khan had recently introduced in the
judicial system. I expected our conversation to last five to six
minutes. When he arrived at Bush House, there was no time left
to pre-record the interview, so I decided to put him on live. A
picture of the two of us was taken by a BBC photographer
because he was an important figure. *Newsreel* came on after the
news and a short commentary on the most important event of the
day. When the red light came on, indicating that we were now
on air, I began by introducing Lari as a former Sindh High Court

chief justice who might be planning to enter politics. I told him that we would be speaking about his future plans and asked for his comments on the judicial changes that had recently taken place in Pakistan.

This is how our conversation went: Question: 'Do you want to enter politics now?' Lari: 'Yes.' I waited for him to say something more but he kept quiet, so I asked, 'You have been judge of a superior court, do you think your decision to enter politics is the right one?' Lari: 'Yes.' I waited for him to add to what he had said, but he kept silent, so I fired my next question: 'The Ayub government, through an ordinance, has restricted retiring judges from taking part in politics. Would you like to say something about this law?' Lari: 'No.' He resumed his sphinx-like silence. I looked at my watch. We had only been on the air for about 30 seconds. I had set aside five minutes. I had not done much home work on my guest, expecting to have a lively to-and-fro conversation with him. I had no prepared script with me either. How was I going to fill the time? I decided to turn the conversation in another direction by asking, 'You have come to London after a long time, so you must have many engagements here,' Lari: 'No.' After uttering this one, single world, he fell silent. All I could do was to bring our exchange, if one could call it that, to an end. I thanked him for having joined us in the studio. How I filled the rest of the time, only I know. Five minutes is a long, long time on the air, I can tell my readers. What I found ironic was that for the fifty pounds the BBC had paid him—I had paid him in advance—Lari had spoken just four words.

When Z.A. Bokhari came to London, he recorded ten programmes for us at my request. Bokhari had been head of Radio Pakistan and the first non-Englishman to be appointed programme organiser of the BBC Urdu service, He was also a fine actor. When I led him into the studio for the recording, I was expecting him to be carrying a script. He had none. When I asked, he told me, 'All you need do is indicate that the recording is now on. Leave the rest to me.' And that was exactly what happened. He had chosen the ten topics he was going to speak on. He recorded those talks without a script and each word was perfect, each sentence complete. He spoke with great eloquence and fluency, showing complete mastery of the medium. There can be no two opinions about it: he was a legendary radioman. There was simply nobody like him. Later, when I went over the ten talks for editing, I found that there was absolutely nothing to edit. Each talk was precisely four minutes and fifty seconds long.

In 1969, when the Ayub regime in Pakistan was on its last legs, a number of changes were made in the Eastern Section of the BBC. The Pakistan section was renamed the Urdu section and the Bengali programme for East Pakistan was merged with the Bengali programme beamed at India. We were unhappy that the name of the Pakistan section had been changed, but we realised later that the lords and masters of the BBC knew that Pakistan would break in two. And they anticipated it nearly two years before it happened.

13 Flying Libel Writs

After I left the BBC, I worked for *Jang*'s London edition but left it to start my own newspaper, *Millat,* in September 1974. Zulfikar Ali Bhutto was in power in Pakistan. In our third or fourth issue, we carried a letter that Air Marshal Asghar Khan, a bitter Bhutto foe, had written to members of the Azad Kashmir Assembly, which virtually urged them to rebel against the government of Pakistan. The story had been sent by our Rawalpindi correspondent along with a facsimile of Asghar Khan's letter. We published both the story and the facsimile. Two days later, there was a phone call from Rawalpindi saying that our office there had been surrounded and nobody was being allowed to leave. The call had come from our chief reporter who was at home. He told me that unless *Millat* retracted the story, the siege of our office would continue. This threat had come from Saeed Ahmed Khan, chief security officer to Bhutto, whom people called deputy prime minister, so powerful was he. I was told that if we did not do what was being demanded, nobody in Pakistan would be permitted to work for *Millat*.

My first reaction was that we should take a stand because our story was correct. We had simply published what was an authentic document. But on second thoughts, I did not feel that it would be the most prudent course. We were a new newspaper. Our basic operation was based in Pakistan and there were ten people working for us there. If we decided to take on the government, who could tell how it would end? Those of us who were in London were safe, but we had to think of our colleagues in Pakistan. I felt bad about this because I was acting against my instinct and was going to behave like a coward, but I decided to give in and do as asked, though under duress.

Saeed Ahmed Khan was an old acquaintance of mine. I had known him since 1950 when he was the senior superintendent

of police in Karachi. Every morning we would contact him for
the updated report of the previous day's crimes committed in the
city. All the crime reporters of the city visited his office to read
that report. If further information were needed, they stepped into
the adjoining room to speak to him. Sometimes, they had to go
to the police station concerned to find out more. He stayed in
Karachi no more than a year and a half and was then transferred
to Bahawalpur. When the Pakistan cricket team toured the West
Indies under the captaincy of Abdul Hafiz Kardar, the team
manager was Saeed Ahmed Khan. He rose in rank, becoming
deputy inspector general of police. When General Yahya Khan,
after taking over from Ayub Khan, announced a list of thirty-
three corrupt officials, Saeed Ahmed Khan's name was among
them. When Bhutto came to power after the break-up of Pakistan
in December 1971, Saeed Ahmed Khan was living in
retirement.

He told me that when he tried to meet Bhutto, whom he had
known for many years, his staff just would not take any notice
of him. They did not seem to know who he was. One day, he
said, he went to the President's House and wrote his name in the
visitors' book. He had travelled from Lahore and was staying at
Flashman's Hotel, Rawalpindi. The next day, a call came on
behalf of Bhutto, summoning him to the official residence.
Bhutto met him politely and asked him if he needed a job. He
jumped at the offer. When Bhutto asked what he wanted to do,
Saeed Ahmed Khan replied, 'I have always been your loyal
servant and since my past career was police, I should like to be
given responsibility for your security. I will never forget the
favour.' Bhutto said to him, 'Done. Report for duty tomorrow.'
Saeed Ahmed Khan remained in charge of Bhutto's personal
security staff till his overthrow by General Ziaul Haq in a
military coup in July 1977. He was taken into custody and he
agreed to testify against Bhutto as a witness for the
prosecution.

But to return to *Millat*, times were hard for us and after a year
we had incurred so much debt that our closure appeared to be

almost a certainty. We had started with a small amount of capital
and, although our circulation was good, we had hardly any
advertising. Urdu newspapers printed from London were
dependent on advertising from Pakistani institutions such as
banks and the national airline, PIA, that were controlled by the
government. As such, they always stayed on the right side of the
government. We were different. Our publication of the Asghar
Khan story had placed us on the black list. At a meeting of the
Millat's board of directors, when the question of our mounting
debt came up for discussion, one of the directors, M. Shaheen,
said that if the other directors sold their shares to him, he would
stabilise *Millat* and its finances. He also promised to clear
Millat's debt. The only other director of the newspaper, if his
proposal was accepted, would be the editor, me. His offer was
accepted and every director transferred his shares to Shaheen. It
was also agreed that Shaheen would not interfere in the policy
of the newspaper.

Shaheen dealt in electric goods and lived in Scotland. What
he actually did instead of clearing *Millat's* debt, was to open
accounts in the newspaper's name at the Muslim Commercial
Bank first and then the Bank of Credit and Commerce. He
borrowed money from both and paid off *Millat's* debtors. I was
so absorbed in my work that I paid no attention to what he was
doing. When five army officers in Pakistan, including some
brigadiers, refused to carry out government orders—a story we
published prominently—Shaheen called me to say that in order
to further strengthen the newspaper financially, he was planning
to induct three new directors in the company. He told me that
they would make sizeable investments in *Millat*, which would
make the newspaper secure. What this had to do with the
resignations of the five army officers in Pakistan, I only came to
learn later. One day, two good friends of mine, brothers Ikram
Beg Mirza and Ehsan Beg Mirza, came to see me in the *Millat*
office. I learnt from them that under an agreement with Shaheen,
they and three other persons, whom they said I knew well, had

joined the *Millat* board as directors. The managing director of the company would from now on be Ehsan Beg Mirza.

Ikram Beg assured me that he would put as much money into the newspaper as was required but on one condition: no story critical of the Bhutto government would be published in *Millat* from now on. When I protested, Ikram Beg said, 'Your protests are what we expected to hear, but since we are old friends, we dismiss them. Your powers have been doubled and we hope to work like the friends and brothers we are. Ehsan will be spending a good bit of time at the paper and you two have full responsibility to do with the paper what you wish, except for that one condition I have laid down.'

Ikram Beg was a glib talker and when he wanted something, he did not present arguments, but did a soft sell. I pointed out to Ikram Beg that he and his brother were already associated with a weekly paper, so I could only wonder what they hoped to get out of *Millat*. 'Brother, *Millat* is going to provide us all with a living,' he replied. When I asked how, he told me that they were seeking a number of licences from the government back in Pakistan and were getting nowhere. Their bid, could now go their way, if I cooperated. When I asked how, he told me that after *Millat* published the story about the resignations of those five army officers, Saeed Ahmed Khan got in touch with them, asking them to take control of *Millat*, and then come to him for what they had long been seeking without success. 'Now if you are intent on proving how bold, courageous and independent you are, we will stand to lose a fortune,' Ikram said.

The association of the Beg brothers with *Millat* lasted just a few months and after they had what they wanted, they lost interest in the paper. Ikram Beg went to the Middle East where he set up a business and Ehsan Beg opened a restaurant in Seoul, South Korea. They also opened a hotel in Manchester called Mughal Hotel, with a branch in Lahore.

The seven years of *Millat*'s life were nothing if not dramatic. Whereas, on occasion, we showed extreme cowardice in the publication of news, on other occasions we displayed equally exemplary journalistic courage. It was only our financial vulnerability that forced us to act in a cowardly manner, but when we felt that the national interest demanded the publication of a story, we never hesitated to run it. On those occasions we just did not care what its impact on our business and our finances would be. In England the libel laws are strict and journalists have to be extremely careful that they do not cross the line out of enthusiasm. This applies especially to journalists who have come from Pakistan where no such restrictions exist. Personal attacks, common in Pakistan, can only be made at one's peril in England. Independence of the press, of which the British are so proud, does not include what courts and juries decide are libellous attacks on a person's character.

In June 1977, Saeed Ahmed Khan called me from the Prime Minister's House. He said he was calling because Zulfikar Ali Bhutto and his national security chief, Rao Rashid, whom I knew, had asked him to print a story in *Millat* to the effect that restrictions had been placed on travel out of Pakistan by Mir Khalilur Rehman, the owner of the *Jang* group of newspapers, and his family. All government advertising in the *Jang* newspapers had been withdrawn. Investigations were also underway into the financial aid received from the United States and other countries by the opposition parties united against Bhutto for the 1977 elections as the Pakistan National Alliance (PNA). Once the investigations were complete, action would be taken against the wrongdoers, Saeed Ahmed Khan added. I was told that both the prime minister and Rao Rashid would be personally grateful for my cooperation. Since Saeed Ahmed Khan was the 'horse's mouth' itself, I ran the story under a banner headline in *Millat*. It was not my intention to blacken anybody's name and I was satisfied about the authenticity of the source, which was none other than the chief security officer to the prime minister himself.

Bhutto stayed in power only about two months after the publication of that report. Ziaul Haq, the army chief, removed the civilian government, as had happened twice before in

Pakistan's history. A couple of weeks after the coup, *Millat* and its editor were served with libel notices from *Jang*, London. A hearing was held a year and a half later and *Millat* was ordered to pay compensation of twenty thousand pounds to *Jang* plus costs. We filed an appeal, which was heard three months later, and we lost. By now the bill from our lawyers had run up to around ninety thousand pounds, a sum of money it simply was not possible for a small newspaper like ours to pay.

I do not want to go into why the libel laws in England are what they are, nor do I want to delve into the rights and wrongs of the story for which we were punished. All I will say is that such laws seriously hamper freedom of speech and freedom of the press. No matter what the British might say about their free press, the fact is that investigative journalism in Britain is seriously handicapped by the country's libel laws. One example of this was a *Sunday Times* report that showed how two children were born with deformities because of the use by the mothers of the drug Thalidomide. This report was a fine example of investigative journalism but the *Sunday Times* was made to pay a heavy price for this, thanks to British libel laws.

It is also a fact that both judges and juries ignore the truth, depending on the nature of the case. Before the *Jang* case went to court, I met the barrister who was going to represent *Millat*. I asked him if he could cite an instance where regardless, of the gravity of the libel committed, the prosecution's case was utterly disregarded. The barrister, who was a most eminent member of the bar, answered that there were many such instances. For example, despite all the rubbish that was printed against Uganda's Idi Amin in British papers, each word of which was libellous, had Idi Amin taken British newspapers and the electronic media to court, he would not have been awarded a single penny. And why? Because the British media had painted Idi Amin as a tyrant and a terrorist, any case filed on his behalf for libel would have been dismissed in no time. No judge or jury in Britain would have given the matter a second thought. Another example given by the barrister was a libel case filed by a Korean priest who had been given such a bad name in the media that not only did he lose the case but he was also saddled with thousands of pounds in costs.

During Ziaul Haq's rule, *Millat* received a rather interesting libel notice. I should add that no matter what kind of government there is in Pakistan, *Jang* divests itself of its old rags to put on new ones. The average reader is quick to forget what happened the week before, which is why such newspapers thrive under any regime. *Jang* was highly critical of Air Marshal Asghar Khan and his Tehrik-e-Istiqlal, which was foremost in its opposition to the Zia regime. It so happened that the party's London president, barrister Zahoor Butt, called a meeting of his party and asked the police for permission to stage a demonstration. The route for the march was approved and about 150 of the protesters marched up to the *Jang* office and chanted slogans against the newspaper and its hostile coverage of their leader and party. They carried more than a hundred copies of the newspaper which they burnt ceremoniously. After it was over, the marchers came to the office of *Millat* and briefed us on the protest they had mounted bringing their banners and placards with them. We ran a single column story about the event on our back page the next day under a banal headline. A week later, we received a libel notice from *Jang*. Litigation is expensive business and a solicitor charges up to a thousand pounds for drafting a simple reply to a libel notice; if the matter proceeds further, the costs begin to escalate. When I took the *Jang* notice to our solicitor, I asked him what wrong *Millat* had done to be served with a libel notice. I was told that we had done no wrong and it was the marchers who were in violation of the law, but since *Millat* had reported the matter, it had also become liable to action. Were these British laws to be applied in Pakistan, not only would public protests cease, so would the statements which politicians issue every day against one another. That would, of course, take all the fun out of politics.

Another interesting event of those days involved a weekly rag called *Awam* that had started coming out of London. These were

Bhutto's last days in office. The backers of this paper were right-wingers who appeared to be opposed in principle to an elected government in Pakistan. The editor of *Awam* had worked as a translator for some months at *Millat* and his conduct had been judged objectionable on more than one occasion. Finally, he was sacked. We also learnt that he had spent three years in prison for passing bad cheques. Ironically, his paper, *Awam*, had come to assume a sermonising stance, sitting in moral judgment on the Bhutto government. I had his past record looked into and published a story in *Millat* that referred to this man as a former convict. A few days later we received a libel notice. We learnt from our solicitor that if a man has served his sentence, he cannot be referred to as a former convict. When I asked why not, the solicitor said that since by serving his sentence, the man had cleared his debt to society, no one had the right to dig up his past; calling him a former convict amounted to libel. Had the case gone to court, *Millat* would have had to pay a large sum of money in damages. However, I saved the paper from that unbearable financial ordeal by apologising to him.

Another libel case filed against *Millat* involved Chaudhry Zahur Elahi, an industrialist and a politician, who had been a police constable before the creation of Pakistan. However, the man had risen to power and amassed a great deal of money since, and carved out a special niche for himself in the politics of Pakistan. During the Ayub regime, he bought Progressive Papers Ltd. and thus became the owner of the *Pakistan Times, Imroze* and *Lail-o-Nihar*. But it did not last because he was neither able to keep the military rulers happy, given their whims, nor was he willing to pump more money into the publications. When Bhutto came to power, the two initially formed a friendship, which turned into bitter enmity before long. Whenever Bhutto mentioned Zahur Elahi, he never called him by name but 'Number 304', the number he had once borne on his police constable's belt. After Bhutto's execution, Chaudhry Zahur Elahi, who had been a minister in Ziaul Haq's cabinet, but who had since left it, came to London. I put a mischievous story in

Millat headlined, 'Belt No. 304 arrives in London.' I wanted my readers to know that this man, who was such a key figure in Pakistani politics, had once been a police constable. There was no shortage of Zahur Elahi's men in London and there were some who were either on his payroll or ideologically close to him. During Ayub's rule, he had been falsely and ridiculously charged by the government with having stolen a buffalo. There was also a case against him for violating some obscure postal law. He had stood his ground.

A few days after Zahur Elahi's arrival, *Millat* received a libel notice from his lawyers. Once again a to-and-fro correspondence began between his lawyers and ours. While this was going on, I developed heart trouble and required bypass surgery. I took leave of absence from *Millat* because I would get breathless easily, and experienced chest pains and exhaustion after walking or climbing stairs. I was resting at home, waiting to enter hospital, when my old friend Ikram Beg called me from Kuwait, informing me that Chaudhry Zahur Elahi planned to appear in the libel case against *Millat* in person. He also told me that Zahur Elahi would be phoning me shortly and I should speak to him with care. Ikram Beg knew of my heart surgery and he was quite close to Zahur Elahi. Half an hour later, Zahur Elahi called, inquired after my health, and then told me that he had come to London only to appear in the libel case, which would be no fun if I was not facing him across the court. He then said that after Ikram Beg told him about my heart surgery, he had instructed his lawyers to leave my name out and simply proceed against the newspaper and the company that owned it. We chatted briefly about my health before he hung up. Regardless of what kind of man Chaudhry Zahur Elahi was, I never forgot that thoughtful gesture of his.

The London court heard the case for two days and decided the case against *Millat*, asking the company to pay the complainant a sum of sixty thousand pounds. Zahur Elahi returned to Pakistan and a few weeks later, his car, in which he was travelling with High Court judge Maulvi Mushtaq Hussain,

who had ordered the hanging of Bhutto, was fired upon by
assailants. Maulvi Mushtaq escaped, but Chaudhry Zahur Elahi
died. Since the complainant was no longer alive, the judgment
against *Millat* was not enforced.

14 Ziaul Haq

Temperamentally, I have always been a strong and committed believer in democracy and democratic traditions. I have never accepted limits on freedom of speech and writing. During my quarter century in the profession, since I was always a working journalist and an employee, I was never in a position to fight openly against restrictions on the press. What held me back was the anticipated reaction of the newspaper owners I worked for. There were many occasions when I was left with no option but to fall in line. When Zulfikar Ali Bhutto came to power, it was sad to find that his government was not too keen on freedom of the press either. Civil liberties existed but often in name only. *Millat* did not show any temerity in opposing the Bhutto government where it believed it should be opposed. For the first time in my life, I was fully in charge of a newspaper and the only person I was answerable to was myself. As far as I was concerned, my true owners were my readers. I had vowed that I would never cover the truth with a lie.

On 5 July 1977, I found it impossible to support General Ziaul Haq's overthrow of the Bhutto government. It was my belief that no matter how badly an elected government was being run, it was not the army's prerogative to remove it from office. The declared grounds on which General Zia had staged his coup had no basis in fact. While it was true that there was a protest movement in Pakistan against the manner in which the national elections had been conducted, Ziaul Haq's argument that the country stood on the verge of a civil war, was not true. In fact, an agreement had already been reached between the government and the opposition parties grouped in the Pakistan National Alliance (PNA) and it was due to be signed the day after the coup. Bhutto had appointed Zia army chief of staff over the heads of several of his seniors. Zia had also co-signed a statement with the naval and air force chiefs and the chairman of the joint chiefs of staff committee, General Mohammad Sharif, that they would all stay loyal to the government and continue to fulfil their constitutional function of defending the country's borders. I could now see that the purpose of the statement was quite different, namely to put Bhutto off guard and to encourage him to continue negotiating with the PNA while the army made the necessary preparations to take over.

When the first report of the coup reached me, I was at my desk in the *Millat* office. The first thing I did was to open a drawer and pull out my copy of the constitution of Pakistan. I looked up the oath that an in-coming chief of army staff takes, which binds him to remain loyal to the constitution and the government of the day. It also clearly stated that anyone who violates the oath would be punished by death. In other words, Zia's military revolution was in violation of the oath of loyalty to the constitution that he had taken. The grounds he had cited for removing the elected government were no more substantial than a house of sand. My mind also went back to earlier military interventions in Pakistan, the first being the Ayub coup in 1958. During his years in power, Ayub had tried to assure the world that democracy was not workable in Pakistan and the people did not yet deserve it. I remembered that one reason he had given for his coup was the accidental killing of the deputy speaker of the East Pakistan Assembly in a fracas during the session. Such incidents have taken place elsewhere in the world but they have never been used to justify a military takeover of the country. It also occurred to me that whenever a military government had taken power in Pakistan, it had found the media compliant because newspaper owners are more interested in financial gain than in principles.

When General Yahya Khan overthrew Ayub, he tried to cover his illegal act by finding fault with ten years of Ayub's rule. He also revived the principle of one man one vote and announced that the next election would be held on that basis. The system of Basic Democracy was scrapped and the One Unit, under which all the provinces of West Pakistan were clubbed by Ayub into a single entity, was disbanded. I felt that as soon as a serving officer became army chief in Pakistan, the one thought in his mind was: now that I have become chief of the army, all that remains for me to do is to become head of state. After all, what was there to hold him back? One simple command from him could rain fire and destruction from his tanks and heavy guns on his enemies and opponents. I was sure General Zia's mind had worked along the same lines.

That very morning I decided to fight Zia's military rule with everything in my arsenal as a journalist. I did not consult my company's board, nor did I wait for instructions or guidelines from my directors. Initially, I found none of them opposed to my thinking and the policy I had decided to follow. *Millat* challenged every single draconian act of the Zia regime, from his claim to impose Islam, to the establishment of military courts to try civilians, to lashing people, to his pledge that he would hold elections by 18 October 1977. I never believed that pledge because how could a man who had grabbed power on the basis of a lie stand by such a commitment? *Millat* gave wide currency to various stories about Ziaul Haq, including his nickname *Surmay vali Sarkar*—The Master with Kohl Eyes—which became very popular. There were various other *Millat* firsts that remained in circulation as long as Zia was in power. Our defiant and independent editorial and news policy gained the newspaper both fame and following. There was no Altaf Gauhar-established 'advice system' in Britain so we wrote whatever we wished to write.

The re-imposition of martial law in Pakistan was depressing news. I knew from experience that it could only end badly. My mind went back to October 1958 when Ayub became the country's first military ruler. I was news editor at *Jang* in Karachi and after I had sent the last copy and put the paper to bed at about three in the morning, I told Shorish Malik, then one of our proof readers, over a cup of tea, that Pakistan would never be the same again. One martial law will follow another. Being a

Punjabi, he was happy as he saw military rule strengthening the grip of the Punjab over national affairs. He told me that such a martial law had not come to any other country. The people were sick and tired of politicians and if I would only walk across the street and talk to the cigarette seller, he would tell me that everything had now been set right and the people were distributing sweets all over the city. I told him, 'A nation that lives under such delusions is given to such antics. But time will prove me right.'

A few days after the Zia coup, my friend Khalid Hasan, who was press counsellor at the Pakistan embassy, phoned me at work and said that Ambassador Mumtaz Daultana wanted to see me. The matter was important, he added. I promised to meet the ambassador, whom I had known from the days when he was a member of the first Constituent Assembly of Pakistan in Karachi. We had often run into each other in the assembly cafeteria. He had just returned from Pakistan after being summoned there for consultations with the new military ruler. I kept wondering what possible business the ambassador could have with me.

Next morning, I first went to Khalid's office. There was a smile on his face. He told me he knew what Daultana was going to say but I had better hear it from him. When I entered the ambassador's room, he greeted me warmly and when I asked to what I owed his summons, he laughed. 'Let's have a cup of tea first,' he said. I asked him how things were in Pakistan. He said things were all right and General Ziaul Haq was a very nice man and had promised to hold elections in ninety days, which meant that the army had taken power only temporarily, which was a good thing for the country. I replied that the general had made that promise in his very first speech. The only question was: who was going to win those elections? I asked him for his opinion. Looking into the far distance, Daultana replied, 'He will win who has no shoes on his feet and no shirt on his back.' I said to him, 'Daultana sahib, the one who wanted 'roti, kapra, makan' — food, clothing, shelter—for the people, you have locked up in Murree, so what good would martial law's imposition be if he wins the elections?' Daultana's response was, 'Let's not go into that. Tell me if you are ready to go to Pakistan.' 'Whatever for?' I asked.

He informed me that General Ziaul Haq was keen to meet me personally, and all that I needed to indicate were my travel dates. I told him that it would take me a day or two to respond because if I were to go, certain arrangements would have to be made at work to cover my absence. After all, the newspaper had to continue publication. Daultana said, 'Look, my friend, if you are going, then you need to give me an answer now. Perhaps your friend Khalid Hasan has already made your reservations. You will be the general's personal guest, so even if there is martial law in the country, that should cause you no worry.' My reply was, 'No one can have apprehensions about returning to his country, martial law or no martial law.' Daultana said that over dinner with the general, the conversation had turned to *Millat*, and he had asked, 'What enmity does that newspaper bear us? Why don't you send its editor to Pakistan so that we can tell him our side of the story?' Daultana also told me that Ziaul Haq was keen to strengthen Pakistan's relations with Britain, since the two countries had such old links. He also wanted Pakistan to return to the Commonwealth which Bhutto had left. He had asked the ambassador to work on that with the British. With help from the press and the media, it should not be such a difficult task, he added. The ambassador also assured me that Zia was a simple, practising Muslim who offered the five daily prayers and even *Tahajjud*, the special early morning prayers. 'He wants to do his best for Pakistan,' he added. I told Daultana that I accepted Ziaul Haq's invitation. Another London journalist who was also invited to Pakistan at the same time was Habibur Rehman, editor of *Azad* weekly.

When I landed in Islamabad—it was still the month of July, on the 5th of which Bhutto's government had been removed in a coup d'état—it was stiflingly hot. An official from the foreign ministry was at the airport to receive me. He took me to the Hotel Intercontinental in Rawalpindi and informed me that

details of my programme would be worked out the next day at
the Foreign Office, which was where I reported the next day. I
was told that I was going to be shown around Pakistan, as if I
were a foreign journalist who had never stepped into Pakistan
before. A day's visit to the Tarbela Dam had also been arranged.
I had no interest in that sort of thing and told them so. I said I
had only come to Pakistan to meet General Ziaul Haq and if
there was no objection, I would also like to meet several other
people so that I was able to fully understand the changes that
had come about with the removal of the civilian government.
That would help me get a grip on what the future held. I wanted
to form a correct and balanced picture of the current situation in
the country and the direction in which things were likely to go.
My lack of interest in Tarbela seemed to cause some
disappointment to my handlers, but it was finally agreed that
there was no need for them to show me Pakistan, since I was not
an alien. I was also told that a Foreign Office official would be
present during any meetings I might hold while in the country.
Although I did not relish such restrictions, I decided not to
object. I was informed that I would meet the general at his
convenience, but as soon as there was a slot, I would be received.
I told my hosts that I would also like to meet the new chief
election commissioner, Maulvi Mushtaq Hussain, who was to
preside over the trial and sentencing of Bhutto in the Lahore
High Court. I was assured that this would be arranged after I had
met the general.

By the time of my arrival, Bhutto and all members of his
cabinet, along with leaders of the PNA opposition, had been
released from the custody in which they had been taken when
martial law had been imposed. Bhutto was in Karachi and the
PNA leaders were busy conferring with one another at Chaudhry
Zahur Elahi's residence in Lahore. On my return from the
Foreign Office, I called Maulana Kausar Niazi, Bhutto's
information minister and a member of his negotiating team with
the PNA. He drove down to Rawalpindi from Islamabad and
took me to his home. I had come to know him closely when

Bhutto had sent him to London to confer with British officials about race riots in Britain that had caused great anxiety in the British-Pakistani community. A big dinner had been thrown for him in London at which at least two hundred people had been present. I had also toured Scotland, Bradford, Manchester and Birmingham with him. Although he did not share any secrets with me, I felt that his loyalty to Bhutto was not quite what it once was. As we walked upstairs to his dining room, he showed me several pictures hanging on the wall—and in all the rooms, he told me—which showed the Maulana with various important personalities. The dinner was skimpy, just a little meat and a watery dish of lentil. My expectation that more substantial food would be served had been unrealistically optimistic. After the meal, he walked me down to his lawn where we ate mangoes. When I told him that I wanted to meet Bhutto, he asked me to come to Lahore on 8 August, because that was the day Bhutto would be arriving from Karachi.

Kausar Niazi did not tell me much about the PPP-PNA negotiations, except that an agreement had been reached and it was Air Marshal Asghar Khan who had sabotaged it. He agreed that two people—Asghar Khan and Ghulam Ishaq Khan—had influenced Zia into taking the road he did. He said he was not in a position to confirm whether Bhutto had made up his mind to remove Ziaul Haq but he did know that Bhutto had discussed it with Ishaq Khan, who had passed it on to Zia, who in turn had moved with the help of General Faiz Ali Chishti to overthrow the government before he could be sacked. Kausar Niazi complained constantly about the attitude of Abdul Hafeez Pirzada, another member of the PPP negotiating team, during discussions with the PNA. He said Pirzada had been aggressive throughout the discussions and very combative, which had not helped things. The Maulana dropped me at my hotel quite late in the evening. I spent 2 August meeting old journalist friends and returned to my room to rest in the afternoon. Before I could get any sleep, there was a knock at the door. When I answered it, I found three army officers there, who said they had come to escort me to army headquarters, GHQ, to meet their chief. I quickly washed my face, put on a *shalwar-qameez* combination, instead of a suit, and put myself into the hands of my uniformed handlers. Two jeeps were waiting in the hotel driveway, and I was asked to take the front seat in one of them; the three officers got into the other.

I found the GHQ much changed from the time when I had worked there in the military secretary's branch for a few months after independence. There was nothing I could recognise. We used to work in old barracks but what met my eyes were several smart new buildings. We finally arrived at the office of the chief of staff, where a major received me and took me to the room of the military secretary to 'The Chief'. As I sat there waiting, it occurred to me that it was the 29th day after the declaration of martial law and the man I was about to see was now the lord and master of all that he surveyed. The powers of the army chief in Pakistan were immense. Civilians spend a long time establishing institutions to run the business of state so that the head of state or government will be answerable to the people, but what happens? A man in uniform, who has sworn allegiance to the constitution, violates his oath, moves a handful of armed men under his command and takes over the government. With this one single act, he throws into the dustbin law, regulations, the constitution and public accountability. He assumes absolute power because he carries a gun and he commands the only armed force in the country.

I had been waiting only a few minutes when I heard someone say, 'The chief is here'. I rose from my chair as did the military secretary, who led me into the next room where I found General Ziaul Haq standing in his full military regalia. There was a smile on his lips. I could also detect the kohl in his eyes. He stood in front of a large table. A row of sofas stood against the left wall, with space enough for twenty people. Next to General Zia stood Colonel Siddiq Salik, head of the inter-services public relations directorate. I shook hands first with General Zia then with Colonel Salik. Zia pointed to his table and said, 'You can see a newspaper lying there. Are you its editor?' I took a few steps to check, as I could not quite read from that distance. It was *Millat* and the lead story featured the general, and said that for breaking the constitution, Zia should be sentenced to death. The story was based on a statement made by former labour leader and maverick political figure, Mukhtar Rana, who was now in London. The newspaper had been placed there to embarrass or perhaps frighten me. 'Yes, that is my newspaper,' I said. I might have sounded like a man making a confession, but with a great deal of pride. The general laughed and said, 'Now we can talk. Let's sit here in comfort.' I sat down and Colonel Salik joined me on the sofa, but at a respectful distance, while General Zia took a chair. The door opened and another general walked into the room. I did not look at him except out of the corner of my eye. I think it was General K.M. Arif. I knew of him and I knew that he was one of the closest of Zia's advisers. Salik I knew through his book on the fall of Dhaka written after his release from an Indian POW camp. We had published two of the book's chapters in *Millat*, though without the author's permission. He has a simple and likeable style and had had a long association with General Zia. He was later promoted to brigadier and perished with his chief in that mysterious plane crash in Bahawalpur in 1988. Before speaking to me, Zia turned to Salik and said, 'It seems you are now overpowered by Islam because I see from where I am sitting that you have not shaved.' 'Not at all sir,' Salik replied, 'I shaved this very morning. The hair must have sprouted between then and now.' Everyone smiled.

The meeting, which remained pleasant throughout, lasted for about ninety minutes. General Zia pulled out a 555 cigarette packet from his pocket and encouraged by that, I pulled out my packet of Player's, which he noticed. 'I like that cigarette. May I have one?' he said. I pushed the packet towards him and he took one out. We both lit up and began to smoke leisurely. Then Zia began to speak, 'This country, you see, stood on the brink of a bloody civil war. Both sides were armed and if the army had not intervened, there would have been great bloodshed.' Was he trying to justify his action in view of what *Millat* had published? I was quick to respond, 'In the two days I have been here, and going by the number of people I have spoken to, I have not gained the impression that the country was on the verge of civil war.' 'I don't know what people you have met, but I can assure you that our information was well-founded,' Zia said.

Although I knew that the general had promised national elections in ninety days or on 18 October 1977, I impishly asked him if he had any intention of holding elections. Zia was startled, 'Don't you know that elections in Pakistan are being held on 18 October?' 'I know that sir,' I replied, 'but I just wanted to hear it from you that elections are indeed going to be held as promised.' He raised his index finger towards the ceiling and said, 'As a Muslim and as an army general, that is my promise, not only to the nation but to the Almighty. Elections will be held in ninety days and I will honour my pledge.' Then he looked at General Arif and said, 'Mark my words.' 'Does it mean that there will be an elected government in the country?' I asked. 'Go easy now,' he came back, 'but it is my guess that there should be a new government in office by 28 October.' 'But why do you want those ten days in between?' was my next question. 'You are a very sceptical person, but by the night of 18 October or the next day, it will be clear which party has won a majority in the National Assembly. The next step would be for every party to choose its assembly leader and elect other officials. I think that will take ten days and by then everything will be in order and where it should be,' General Zia said. 'We should be able to summon the National Assembly session on 28 October, which will be attended by all the service chiefs. That will be the time when we will hand over power to the people's elected representatives. Can there be a better way than this of transferring power?' he asked.

I shook my head in assent and told him that before I entered his room, I had been informed that the entire conversation was off the record and not to be used. However, since he had named a specific date for the transfer of power, I should like to be permitted to report that in *Millat*. General Zia looked at Colonel Salik and then said, 'You can use that part of our conversation for your paper.' I thanked him. 'Will every party be allowed to participate in the 18 October elections?' was my next question. Zia, who could smile effortlessly, did so again and said, 'The army has taken power not on behalf of or in opposition to any particular party. All we wanted was to prevent civil war and maintain national unity. We took government and opposition leaders into protective custody for a few days. They are all free now and in their homes. We have nothing against any Pakistani leader. We have promised God and the nation that we will hold elections in ninety days and the nation will come to know that those who wear an army uniform keep their word.' Then he added, 'We people have sharp nails but I can assure you that we do not intend to scratch anyone's skin, even lightly.'

I decided to put a direct question. 'Although you have made it clear that you will not impose restrictions on any political party, should one conclude from what you say that in the coming elections, Zulfikar Ali Bhutto and the Pakistan People's Party will be allowed to participate?' 'You are trying to create differences where none exist. Every person and every party will be entitled to take part in the elections, as long as there is no constitutional bar on them doing so,' Zia replied. 'What constitution?' I asked, 'The one there was, you have abrogated.' He looked offended. 'Listen my friend,' he said after a pause, 'I only suspended the constitution, but many of its provisions have been revived. What is left will be restored too when martial law is brought to an end. When there is martial law in the country that means there is no constitution. When we approach the point where martial law is to be removed, everything will become clear. You need have no worry on that count.'

He did not appear to be keen to spend anymore time talking about domestic affairs and began to talk about *Millat*. He said younger Pakistanis in Britain could not read the paper because their first language was English. I agreed with him but added that it would need money to add English language pages, which

at present we did not have. Zia said I had his sympathies because
although he felt that we should be helped, his government was
temporary and in no position to make any promises. My reply
was short and quick. 'I have been misunderstood. We are not
asking for any help from the government. All I was trying to say
was that the company that publishes *Millat* is not financially in
a position as of now to add an English language section to the
paper.'

The name of Moazzam Ali cropped up at one point. General
Zia said, 'A gentleman by the name of Moazzam Ali lives in
London. Do you know him?' I told him that I had known him
for many years. At this point, Siddiq Salik, who seemed ready
with his homework, quipped, 'Moazzam Ali founded the Pakistan
Press International (PPI) in Pakistan but Bhutto snatched the
agency from him, so he went to London. He is a very nice man
but Bhutto was most unkind to him. He deserves to receive
justice.' General Zia replied, 'I think you and Brigadier Siddiqi
mentioned that to me earlier. I think we should call him from
London and I would like to meet him to see what can be done
to undo the injustice done to him.' (I should add that after I
returned to London, Moazzam Ali was appointed General Zia's
adviser for overseas Pakistanis with the rank of minister of state.
He was also given certain diplomatic privileges.) When the
meeting ended, General Zia rose to say goodbye. Behind me
stood Siddiq Salik. I noticed that General Arif had already left
the room. I also noticed that General Zia was bandy-legged and
wondered how a man with those legs had been accepted into the
army. General Zia could be called simple, polite, courtly or
whatever, but I will say without hesitation that he did not impress
me as a head of state, many of whom I had had the privilege of
meeting, including Quaid-i-Azam Mohammad Ali Jinnah,
Liaquat Ali Khan, Iskandar Mirza, Field Marshal Mohammad
Ayub Khan and Zulfikar Ali Bhutto. I had also met Pandit
Jawaharlal Nehru, Adnan Menderes of Turkey, Ahmed Sukarno
of Indonesia and Zhou En-lai of China. All of them had a certain

air, a certain grace and gravitas, but Ziaul Haq struck me as an empty vessel. Why, I am unable to say.

Before we left the general, he said to Siddiq Salik, 'Look, these gentlemen are my guests and they should be treated, not as VIPs, but as VVIPs. They should be comfortably lodged in their hotel and they should encounter no difficulty in terms of air travel reservations.' Then he turned to me, 'I want to make one thing clear. There is no censorship in the country. Whatever you observe, you can report freely in your newspaper. No one is going to bar you from doing that.' I thanked him and asked if he would mind my meeting leaders of the opposition parties. He laughed and told me that all opposition leaders were currently gathered at Chaudhry Zahur Elahi's house in Lahore and since I was going to Lahore, I should most certainly meet them. I assured him that while I would meet them, there was another opposition leader I was keen to see. 'Is anyone left out?' he asked. I replied, 'Zulfikar Ali Bhutto.' He laughed heartily and asked, 'You mean our Quaid-i-Awam. My dear, he is among our most respected leaders and I respect him deeply. You must meet him. I believe he is due to come to Lahore soon.' Then he turned to Colonel Salik, 'Please make arrangements for the meeting with Mr Bhutto. I think such a meeting would be most desirable.' 'But all I wanted was your permission,' I interrupted him. 'I will arrange to meet him myself. I would appreciate that.' He gave me his hand to shake, then walked up to the door to say goodbye.

When I stepped out of General Zia's office, it was about 4:45 in the evening and the officers who had brought me over were waiting for me. It was still hot but the intensity of the heat had diminished somewhat. I was asked to get into a jeep and arrived back at the Intercontinental in a matter of minutes. In my room I stretched myself on the bed, trying to go over the conversation I had just had with General Zia. His manners were impeccable but there was something rustic about him which did not sit well with his present office. Suddenly, there was a knock on my door. It was a middle-aged man whom I had not seen before. When I asked him what I could do for him, he asked if he could come in. I threw the door open and invited him in. I asked him to take a chair and phoned room service for tea. The man did not tell me his name but told me that he worked for a chemicals company and he had come to see me because he wanted to hear my impression of General Ziaul Haq, whom I had just met. Before he could say anything more, I knew that he was an intelligence agent, otherwise how would he have known that I had just returned to my hotel after meeting the general. I told him that I had had an excellent meeting with the general and he was most kind and courteous. I had been with him for more than ninety minutes. I asked him what else he wished to know. He replied that he did not want details; all that he wanted to know was whether the meeting had gone well.

Tea arrived and I poured each of us a cup. I told him that I was a working journalist and I had been summoned from London for this meeting. I was not sure what he meant by asking if the meeting had gone well. I wasn't here to get a plot of land or a residential house, so his question was irrelevant. He said, 'My information is that the meeting was not a success because the general has banned your newspaper.' I could not stop laughing on hearing this. 'Why are you laughing?' he asked. 'Our newspaper publishes from London and if the general has banned *Millat*, then he is welcome, except that our newspaper does not come to Pakistan, so there is no question of banning it. As I said this, I remembered that we did airmail sixteen copies every day, eight of them to our Rawalpindi office, one for Zulfikar Ali Bhutto, one for Mufti Mahmood and the rest for advertising agencies. Did the man who had come to see me out of the blue mean that there was now a ban on the entry of those sixteen copies? My guest confirmed that it was so. He said he had learnt that orders to that effect had been issued already. I thanked him and he left. I asked the hotel reception desk if I could use one of their typewriters. They said I was quite welcome and I typed out my story, leading with General Zia's decision to hold general elections in Pakistan on 18 October 1977 and transfer power by

28 October. I also mentioned some of the things that had come up during my conversation with him. I went to the telegraph office and using my ITU card telexed the story to the *Millat* office in London.

The next day, the Reuters correspondent came to see me at the hotel and asked where I had got the 28 October transfer of power date. I asked him how he knew about that. He replied that he had had a message from London asking him to check the report published in *Millat*. I told him that I had met General Ziaul Haq and it was he who had told me what I had filed. I also gave him more details, such as the decision not to ban any political party and General Zia's plan to go to the National Assembly with all his service chiefs to ceremonially hand over power to the people's elected representatives.

That of course did not happen. General Zia set up a cabinet of advisers, one of whom visited me in the *Millat* office and, after a quick introduction offered to buy the newspaper. I suggested to him mischievously that while he could get a copy from me, the rest he could buy from a news agent for twenty pence each. He said, 'You are joking. I am serious about buying not only your newspaper but your press as well.' I told him he was welcome but he should go upstairs to get some idea of the financial position of the paper from our accountant. I told him that we had a lot of debt and only after learning more about us, should he make us an offer, which I would take to my board of directors for approval. The man, who was a Karachi businessman and was later chosen to 'advise' Zia on health, was offended. 'We are prepared to pay the asking price. We will also make up the newspaper's losses and recompense the directors for their holdings,' he said. I told him I was ready and willing and he should make me an offer. I also told him that if *Millat* closed down, another paper would take its place because, unlike Pakistan, it was not necessary to obtain a declaration to publish a newspaper in Britain. That seemed to surprise him but he offered to pay us the asking price, as long as one condition was acceptable to us. When I asked him what that was, he replied

that since the newspaper would be in his ownership, I would
have to work for it. Actually what he was trying to buy was not
the newspaper but the editor. I told him that while he could buy
me, the Biro pen I was holding in my hand was not for sale. This
was the end of our conversation. He got up, shook hands and
said, 'You are the loser. I will inform my people about our
meeting.'

15 Zia Digs In

When I returned to London after my meeting with Zia in Rawalpindi, the *Millat* had come to establish its image as a newspaper dead set against the military regime. While we were not the supporters or followers of the Pakistan People's Party, it had our full backing because it was arrayed against the Zia military dictatorship. We were prepared to print anything that would weaken the foundations of the regime in power. And on that count, we were not willing to make any compromises.

Not long after the coup, a former member of the Pakistan National Assembly, Mukhtar Rana came to our office. He was in the doghouse as far as Bhutto was concerned, having been divested of his assembly and party membership. After spending some time in jail, he had landed in Britain where he had applied for political asylum, which had been given to him, but on a temporary basis. When the army took over, the British Home Office wrote to Rana, saying that since he had sought asylum when Bhutto was in power, now that he was gone, the asylum application was going to be reviewed. He had been told that it would be advisable for him to return to Pakistan. Rana showed me the Home Office letter, saying he was unwilling to return home and he would appreciate my help. He then handed me a statement, which he asked me to publish, arguing that it would help him maintain his stay in Britain. The statement was well written, logical and based on sound legal arguments. He had got it drafted by a lawyer. I ran it as the main lead, something I was reminded of when I met Ziaul Haq.

When the murder case against Bhutto was being heard at the Lahore High Court, I received a phone call from a man who said he was at Heathrow and would like to see me. I told him to come to my office but he was not willing to do so because, according to him, our office was a most dangerous place. He said he was an army officer and he had brought a letter for me from Pakistan. His manner was rather mysterious but I just could not understand what sort of a letter an army officer would bring me. I asked him several times to give me his name but he was not willing to do that. He asked me to meet him at the PIA counter at Heathrow Arrivals. He added that he would wait there until I turned up. Curious because of my caller's insistence, I phoned for a minicab and was at Heathrow in an hour and a half. Heathrow was about twenty miles from my office. The traffic was heavy because of the time of day. All I found in the Arrivals hall at Heathrow as I stood in front of a PIA sign was a single window, only kept manned at the arrival of a PIA flight. Then I noticed a man in a rather good suit standing there. Being quite sure who he was, I greeted him and he unzipped his leather bag and asked me if I was Inam Aziz. 'I have an envelope for you,' he told me. I asked him who the sender was. He replied that two days earlier, he had met the 'Bara Sahib' in jail who had ordered him to carry this envelope to me. I took the envelope and without opening it, invited him for a cup of tea. 'I have done my job, so there is no need for our meeting to continue.' With those words, he walked towards the exit. I tore open the envelope and found it to contain an affidavit that Bhutto had filed before Maulvi Mushtaq Hussain, the chief justice, who had forbidden its publication.

On my way back to the office, I kept reading the affidavit, which was a good indicator of Bhutto's politics and his state of mind. Later, this long affidavit was included in a book by an Indian journalist. *Millat* published the entire document in twelve instalments under the running headline: 'The Bhutto affidavit whose publication Maulvi Mushtaq Hussain banned, a ban that *Millat* rejects with contempt.' After the Bhutto trial was over at the Lahore High Court, with the court reserving judgement, I happened to meet a judge of the same court at the Pakistan embassy and found him reading the day's issue of *Jang*, London. After some time, he put it aside and said, 'No, not this newspaper. I want that rebel newspaper about which I have heard so much in Pakistan.' The gentleman on whom I had gone to call and in whose room the judge was sitting, said to him, 'Why just the rebel newspaper, why not meet the rebel editor?' I invited the judge to visit me at our office that evening. He turned up at around seven, looked through several of the back issues and said, 'I must say you have great courage.' I don't recall what I said in reply, but I do remember asking him what was going to happen to Bhutto. 'The judgment has already been written,' he replied, 'Bhutto is gong to be sentenced to death.' This was a big surprise because the impression outside Pakistan was that Bhutto would not be sentenced to death. At most, he would be given a life sentence. Nobody could imagine that the man who had himself committed treason, would liquidate an elected prime minister because although he was no longer in power, he was still viewed as an obstacle.

The judge told me that a meeting was held at Gen. Ziaul Haq's residence to discuss the verdict in the Bhutto case. It was attended by Gen. Faiz Ali Chishti, Supreme Court Chief Justice Anwarul Haque and Maulvi Mushataq Hussain, Chief Justice of the Lahore High Court. The decision was that Bhutto should be sentenced to death and Anwarul Haque was asked to draft the decision because ultimately the appeal was going to land in the Supreme Court. It was also decided that the Lahore High Court judgment sentencing Bhutto to death should be signed by Justice Aftab, with the two other judges on the bench, including Maulvi Mushtaq, signing concurrence. Since what the judge was saying amounted to lifting the veil on this court drama, I began to take notes, as is my routine. He sat for some more time and then took his leave. I thought long and hard over what I had been told before deciding to run the story. We published all the details that I had learnt from my visitor, including dates and the names of all those who had conspired to eliminate Bhutto. The story was not well received by our readers because they just did not wish to believe that Bhutto was going to be hanged. A few days later, the Lahore High Court sentenced Bhutto to death and the same people who were critical of *Millat* realised that we had been right all along.

The military regime tried everything to have *Millat* either closed down or change policy. There were no holds barred. A drug mafia figure was infiltrated into our managing board, largely because of our own carelessness; and before we knew it, the man had become the company's chairman, taking financial control of the newspaper. Shortly after that, the *Financial Times* printed a report showing the man's links with the Italian mafia. Our bank manager told me that as long as that fellow was head of the management, the bank would not be in a position to host our account. Without consulting the board, I wrote to the bank manager cancelling the chairman's authority to deal with the bank on *Millat's* behalf. I took over those responsibilities myself; something that was against both regulations and law. Later, the board lent its assent to my decision. There were several other attacks against *Millat*, but let me narrate one of the most serious. A month and a half after taking power, Gen. Zia appointed Moazzam Ali as his special adviser for overseas Pakistanis. Moazzam Ali and I had known each other over many years and we often used to have evening chats on the phone. One day he arrived at our office unannounced and offered to appoint me as his London-based adviser. That was a most astounding offer, but he did not stay long after I told him that while I had many faults, I had yet to hit the low point where I would agree to become an adviser to an adviser. He was quite upset by my response and we never met again, nor did we ever speak on the phone. When I fell ill in 1980, Moazzam Ali swung into action and was at last able to get *Millat* closed down. I am sure until his dying day, Ziaul Haq never forgot his adviser's achievement.

Another such episode involved Qutbuddin Aziz, who had been sent to London as press minister at the embassy. He was one of the three owners of the United Press of Pakistan, a so-called news agency that was known in Pakistan as 'the father, the son and the holy ghost.' He and I were good friends, however, since my Karachi days. The day he arrived in London, his first port of call, according to him, was 'my friend Inam Aziz' at *Millat*. He told me that he had not even opened his bags yet. In the 1977 elections, he was keen to run on a PPP ticket but party leaders from Sindh had opposed him and he had been refused a ticket. After this disappointment, he had turned against the PPP. As soon as Bhutto was overthrown, Qutbuddin Aziz landed in the lap of the army. He was offered the London post, which he took, hoping to become an ambassador before long. We chatted about this and that and then I took him to a Turkish restaurant for a meal. He told me as we were eating that he had been given the London post because it was thought that he would be able to bring *Millat* in line. He said Gen. Zia was very happy to learn from him that the two of us were old friends. And when he learnt that I had once worked as UPP correspondent in London, he signed Qutbuddin Aziz's posting orders. He told me that before setting out for London, he had looked at *Millat* files available in Islamabad and come to the conclusion that the newspaper was not getting its due share of government advertising. He said he had come to London with the mission of pulling *Millat* out of its financial difficulties and enabling the newspaper to join the 'national mainstream'. I kept eating my delicious Turkish food while he talked in a charged voice. After he had finished, I thanked him for having spent so much time in Pakistan worrying about *Millat's* financial health, but assured him that the *Millat* issue that he had come to resolve was beyond his capacity because my newspaper was on the side of democracy and opposed to military rule. As for advertising, I added, we would carry grocery store ads, even if they pay five pounds each, and we will be happy in the bargain. Let me add here that the Pakistan government has long used advertising from the seven or eight national institutions, such as PIA and the banks, as bribes. Qutbuddin Aziz kept arguing with me for some time, but in the end, realising that I was a lost cause, he left. I met him several times after that but our old friendship could never be revived.

We printed the news of Bhutto's hanging three days before it took place. This is how I landed that great exclusive. A Pakistan army brigadier dropped in to see me one day and said, 'You keep

harping on Bhutto's name, but the man is going to be hanged in
three days. I can confirm it because his grave at Larkana was
dug under my supervision.' After listening to this sensational
news, I made a few inquiries about the brigadier and learnt that
he had been sent to London on 'special leave.' Although it was
risky to print such a big story—as it could be wrong—I felt that
it would help the movement to save Bhutto's life which was
already afoot. Our story said that Bhutto would be hanged at
Rawalpindi and his dead body would be sent to Larkana for
burial. We had also said that his wife Nusrat and his daughter
Benazir would not be allowed to be present at the burial. In the
end, everything happened precisely as we had predicted. The role
that *Millat* played to highlight Bhutto's 'political murder' will
not be forgotten when the history of the democratic struggle in
Pakistan is written. *Millat* was the only newspaper that made it
a mission to keep alive the movement for democracy among the
overseas Pakistani community. Despite many tempting offers
dangled before us, we remained committed to the hard and
difficult path of truth that we had chosen for ourselves.

Some time after the arrival of the Zia regime, Ambassador
Mian Mumtaz Daultana returned to Pakistan, to be replaced by
Maj. Gen. Muhammad Akbar, a senior Pakistani army officer.
He belonged to Azad Kashmir and since most of our people
living in Britain come from Azad Kashmir, Gen. Zia had sent
Gen. Akbar to bring them to the 'straight path.' One day,
Qutbuddin Aziz called to say that Gen. Akbar would like to see
me. When I asked why, he replied that since the new ambassador
had not met me so far, he would like to do so now. 'Please do
come over in a couple of hours,' he added. I had no problem with
that and I arrived at the embassy and was taken to Qutbuddin
Aziz's room. He shuffled through his papers, picked them up and
asked if I had any objection to his presence during the meeting
with the ambassador. He wanted to know perhaps what Gen.
Akbar was going to say to me. The ambassador's office is quite
commodious. Behind the ambassador's large table, there hangs
on the wall a portrait of the Quaid-i-Azam. There are a couple

of sofas in front of the ambassador's table, but at a respectful distance of fifteen or twenty feet. There are side tables on which I found small ashtrays. The ambassador rose from his chair and plonked himself in the sofa placed to the right. There was a buzzer for which he reached, and in walked an office assistant whom he asked to bring tea. Gen. Akbar began by saying that he had been in London for quite some days now but we still hadn't met. 'Maybe because my name is on a blacklist, which is why I never visit the embassy,' I replied. 'There is no blacklist. You are most welcome any time,' he said. Then he turned to Qutbuddin Aziz, 'If there is such a thing as a blacklist, I want it torn up.' Qutbuddin Aziz smiled.

This was how our conversation went: Gen. Akbar: Where do you come from in Pakistan? I: I was born in Gujrat, Punjab. Gen. Akbar: Then you are very close to our area. Do you have a home of your own in Gujrat? I: No. Gen. Akbar: Surely, the home of some close member of your family? I: It is just one of those things but although I was born in Gujrat, we have no property there. Gen. Akbar: But, my friend, you must have a home somewhere in Pakistan. I: None. Gen. Akbar: Do you have a factory or a mill in Pakistan? I: Not that I know of. Gen. Akbar: It is strange that you have nothing of your own in Pakistan. His questions startled me but I could well imagine what he was driving at. Sipping my tea, I said to him, 'General sahib, if you are worried about my properties, I can furnish you with all the details right here and now, but I am afraid there is nothing you would be able to do about it. I have my own home in the Hounslow area, whose monthly mortgage I pay regularly. My wife and children also live in this country. Since the house where I live happens to be here, it may not be possible for you to do anything to it. As for Pakistan, I don't even have a reserved burial spot there.' He was not at all upset by what I had said. 'I am glad you told me all this. You know how foolish our governments are. Perhaps all they wanted to know was if you had a home in Pakistan which they could grab hold of. I am glad you have given them the slip as far as that goes.' He seemed to be mentally unprepared to complete the task that he obviously had been given. When we began to talk about our opposition to the Zia regime, I told him that we were only opposed to this government because we wanted to have people's rule in Pakistan, just as the Quaid-i-Azam had laid down. We were not willing to accept army rule. Gen. Akbar said, 'But you can have a ceasefire?' I replied, 'The war hasn't even begun, when it does, I will certainly get in touch with you about a ceasefire.' Gen. Akbar then began to talk against army rule. He said he had advised Gen. Ziaul Haq to hold elections as soon as possible and transfer power to the people's representatives. He assured me that a date for elections was to be announced soon and all my questions would be answered.

One story that *Millat* ran in those days will be long remembered. The story said that Bhutto had been killed before he was hanged. This was also reported by Bruce Louden of *Daily Telegraph* and later Benazir Bhutto issued a statement from Karachi confirming that her father was killed before he was hanged. This is how I came by the story. One day I was busy going through my mail, when I noticed a letter mailed from Pakistan. All it said on the envelope was: Editor, *Daily Millat*, London. I couldn't help complimenting the British postal authorities who had delivered a letter that bore no street address. When I opened the envelope, inside was a letter from an ex-army man from Quetta (because the postage cancellation stamp said Quetta.) Without revealing his name, the man had written that Zulfikar Ali Bhutto was not hanged at the Rawalpindi jail but murdered by Capt. Aziz and Brig. Rahat Latif, who were in charge of Bhutto's security in jail. While this kind of charge could be made by anybody, as I began to read the letter, what struck me was that so many of the things it said tallied with what I had myself witnessed. The man had written that when Bhutto was released from Murree in August 1977 and came to Lahore, a section of the welcoming crowd, somewhere between Gulberg and the airport, came upon Shah Ahmed Noorani, who was out there with some companions to watch Bhutto's reception. The people pulled out Noorani from his car when they recognised him, made him stand on top of the car's roof, pulled off his turban and tore it to bits. The letter writer had written that it was because of this incident that on 10 August, an enraged Gen. Zia had rung up Bhutto at White House (Nawab Sadiq Hussain Qureshi's Lahore residence) and told him in a bitter tone that he or his people had insulted and roughed up a respected religious leader and he won't be forgiven for that. The letter writer had said that he knew this because he was Zia's orderly. He had added that it was a very unpleasant conversation because after hanging up angrily, Gen. Zia had kept muttering abuse under his breath.

The letter had gone on to say that on the night Bhutto's was hanged, before dinner, Zia, Gen. K.M. Arif and he had flown in a helicopter from Army House in Rawalpindi to the Central Jail where Bhutto was lodged. The two were received by Capt. Aziz and Brig. Rahat Latif who had taken them to Bhutto's cell. They had placed certain papers before Bhutto and asked him to sign them and his hanging would be called off. Bhutto had refused to sign anything. One of the documents said that Bangladesh had come into being with his, Bhutto's, consent. Another stated that he had ordered the rigging of the 1977 elections. The third document said that he, Bhutto, was personally responsible for all the rioting and upheaval in the country and he was also behind the murder for which he had been sentenced to hang. Bhutto had kept saying no repeatedly, which had enraged Gen. Zia who had shouted, 'Kill this bastard.' That was the signal for Capt. Aziz and Brig. Rahat Latif to unlock Bhutto's cell door and jump in and start to beat him up with kicks and blows. Bhutto had fallen to the ground at which point Zia had screamed, 'Are you going to sign or not?' There had been no reply from Bhutto. The two officers who had been beating him were told to see what was wrong. They had shaken Bhutto's body from side to side but he had shown no sign of life. One of them had said that Bhutto had probably fainted. Zia had asked them to summon the jail doctor quickly. The doctor had arrived and pronounced Bhutto dead.

However, he had still given him an injection but Bhutto had not stirred. Gen. Zia and Gen. Arif had then got into their helicopter and returned to Army House. My correspondent had written that the next day the news of Bhutto's death by hanging had been made public. He had added that the same day he had run away from Rawalpindi because he was not willing to live with a lie. He was now in hiding in Balochistan and he might escape to Afghanistan to be safe.

The phone conversation that my correspondent had reported between Bhutto and Zia was significant for me because I was present at White House on 10 August, interviewing Bhutto. After taking the phone call from Zia, he had told me what Zia had said to him, which was what my anonymous correspondent had confirmed. That had led me to believe that the rest of the story was also correct. The *Daily Telegraph* correspondent in his report from Pakistan had also mentioned three people who had met Bhutto before his death. Those who had been allowed to see Bhutto's face before burial were his first wife, Amir Begum, one of his family servants and his uncle. His first wife had said later that he was not hanged. There was no mark around his neck and his eyes and tongue were not bulging out, as they invariably do if a person has been hanged. Bhutto's face was calm and peaceful. One of his servants had also confirmed that, saying that he had once viewed the face of an enemy of his who had been hanged but none of the signs he had seen on that man's face and neck were visible on Bhutto's face and neck. One of Zia's right-hand men, Gen. Faiz Ali Chishti, whose book was published in India, has expressed his lack of involvement in Bhutto's death, holding Zia and Arif entirely responsible. What he has forgotten to mention is that before he went on a tour of Gilgit on 2 or 3 April 1977, the cabinet had decided to hang Bhutto. In 1989, during a TV interview in London, Gen. Chishti was asked if Bhutto had been killed rather than hanged. He had replied that at the time of his hanging, Gen. Arif was present in the jail, which at least proves that even at midnight Gen. Arif was present in Central Jail, Rawalpindi. Gen. Chishti had also claimed that

Bhutto that had walked to the gallows. He had, however, failed to explain why Bhutto had been hanged at midnight in violation of standing jail regulations.

16 How Bangladesh Came to be Born

I had more than a nodding acquaintance with Zulfikar Ali Bhutto since his days as a young minister of trade in the Ayub government. He was the youngest member of the cabinet and he was quick to make his mark as a handsome, bright and upwardly mobile minister, far more prominent and in the public eye than his other colleagues. He began his political life under a military government and it was a military government that sent him to the gallows. So in a strange way his past and future were stringed together. After the Tashkent Declaration, his relations with Ayub became tense. It was during those days that he came to London. I was with the BBC in those days and my old friend and BBC colleague, Athar Ali, and I went to meet him at Dorchester Hotel. He told us right away that he had resigned as foreign minister and on return to Pakistan, he would formally part ways with the government. He was caustic in his comments about Nawab Amir Muhammad Khan of Kalabagh, the West Pakistan governor. He told us, 'This bastard has cancelled several of our family gun licences and he got all that done through Qazi Fazlullah, who has been jacked up as the interior minister of West Pakistan. I will never forgive this dog.' The way he spoke about this clearly showed that the enemies he had made in his political life as a *wadera*, would never ever gain his friendship. One thing I noticed about him was that while he was intensely patriotic, as far as his political opponents were concerned, they occupied the same position as Hindu politicians did in the eyes of the Quaid-i-Azam. While there was something subtle and sophisticated about politics in the Quaid's time, the politics of Bhutto's day oozed crude hatred. However, he was a person whose company one did not like to leave.

When Ayub Khan visited Britain, the BBC put me on duty at Heathrow, though in a portion where the old airport used to be. I had to do a running commentary on his arrival. A number of local people had been gathered there to welcome him; others had travelled from Pakistan to be seen and counted. Around the same time, there was an announcement that Zulfikar Ali Bhutto would be addressing an open meeting at the London School of Economics. A crowd of three to four hundred at a London meeting is something not witnessed every day. I wanted to record Bhutto's address. After obtaining permission from the School, I had two engineers set up the necessary equipment. When the meeting began, not only was the auditorium full but a hundred or more people were standing outside because they could not find seats. The moment Bhutto stood up to speak, hostile slogans began to be raised from all points in the hall. Since I was on the stage, I could see that those screaming the slogans were the same people whom I had earlier seen at Heathrow as Ayub's welcoming committee. Almost all of them appeared to have come all the way from Pakistan. However, I was able to record Bhutto's entire speech, which no doubt remains preserved to this day in BBC archives.

I also met Bhutto in Karachi in 1969 when he was leading a movement to topple the Ayub regime. When I arrived from London on home leave, political agitation was in full swing in Karachi. No day passed without unruly crowds hitting the streets, and invariably smashing traffic lights and damaging government property. Buses were also being burnt. Maybe because there were orders from 'above,' nobody ever got arrested by police. Off and on, army soldiers were brought in, but they too appeared to be unwilling to do much. While I was happy in one sense because a military dictator appeared to be on his way out, I also felt like a stranger in this utterly uncontrolled situation. Television was new to Karachi but it was rapidly coming into its own. A close friend of mine, Mukhtar Zaman, with whom I had worked at the BBC in London for three years, called me one day to say that he was producing a discussion programme for

television and asked if I would like to take part in it. I was, so
he asked me to get to the studio right away. The topic of the
discussion was: The current political situation and how it might
be resolved. On arrival, I was told that since the programme was
going live, we would need to be careful in what we said.

There were five of us, all journalists. Everyone was bending
backwards to ensure that nothing critical was said about Ayub
Khan, something I found unacceptable. I felt that the plain,
unvarnished truth should not be held back and one should not
play around with facts. So, when a question was put to me, I said
unhesitatingly, 'Look, Field Marshal Ayub Khan gave the
country a new political system, which the people know as Basic
Democracy. The last few weeks have proved that the Basic
Democracy system has failed. It is my view that when a system
fails, the author of that system should admit defeat. That is why
I believe the Field Marshal has been politically defeated and it
would be best for him to resign as president. In the interim, the
control of the government should pass on to the one specified in
the constitution. The new caretaker head of government should
be duty bound to hold fresh elections for a new constituent
assembly, so that Pakistan can be rid of the discredited Basic
Democracy system.' When I finished, I noticed that the faces of
my fellow discussants were red, either with anxiety or
embarrassment or anger. As we stepped out of the studio, we
found station director Aslam Azhar waiting in the corridor. He
expressed annoyance at my observations. He said the switchboard
was flooded by viewers' calls, some of them abusing me, others
expressing praise. He also said that he might lose his job because
of the programme. He also told me to take care as I might be
picked up by 'the boys.' I was with him in his room when the
phone rang. He took the call and then handed the phone to me,
saying it was a friend of mine on the line. The friend turned out
to be Mustafa Zaidi who began by saying, 'Why strike a man
when he is already dead? What will you gain by dragging around
his carcass?' He invited me to spend the evening with him at
Hotel Metropole where he was arranging a sitting, a 'mehfil', as

he put it. I had spent a lot of time with Zaidi in London when he was once there for several months, having stepped down as deputy commissioner of Lahore and come out on a course of study in Britain and Germany. His wife was a very nice and beautiful German but he was not a one-woman man, being given to flitting around. This ultimately led to tragedy. He was found dead at the home of a Karachi beauty with whom he had fallen in love. He was a wonderful poet and a man of great warmth who loved his friends.

On my 1969 visit to Karachi, one day Athar Ali and I decided to go see Bhutto. With that in mind, we arrived at his fortress-like Clifton residence. There were at least three thousand people outside the house, all hoping to catch a glimpse of the man who had suddenly taken their fancy. It seemed difficult even to get to the front door but we did manage to do so. Our persistent knocking on the large steel gates produced no result, till someone opened the gate to step out. We wrote our names on a piece of paper and asked him to kindly take it inside to Bhutto sahib. A short time later, we were called in and there was Bhutto to greet us. He led us into the garden and promised to be with us as soon as he was done with the two or three television camera teams that had come to interview him. Athar Ali and I kept sitting in the garden for hours. We noticed sandbags all along the four boundary walls of the house, as well as half a dozen men, with guns on the ready. Bhutto appeared to be living in danger of his life, which was why he had taken so many precautions. He was in jail until a few weeks earlier, but so helpless had the Ayub regime become that the courts had stopped siding with him. Bhutto's trial had been held inside the jail and he had been acquitted, ironically, by Maulvi Mushtaq Hussain who was to order his hanging ten years later.

Bhutto joined us close to midnight and asked about our future plans. We told him that we were both working with the BBC. 'Quit your jobs and work for me. I am going to come to power in this country very soon. No one can stop me now; nor can the army disregard the people's wishes,' he advised us. We promised to think about his offer before taking our leave. When I had met him in London, he looked depressed and he could not see his political future clearly, although the movement he had started against Ayub's dictatorship had already taken root. Retired Air Marshal Asghar Khan, who had been preparing to enter politics had also jumped into the fray and become part of the anti-Ayub movement with Bhutto. However, the two did not stay together for long, perhaps because their political views were not identical, or more probably because Bhutto wanted everyone to accept him as a political superior. From Karachi I went to Rawalpindi. I can never forget the evening of 22 March 1969, when it was announced that Ayub Khan had resigned because of ill health and transferred power to Gen. Yahya Khan, chief of army staff. While the politicians were confident that they had brought down Ayub, he had had the last laugh as he had handed over power not to them but to the army.

I returned to Karachi where I held several long meetings with Mir Khalilur Rehman, who instructed me to look for suitable office space in London for *Jang's* London edition. Mir and I went back a long way. I had joined his paper as a sub-editor and risen to become news editor. He told me that it was now increasingly difficult to publish a newspaper in Pakistan and he wanted to develop an option abroad so that if one day, he found it difficult to carry on his business in Pakistan, he should have something to fall back on. This lecture from Mir Khalilur Rehman was rather surprising for me because I had never known him to be critical of any government. No matter what government came to office, there never was a diminution in the privileges that he enjoyed. I simply could not understand why he was in such despair with conditions in the country. After I returned to London, Mir sent me several letters in which he urged me to do the necessary so that a newspaper could be published from London. A few months later, he came to London himself and the two of us went from one corner of the city to another, looking for a suitable place. Mir Khalilur Rehman is one of Pakistan's richest people, although I have known of times when he would go around on the streets of Karachi on a bicycle in search of advertising. I also remember the used Ford car that he had once bought and which he showed to the entire staff with great pride. In those days, Mir Khalilur Rehman used to live in a third floor flat, which he had quit after suffering a heart attack. In its place, he had bought a house in Lyari because his doctors had forbidden him to climb stairs. 'How do you fellows manage to live here?' he said to me, implying the prices in London. One day we saw several properties to which we had been guided by estate agents. I felt very tired because we had done a lot of walking. When I tried to hail a cab, Mir said, 'That cab is going to cost hundreds of rupees; let's just keep walking.' Even the nearest Underground station was quite far when he said that, but I had no choice so I kept trudging along. In the end, we were able to find office space in Hoxton Square, near the city's Old Street tube or Underground station, which was where the first office of *Jang*, London was set up.

Three months before *Jang*'s appearance, I asked BBC to permit me to terminate my contract. The head of the Eastern Service backed my request on the ground that I was being offered the editorship of a newspaper and my contract should not be made to stand in my way. After quitting the BBC, I paid a short visit to Pakistan where I set up a London desk at *Jang*, Karachi, putting Hafiz Islam in charge. I briefed him on my requirements and when I went to see Mir, he asked me how many pages I planned the newspaper was to have. I replied that since he had bought small-size printing machinery, I would bring out a 12-page paper. He was surprised and wanted to know how I would fill all those pages. I asked him to leave that to me. He told me that during Haj, there is an Urdu newspaper produced in Jeddah, which is just two pages. He had thought I was also going to produce a similar newspaper. I told him to relax on that count because we were not going to produce a newspaper that would leave the reader unimpressed. I informed him that I had left all necessary instructions with Hafiz Islam. All he would need to do would be to make sure that my instructions were carried out. That decision, namely the production of a 12-page newspaper from London, has become a landmark in Pakistani journalism. Even today, every Urdu newspaper coming out of London is following the lead we set. I had told Hafiz Islam that without fail he should ship by PIA every day two copies each of every Pakistani newspaper in print. He should also send me any calligraphed material available with *Jang*. The idea was to reprint selected stories that had appeared in Pakistani newspapers, quite disregarding the niceties of the copyright law. Ten of our pages were made up of these cut-and-paste stories, while the other two consisted of calligraphed material from Karachi, plus news agency copy. It was I who invented the term 'scissor: or *qainchi* editor.' The only problem was that the material we printed on the inside pages was beyond our editorial control, because it was not produced by us. We had to reproduce the story and the headline as in the original. Our calligraphy staff, in any case, was just three people, which was insufficient for a daily newspaper.

The first issue of *Jang*, London came out on 23 March 1971, the day Sheikh Mujibur Rehman declared the independence of Bangladesh in Dhaka and raised the flag of the yet-to-be country. That was the day the Pakistan army launched its operation against 'rebels', setting in motion a fratricidal and bloody war. Being an employee of *Jang*, I kept to the policies chosen by the newspaper's owners. Had I done otherwise, our paths would have taken separate turns. As time passed, the struggle for Bangladesh intensified and India threw its army into the conflict, triggering a war between the two countries. I will never forget what our newspaper in London went through during those trying days. All our links with Pakistan had snapped; it wasn't even possible to make a phone call to Pakistan. We had to subsist on what we got from Reuters, whose stories, it goes without saying, were not tailored to our requirements. I got in touch with Gen. Muhammad Yusuf, our high commissioner, asking him to help us make a phone call to Mir Khalilur Rehman so that we could know what really was going on. I was asked to come to the high

commission the next day and Gen. Yusuf phoned the General
Headquarters in Rawalpindi. Mir Khalilur Rehman had already
been informed and he was waiting for the call from London. We
talked and he read out a communiqué issued that day by the
defence ministry. I took notes as he spoke. The communiqué
claimed that the Pakistan army was winning not only in the East
but also in the West and the enemy was retreating on every front.
I returned to the office and based on what I had been told, wrote
the lead story, which ran under the headline: Pakistan winning
the war. The story also detailed the 'heroic exploits of our
soldiers.'

After putting the paper to bed, I left the office to go home,
feeling quite happy. On the way, I ran into some friends and by
the time we were done gossiping, it was 11 in the night. I got to
the King's Cross tube station to board my train, when I noticed
the next day's issue of the *Times* which was already on the
streets. One glance at the headline and I felt as if a slab of ice
had fallen on my head. The headline said, 'Pakistan Army
Surrenders.' I immediately jumped into a cab, rushed to the
office but found it locked. The paper had been printed and
distributed. I got home somehow but just could not sleep. Next
day, I had to field scores of calls from readers who accused the
newspaper of being a dishonest liar. The gist of most calls was,
'You report that Pakistan is winning the war, while the fact is
that our army has surrendered.' We were so ashamed of ourselves
and of what had happened that we simply had nothing to say in
our defence. After the war, in order to assuage our conscience,
we began to fling mud on Yahya Khan's, the idea being to find
some explanation for the defeat Pakistan had suffered. We ran
stories about General Rani and Madam Noor Jehan and how
Yahya was cavorting with them while the country was breaking
up. Not that people were not already aware of Yahya's excesses;
but we had to revive those stories in lurid detail in an effort to
rationalise the disaster Pakistan had suffered. By the time, the
dust settled, the head of the Eastern Command Gen. Niazi,
Governor Malik and his army adviser Gen. Farman Ali, along

with thousands of officers and men—the overall number was
close to 100,000—had been taken prisoner by India.

17 Bhutto's Hangman

Three of Pakistan's judges will always find a mention in history. They are Justice Mohammad Munir, Justice Maulvi Mushtaq Hussain and Justice Anwar-ul-Haq. All three compromised themselves and their august office. The destruction of constitutional rule was performed by Justice Munir. He was the author of the infamous Doctrine of Necessity, which lent legitimacy to illegitimate governments. This judgment dates back to 1955 and ever since then has been used to justify military coups d'état, which have become Pakistan's recurring fate. When Ghulam Mohammad dissolved the Constituent Assembly illegally, the Speaker Maulvi Tamizuddin Khan, who came from East Pakistan, challenged the dissolution in the Sindh High Court and won. Ghulam Mohammad went to appeal in the Federal Court and had the lower court judgment overturned. Justice Munir wrote that Pakistan stood at the edge of an abyss and there were three options before the country. One was to retrace our steps, the other was to build a bridge of legality over the abyss to get across and the third was to leap into the abyss. He wrote that he had opted for the second course and provided a legal bridge so that the nation could overcome the crisis it faced. The Doctrine of Necessity has haunted Pakistan ever since. Justice Anwar-ul-Haq, who presided over the Supreme Court of Pakistan which hanged Bhutto, also went along with that infamous doctrine, although earlier he had declared Pakistan's military rule under General Yahya Khan, illegitimate and illegal. Pakistan's higher judiciary has always gone along with illegitimate rule while it has lasted and only declared it illegal after it is no more.

But it is about Maulvi Mushtaq Hussain, chief justice of the Lahore High Court, which sentenced Bhutto to death, that I wish to share my experiences with the reader. I met him in Rawalpindi after he had taken over from Justice Sajjad Ahmed Jan as chief election commissioner. Before this appointment, he had spent some time in Cambridge, England, with his 'daughter' (at least that was how he referred to her). He was summoned to Pakistan after the Zia coup and made chief election commissioner. He was also assured that he would be made chief justice of the Lahore High Court, an office Bhutto was not willing to give him, hence his bitter enmity with the deposed prime minister. But let me return to my meeting with him after my interview with General Zia. Since the Foreign Office had approved of my meeting with him on 13 August, I was escorted to Punjab House where he was staying.

Among his advisers at that time was my old Karachi friend, the journalist I.H. Burney, who had developed an intense dislike for the Bhutto regime. That very day, it so happened, the chief election commissioner had announced a list of regulations that were to govern the conduct of the promised elections. I asked the Foreign Office official who was to take me to see Maulvi Mushtaq Hussain if we could stop off at the election commission as I wanted to take a more careful look at the new regulations, having gone through them only cursorily in the morning papers. I was told that whatever I was looking for would be available at Punjab House. When we arrived there, I asked an official of the commission if I could take a look at the new regulations and schedule. He was under the impression that the regulations were still confidential and was not fully reassured when I told him that they had appeared in that day's newspapers. He finally produced a booklet and said that I could consult it for about five minutes. Any trained journalist is quick to spot what is newsworthy and I had no difficulty doing that in less than five minutes. Armed with what I had read, I returned the booklet to the official who put it in his drawer, which he locked, as if guarding a state secret.

At 11 o'clock, we knocked at the door of Maulvi Mushtaq Hussain's residential suite. The door was opened by a huge man wearing a muslin shirt, who turned out to be the chief election commissioner himself. I walked into what was his makeshift office containing a table on which various papers lay in some disarray. I was offered a chair. The conducting official found a corner of the sofa for himself. I began by raising the question of the constitutional situation existing in the country. He cut me short. 'There is no need to speak of constitutional matters here,' he said in a commanding tone. Then he said that the man this country needed to be rid of had been removed. It was therefore necessary that an orderly atmosphere should be established all around. The new rulers were fully aware of the existing situation and would succeed in improving it. The way he had cut me short, had left me wondering what I should ask him next. As chief election commissioner, it was most inappropriate on his part to be making such partisan comments. His sole task was to oversee the holding of elections, not to pass political judgments. His manner was aggressive.

I let him talk for some time before referring to the regulations issued that day by the commission. I told him that one of the regulations was beyond me and I should be grateful if he would explain it to me. He asked me to go ahead. I said that according to one regulation, if a candidate or his agent feels that an irregularity has been committed in his constituency, he is required to report it to the election official in charge of the area, and if he is not available, to bring the matter to the attention of the chief election commissioner, who is expected to take one of three steps: order the voting to be stopped. If the votes have been already cast and counted, he can stop the results from being announced. And if the results have already been announced, he can suspend them. 'What is your objection?' Maulvi Mushtaq asked. I replied that while the chief election commissioner had been imbued with wide powers, nowhere did the regulations make any mention of his obtaining proof that irregularities had in fact been committed. That being so, would not every losing candidate challenge the results?

A wicked and triumphant smile appeared on Maulvi Mushtaq's face, 'I already know that you support a certain political party.

The purpose of these regulations is to create such conditions in the country that the party that you favour will never win elections. The time when elections were rigged is gone.' I stopped him right there and complained that he had associated me with a particular political party when my question was only an attempt to understand how the system put in place would actually work. What I could make out was that the chief election commissioner could act to nullify any election without requiring evidence. He replied that I had got it all wrong and what the regulation meant was that the chief election commissioner should use his discretion and would not require any immediate proof before taking action. He gave me a dirty look, as if I were a thief or a robber whom he had just caught. Then he said, 'Perhaps you do not know my powers. Since you are here as a guest of General Ziaul Haq, I will say nothing, but you will have to be careful in future.' The Foreign Office man was taking all of this down in his notebook. Maulvi Mushtaq noticed that. 'What are you writing?' he asked. 'Sir, I am doing my duty,' he replied. 'Cut that out. If you want to sit here then you will have to stop taking notes. My conversation is personal and you are hereby instructed to make no written report about this to your superiors. If you are asked, just tell them what I have just said.' The Foreign Office man put his pen back in his pocket and closed his notebook.

Maulvi Mushtaq then turned to me, 'You perhaps do not know that journalists in this country are mortally afraid of me. I have punished a couple of them for contempt of court. During General Yahya's time, I was the federal law secretary. The government announced the names of 303 officials who were found to be corrupt. When this list was issued, I was in Cambridge. I was told that a London weekly, *Mashriq*, had added my name to that list. I phoned the editor and when I returned to Pakistan, I learnt that it was all a mistake. But I never forgave that editor and once, when I learnt that he was visiting Pakistan, I had him hauled up in my court and I gave him hell, something he would remember till his dying day. As far as you are concerned, I want to warn you that you may be a journalist, but if you don't take care, you will get it in the neck. I will let you go this time because you are somebody's guest, but next time you are in the country, I will have you summoned to my court and what will happen to you then, I leave to your imagination.'

As soon as he had finished, I rose from my chair and said in a calm voice, that all I had asked was a simple question about election regulations and he had not only threatened to haul me up before his court but also associated me with a certain political party. I told him that I did not expect such threats from him. As far as his promise to deal with me when I visited Pakistan next, all I would like him to know was that as long as he remained in the position he currently held, I would not return to Pakistan, so he could remain satisfied on that count. As I was about to walk out of the room, he said, 'You can't go like that. You have come to visit me so you must have a cup of tea.' I did not wish to spurn his gesture, so I sat down. He went into the next room where an attendant was preparing tea. He surprised me when he re-entered the room, carrying a tea tray with three cups and a plate of biscuits. He poured out the tea and asked me how much sugar I took. I pulled my container of artificial sweetener from my pocket. He asked me for one because he too, he added, did not take sugar. When I lifted my cup, he insisted that I should eat a biscuit. 'I want you to have no misgivings about my hospitality,' he said. 'How can I,' I replied, 'unless I want to land in jail? And since I have no intention of ending up in jail, you should feel no anxiety on that point.' For the first time, he smiled, 'So, you haven't forgotten,' he said. The meeting ended and the Foreign Office official and I left Punjab House in a hurry.

When I returned to London, I saw a Pakistani journal which carried a profile of Maulvi Mushtaq Hussain that compared him with an angel, who 'fills the room he enters with light'. As far as I was concerned, he looked to me like one of those free-style wrestlers who knock each other all over the place on television. What was more, he was a particularly ungainly wrestler. What could be more ironic than to compare a man like him to an angel? There could be no greater indecency! About eleven and a half years later, when I returned to Pakistan, much had changed. Maulvi Mushtaq, after Zia used him to hang Bhutto, was dead, having been eased out by the dictator. When the time had come to raise him to the Supreme Court of Pakistan, Maulvi Mushtaq's name was not even on the short list of probables. And General Ziaul Haq was dead too, having met a flaming end in a mysterious air crash.

My visit to Pakistan took place in November 1988 because I wanted to straighten things out with *The Pakistan Times* for which I had begun working. Some time later, I took another trip to the country for the wedding of my eldest son. On both occasions, I could not help feeling that I was returning in triumph, while the man who had threatened to jail me was not even alive. In Lahore I learnt that Maulvi Mushtaq's funeral procession had been attacked by wild honey bees. The pall-bearers and the party of mourners had had to put the body down and seek cover to save themselves from the furious bees. They could return only after several hours when the bees had fled the area. Maulvi Mushtaq's body was lifted from where it had lain abandoned and buried in a local graveyard.

18 Zulfikar Ali Bhutto

I arrived in Lahore on 7 August and stayed at the Hotel Intercontinental, where a representative from the federal government came to call on me. I told him that the official part of my visit was over and he need not follow me around any longer. I promised to inform him when I planned to leave for Karachi so that he could find me a seat on PIA as I wished to return to London by 12 or 13 August.

My sole purpose in Lahore was to meet Bhutto and to find out from him what his plans were. While in the city, I met several journalists and political workers, all of whom were of the view that it would be difficult for Bhutto to survive now. Everyone also said that if elections were held in ninety days' time, Bhutto and his party would score a massive victory, which would mean that Zia and his fellow generals would not escape punishment. Since the army was holding power, it would never permit Bhutto to return. Here and there, without quoting Ziaul Haq, I argued that the army wanted to remain strictly neutral during the elections and had no interest in who might win, but no one was prepared to agree with me. One person said to me, 'You do not know the feeling of euphoria a person experiences when he gets into a bullet-proof Mercedes with forty outriders at his front and rear. Who is going to pass up that kind of glory? Anyone who thinks Ziaul Haq will return to the barracks, lives in a fool's paradise.'

On 8 August, I drove to the airport in a car that had been provided by the government. As we approached Gulberg, we had to stop because of the crowd. It seemed as if the entire population of the city had decided to go to the airport. We moved ahead, but at snail's pace, so thick were the crowds on all roads leading to the airport. We also heard reports of rioting here and there. My driver got out of the car to find out what was going on, only to come back and report that the police were lobbying tear gas shells into the crowd. There were clashes going on between the police and the people. He asked if we should return to the Hotel Intercontinental but I told him to drive to Mughal Hotel on Gulberg Main Boulevard, which belonged to my old friend Mirza Ikram Beg. I learnt that there were more than half a million people in and around Lahore airport. There were many smaller processions around the Mughal Hotel who were shouting anti-Zia slogans such as *Zia Bey-haya* (Zia the shameless). I asked the driver if he knew of a route that would take us to the airport, but he did not think there was one. There were people everywhere. After about an hour, I asked him to return to the Intercontinental, promising myself to find some means of meeting Bhutto in the evening. However, we got caught up in the milling crowds. Two or three tear gas shells also landed close to our car and although the window was up, I felt suffocated with tears running down my face. The driver was smart and managed somehow to find his way out and get me to my hotel.

By evening it was clear that only once before in Lahore's history, when Liu Shao-chi visited, had a million people turned up to welcome a visitor. It was an historic occasion. Bhutto was staying at White House, Nawab Sadiq Hussain Qureshi's residence. I hailed a taxi and asked the driver to take me to White House (which bore no resemblance to the one in Washington). It was around nine in the evening. I was sure Bhutto knew that I wanted to meet him as Maulana Kausar Niazi had promised to tell him. I found one procession after another of Bhutto supporters arriving to greet their leader. Every now and then, he would come out onto the balcony of the house, deliver a short speech and disappear till the next group came along. Emotional slogans were being chanted wishing him a long life and declaring that he and the people of Pakistan were one and they would live and die together. In one of his brief addresses, he said the PNA and the PMA (Pakistan Military Academy) were one and if the people of Pakistan were with him, the military junta could do him no harm.

Interviewing Zulfikar Ali Bhutto, Lahore, 1971.

White House was still under construction, or parts of it were, as one could see from the building materials piled up around it. Some of the windows were still without glass, but the lawns were immaculate. However, it did not take long for them to be ruined by the crowds. I tried to get into the main house a number of times but did not succeed. Disappointed, I returned to my hotel at about ten. I called the daily *Musawat*, the PPP daily, and some other newspapers to get more details of Bhutto's arrival, and once I had them, I went to the telegraph office from where I sent a short news story to the office in London, asking them to pick up agency copy to pad it out. Meanwhile, I had learnt that Shah Ahmed Noorani, head of the Jamiat-i-Ulema-i-Pakistan, a member of PNA, the anti-Bhutto front, had been in a car with some companions on his way to the airport. He had been recognised; his turban had been torn and he was made to get on the roof of the car and shout 'Bhutto *Zindabad*!' I mentioned that in my story.

I tried to get hold of Noorani the next day but he had already left for Karachi. In the afternoon, I went to White House and found people gathered here and there in small groups. One group was being addressed by General Tikka Khan, the PPP secretary general and former army chief. I asked around to see if it would be possible to meet Bhutto, but was told that he had an upset stomach and was not receiving visitors. It was suggested that I come the next day. I was able to have a word with Nawab Sadiq Qureshi whom I told of my planned meeting with Bhutto. He assured me that if he had agreed to meet me, then he would certainly do so. However, because of his indisposition, he was receiving no visitors. It would be better if I came the next day, he suggested. When he was in power, it had been impossible to meet him; and now that he was out of power, it was no different. The next day, I went to White House in the afternoon, met Nawab Sadiq Qureshi and asked him to take my message to Bhutto. He said to me, 'Are you under the illusion that I can just march into Mr Bhutto's room? I do not have that kind of courage, brother. But if he sends for me, I will tell him that you are here and waiting in the lounge to see him.' I felt sorry for the man whom Bhutto had made governor of Punjab and who was afraid to knock on his door, unless summoned.

At about seven in the evening, Maulana Kausar Niazi entered the house. He asked me if I had met Bhutto already. I told him that it was difficult even to get word to him; the question of meeting him had not even arisen. He asked me to go with him and the two of us walked into Bhutto's room. He immediately recognised me. I had met him three or four times before. He called me by my name and asked me to take a seat. It was a big room and as you entered, there was a large sofa to the left, on which Bhutto sat, half-sprawled. Niazi left me with Bhutto and walked across the room to take one of the sofas lined against the wall. I asked Bhutto how he was feeling. He said he had eaten something the night before that had a lot of chilli, which had upset his stomach. I had bought a box of cigars on the plane for him because I knew he liked to smoke fine cigars. When I gave him the box, he asked, 'You brought them for me?' 'Yes,' I replied, 'I have been carrying them around for days and had I been unable to meet you, I would have given them to someone else.' He thanked me, opened the box, pulled out a cigar and lit it. He asked me whom I had met since my arrival. I told him that I had met Ziaul Haq and Maulvi Mushtaq Hussain. He said it was good I had met the two people who could give me some idea of what was going on. We had barely started talking when a side door opened and a servant told Bhutto that there was a call for him from Rawalpindi. He did not ask who the caller was, but went into the next room.

After about fifteen minutes, during which no one spoke, not even Maulana Kausar Niazi who sat across the room from me staring into empty space, the door opened and Bhutto came in. He was visibly angry and muttering under his breath, '[he] says he will take my life. I have told the fellow that I have a list of thirty-five generals, none of whom will survive.' Taking my cue from that, I asked, 'Why are you so upset? What's the matter?' He replied, 'Zia was on the phone threatening to kill me. I have told him that if I survive, I will have thirty-five of his generals put to death for abrogating the constitution.' 'But why did he threaten you?' I asked. He looked at his cigar, which had gone out, re-lit it and said, 'I hear Noorani Mian was surrounded by the people yesterday and roughed up. It was a sorry affair. The general said that I was responsible for the incident and I will have to pay the price. This is the first time he has spoken impertinently to me. Every time he came to see me in Murree, he just could not stop 'sirring' me. Today he was full of arrogance. But forget about it, let's talk about something else.' I said, 'This does not sound like an empty threat. Everyone I have talked to here fears for your life.' He drew on his cigar and said, 'I am not afraid of death. I am a man of history and you cannot silence history.'

I told Bhutto what Zia had said to me about holding elections in ninety days. I added that he had chosen 28 October as the day power would be transferred to the elected representatives. Bhutto smiled. 'You expect elections from these people? Don't expect the truth from liars,' he said. 'But he says that is his promise to God and he has also told me that the elections will be free and unrestricted,' I said. 'That is another lie from this general. I have just shared with you the gist of my conversation with the fellow; so you can work out for yourself whether elections will be held in this country or not. If they are held, then what about Zia's threat to me and my counter-threat to him?'

To change the subject, I asked him what had led to the overthrow of his government. Bhutto smiled. 'If you want the truth, then I would say that I chose the wrong advisers. It is also true that a person who reaches the highest office gets caught up in intelligence agency reports and the misleading advice of those he has picked as his lieutenants. Although he knows what the masses want, those around him do not let him take the right road. The class I hate most is that of the semi-intellectuals who drew enormous benefits from me and who are foremost in the ranks of my enemies today. They have ganged up with the army.' When I raised the question of the elections he had held, he replied that there was no organised government plan to rig them. The constituencies where irregularities had taken place were not more than seven in number. But the responsibility lay with the candidates, not the government.

I asked him about the findings of the inquiry he had ordered into the PNA agitation. He replied that he was glad I had asked him that question. The inquiry report was just ten pages long and the military government had a copy, he told me. The investigation had clearly established that the US government was involved in creating countrywide unrest. The Americans had not only spent dollars but the PL-480 reserves in rupees that they held, running into hundreds of millions, had also been thrown in to fuel the agitation. There were incidents where dollars were found tucked into the waist-bands of mullahs. If anyone suffered an injury or died during the protests, opposition leaders rushed to his family with immediate cash compensation. All this money, he added, had come from the American embassy. I asked him what action the government had taken if it had evidence of blatant American interference.

'Let me give you some details,' Bhutto said. 'After we received the results of the investigation, we told the US embassy that we had evidence of its interference in Pakistan's internal affairs and a high-level Pakistani representative would like to discuss this matter with the US secretary of state. We asked for a meeting to be arranged, and to be notified of it expeditiously. After a few days, we were told that the secretary of state was proceeding to Paris to attend a NATO ministerial conference and if a Pakistani representative wished to meet him, he would be welcomed. I decided to send Aziz Ahmed, minister of state for foreign affairs, to Paris with the necessary instructions from the cabinet. He flew to Paris with our investigation report and some other important documents. He was also instructed to confer with the French government in Paris about the nuclear reprocessing plant that we had ordered.

'When he met the secretary of state, he found that the man was not willing to talk about US interference in our affairs.

Whenever Aziz Ahmed brought up the subject, the secretary told him that Pakistan and the US were old allies and what had happened after the 1970 elections should be forgotten; US-Pakistan ties must not be affected by that. Several times, Aziz Ahmed tried to open his briefcase to hand his counterpart our report and other documents and every time he was told to close that chapter and return home satisfied that Pakistan would have no cause for complaint in the future. Aziz Ahmed returned to the embassy, handed over his briefcase to Ambassador Muzaffar Ali Qizalbash, asking to have it safely lodged at the embassy and returned to him at the time of his departure for Pakistan.

'That evening there was a dinner for NATO ministers to which Aziz Ahmed had also been invited, and to which he went. When Aziz Ahmed returned to his hotel,' Bhutto told me, 'he found that his room had been turned upside down, obviously by the CIA. They had been looking for his papers. The mattress and pillows had been ripped open and the even the bathroom had been vandalised. Aziz Ahmed summoned the manager to his room, who was taken aback by what he saw. He was about to call the police when Aziz Ahmed told him not to, but to shift him to another room.' Bhutto drew on his cigar again and said, 'This should give you some idea of what a clash with a superpower can lead to.' I asked him which foreign elements were involved in overthrowing his government. He laughed, 'I don't want to say anything at this point, but I will when the time comes so that the people know the facts.'

When I asked him about Zia's promised elections and what political picture would emerge if they were indeed held in ninety days he replied, 'Let me repeat: there is no chance of elections taking place in ninety days. But if I am wrong, then the elections would wipe out the *waderas*, landlords, *jagirdars* and feudal bigwigs.' I told him that he himself was considered a *wadera*. He replied that as a *wadera*, he too would be finished, but if he continued to reflect popular aspirations, he was confident the people of Pakistan would not reject him. He said his objectives would remain unchanged. He was determined to provide the people of Pakistan with food to eat, money to clothe themselves and a home where they could shelter.

I put it to Bhutto that while both India and Pakistan had inherited the same system of administration and the same army, there had been several coups in Pakistan but none in India. He said in Pakistan there were two basic weaknesses. One was that 85 per cent of the army came from a single province, Punjab, which consequently controlled it. Add to that the fact that the bureaucracy was also largely Punjabi. Both these classes had derived every benefit by dint of the position in which they found themselves after independence. When these two classes, the army and the bureaucracy, join hands in defence of their interests, political forces become helpless in fighting them, he pointed out. Political forces lack confidence and therefore become the tool of these two powerful groups. For the protection of their interests, political forces become dependent on unconstitutional vested interests represented by the military and the civilian bureaucracy. As for India, he added, the bureaucracy and the army did not derive their legitimacy from any particular lobby or constituency. No attempt had been made in India to divide the army on regional lines because that would break up that vast country into dozens of states. The people of India had witnessed the emergence of Pakistan on religious and geographical foundations and learned their lessons. India, he added, was not likely to face a situation where the army chief took the risk of overthrowing the government only to see the country dismembered.

We had been talking for a long time and I therefore sought his permission to leave. He said, 'When you return to London, and if you find me alive here, then do return to Pakistan and we can meet.' I replied, 'I thank you for your offer but if you become prime minister after the elections, people like me would be at the end of a very long queue.' We shook hands and he said, 'Try, I don't think that would happen this time.' Today, when I recall that day, it occurs to me that it was a historic meeting in the sense that it was his last formal interview. On 13 September 1977, he was arrested from his Karachi residence and brought to Lahore, where Justice Samdani released him on bail, but he was rearrested a few days later. He never came out of prison. He was permitted to appear before the Supreme Court of Pakistan when his appeal against the death sentence handed down by Maulvi Mushtaq Hussain was heard and rejected. Scores of mercy petitions, none lodged by him, were rejected by Zia and on 4 April 1979, Zulfikar Ali Bhutto was hanged in Rawalpindi Central Jail.

I was leaving for London the day after the interview and took a flight to Karachi. Before boarding the plane, I decided to file the Aziz Ahmed story; the full Bhutto interview could be written up once I got home. I wrote the story in my hotel and took it to the telegraph office where I handed over the dispatch and my ITU card to a bearded clerk. Since General Zia himself had assured me that there were no censorship restrictions in Pakistan, I was expecting no problems. In fact, instructions had been given to Colonel Salik that I should encounter no difficulties. I noticed that the clerk was reading my dispatch with some care. When I asked him why, he replied that since what I had written was important, he would like to show it to his supervisor before sending it. He noted down my ITU card number and returned the card to me. Then he disappeared.

I stood there waiting for at least forty-five minutes but there was no sign of the bearded gentleman. I asked one of his colleagues if he knew where the man had disappeared to. He smiled and assured me that he had gone upstairs and would be back soon. I requested him to call someone upstairs or phone and ask when the man was coming back since I wanted to return to my hotel. He made the call and informed me that the bearded gentleman would be back shortly. It was another fifteen minutes before he returned, only to tell me that my message could not be sent because it had been blocked. I did not want to get into an argument and therefore asked him to return my dispatch. He replied that he was helpless because my dispatch was with the brigadier sahib. I told him to take me to his brigadier so that I could talk to him. He picked up the phone and spoke to someone.

Then he told me that although it was not easy to see the brigadier, he had agreed to receive me. He stepped out of his cubicle to escort me upstairs.

It was quite a trip because there were at least a dozen armed soldiers standing guard on the stairs. I had no security pass but my escort assured the soldiers that I had been summoned by the brigadier sahib. This took about ten minutes because every soldier on duty had to be assured that I was not an interloper. We stepped into a huge hall containing hundreds of telex machines and printers. It was quite an impressive sight. I was taken to the office of the brigadier who asked me harshly, 'I have blocked your news report, so why are you here?' I told him that while that may perhaps have been his right, all I wanted was to have my story returned. He replied that it was now part of his record. I asked him out of mischief, to at least tell me what particular part of my report he had found objectionable. He opened a drawer and handed me the three pages on which I had typed my dispatch. I tore them up while he watched in disbelief. My escort practically ran out of the room. Dumping the torn paper on his table, I told him that every single word that I had written was safely lodged in my memory and I would rewrite my story in London where there would be nobody to stop me. 'You haven't done the right thing,' the brigadier said, trying to hide his anger and embarrassment. I replied that General Ziaul Haq had personally assured me that there was no censorship in Pakistan and in my presence, he had instructed Colonel Siddiq Salik that nothing that Inam Aziz filed to his newspaper should be stopped. I assured him that I would write my report once I got to London. I would even tear up the notes I had taken during the interview because everything was safe and secure in my mind. The brigadier who had earlier perhaps decided to punish me, now melted at the mention of Ziaul Haq's name. I was still standing, but now he insisted that I take a chair and drink a cup of tea with him before leaving.

The two of us had a fairly interesting conversation. I told him that I was here at General Ziaul Haq's invitation and had held a long meeting with him at GHQ in Rawalpindi after which he had instructed Colonel Salik to make sure that all facilities were available to me. I also told the brigadier about my 11 August meeting with Bhutto in Lahore. I tried to convince him that my story, based on what Bhutto had told me about what happened to Aziz Ahmed in Paris, had nothing to do with the present regime, so there should have been no need to block it. Chucking the torn pieces of my three-page dispatch into the dustbin the brigadier wanted bygones to be bygones. He also told me that General Zia was arriving in Karachi that evening and he would abide by any instructions that may be given by him. I told him not to worry. I was on my way to London anyway, from where I would be able to write my report in perfect peace. The brigadier's last words to me sounded like an appeal, 'Please do not mention what happened here to anyone.'

19 Exile Politics in London

With the arrest of Bhutto from his residence in Karachi on 13 September 1977 for the murder of Nawab Mohammad Ahmed Khan, prominent PPP leaders began to arrive in London, all seeking political asylum. They were afraid that if they had not left, they would have been arrested on one excuse or another. The first to arrive was Malik Ghulam Mustafa Khar, former chief minister and governor of the Punjab. When the coup took place, he was Bhutto's political adviser. He was taken into custody along with nine of his colleagues and locked up in Murree with some leaders of the PNA, the opposition grouping. One evening Khar called me and we decided to meet at his flat in Marble Arch, where he was staying with his new wife Tehmina Durrani. Tehmina had just given birth to a daughter. It was her second marriage and she had become Khar's fifth, if not his sixth, wife. Her father, S.U. Durrani, was now in London as head of an Arab-sponsored bank. He had been chief of the Pakistan International Airlines and the State Bank of Pakistan but had suffered imprisonment and much humiliation under Bhutto. Marble Arch was one of London's most expensive areas. Opposition people accused PPP leaders of having decamped from Pakistan with large sums of money, but I saw no sign of any such wealth during the eleven years Khar stayed in London after the Zia coup.

Khar left the PPP twice, once during Bhutto's days in power when he was removed as governor of the Punjab. At that time, he had raised the issue of Punjabi nationalism and the government had tried to charge him with various offences. He had run against a PPP candidate (Sher Mohammad Bhatti) in a by-election in Lahore and lost. It was Maulvi Mushtaq Hussain who had bailed him out after giving him a hearing in his chamber. He had also directed that, regardless of the nature of any future charge

AN APPEAL TO GENERAL ZIA UL-HAQ, MILITARY RULER OF PAKISTAN

No-one of course, has the right of intervention in Pakistan's internal affairs. But sometimes good friends – who believe in the democratic process, together with a free press and independent judiciary as its essential pillars – might be permitted to put in a timely word.

You assured Mr. Callaghan, as you have sincerely assured other world leaders, of your intention to bring back democracy to Pakistan. Yet there is no doubt (at least in the view of the rest of the world) that if Mr. Bhutto's appeal against his death sentence is denied and he is executed, democracy may face a further and perhaps fatal set-back in troubled Pakistan.

No papers in Pakistan have been permitted to publish details of Mr. Bhutto's appeal against his death sentence. (The Court record of his trial is incomplete and is unavailable in complete form to the press or the Defence.) No paper in Pakistan, except one, whose Lahore editor has since been imprisoned, reported statements in Bhutto's defence at his trial. The Government-owned TV and radio stations were silent.

Bhutto is the target: but is the victim democracy? That is the question people are asking.

We wish Pakistan well. We wish stability, not division. We long to see the return to democracy and freedom you promised last year.

Yet what will happen to Pakistan if :.

observers agree, is that all his (General Zia's) calculations could go awry because of ferment over the Bhutto death sentence".

The Wall Street Journal (March 28 editorial): – "If, in the weeks ahead, his (Bhutto's) neck is stretched by the hangman's noose, there will surely be a lot of blood spilled in Pakistan.... It is too late in the twentieth century to be hanging democrats".

The Daily Telegraph (David Harris March 30): – "There seems certain to be a marked deterioration in Britain's relationships with a country which is still treated as something of a special care".

The Guardian (April 1 editorial): – "The outlook for civil strife in Pakistan will be grim. Accountability, on the Zia model will not have operated because many millions will see it as retribution".

The Daily Telegraph (April 6): – "More than 100 MPs of all parties have signed a Commons motion that the execution of Mr. Bhutto would cause revulsion and do immense damage to the standing of Pakistan abroad".

The Observer (Simon Henderson April 9)

Signed
Jonathan Aitken, M.P.
Rt. Hon. Julian Amery, M.P.
Ronald Bell, Q.C., M.P.
Christopher Brocklebank Fowler, M.P.
Rt. Hon. William Craig, M.P.
Julian Critchley, M.P.
Sir Nigel Fisher, M.C., M.P.
Peter Gallner
Q.C., M.P.

Britain protests the sentence against Mr Bhutto in an advertisement published in the *Times*, signed by prominent politicians and journalists.

Banner headlines in the Urdu daily *Millat* under the editorship of Inam Aziz.

Banner headlines in the daily *Millat* during the editorship of Inam Aziz after Zulfikar Ali Bhutto was hanged on 4 April 1979.

Zulfikar Ali Bhutto's hanging on 4 April 1979 as reported in some papers in London.

against Khar, he would not be arrested. After some time Khar
made up with Bhutto and in his last days, he became the prime
minister's adviser. He left the PPP for the second time when,
despite his protests, Benazir Bhutto, who was herself in exile in
London, appointed Jahangir Badar as president of the Punjab
PPP. His friend and fellow politician Ghulam Mustafa Jatoi was
also browned off with the new leadership of the PPP, and thus
led to the formation of a Khar–Jatoi alliance in London. Jatoi
returned to Pakistan and set up the National People's Party,
which Khar joined.

When Khar returned to Pakistan after ending his political
exile, he was arrested in the Liaquat Bagh firing case, dating
back to 1972 when an opposition public meeting in Rawalpindi
had been attacked and fired upon, allegedly on Khar's orders.
While he was in London, a military court had sentenced him *in
absentia* to a prison term of fourteen years and ordered the
confiscation of all his landed property. In November 1988, he
was elected to the National Assembly from his Kot Addu
constituency. He had also got his friend Jatoi elected from one
of his old constituencies. He did not stay with the enemies of his
old party for long and returned to the fold of the PPP, which he
had left while in London. He used to tell me in London that he
was unwilling to accept Benazir Bhutto's 'dictatorial' attitude.
He once asked me, 'How can I accept the leadership of a girl we
used to call Baby?'

During my meeting with him at his Marble Arch flat, he told
me that from custody in Murree, he had been taken to Rawalpindi
to meet Zia and General F.A. Chishti and urged to take the field
against Bhutto and cooperate with the military regime by
providing evidence of Bhutto's misdeeds. He said he had
returned to Murree and told Bhutto of his meeting. Bhutto had
advised him to go abroad on one excuse or another or the
generals would entrap him on some trumped-up charge. In a
second meeting with General Chishti, Khar told him that he had
once deposited certain tapes and secret documents implicating
Bhutto in a London safe deposit vault, which only he personally

could retrieve. He assured the generals that he would hand over that damning evidence to them to avenge himself on Bhutto, who had subjected him to great humiliation. He pledged loyalty to the regime, which the naïve generals believed. He told them that he would return from London after two to three weeks with all the evidence against Bhutto. Khar hinted that the rent for the Marble Arch flat was being paid by the military government. His wife had been allowed to come with him also. He said that what he really intended to launch in London now was an international campaign to save Bhutto's life, which was in grave danger. He told me that the murder case was going to be heard by Maulvi Mushtaq Hussain, who was a bitter enemy of Bhutto. I knew this was true because I remembered all the abuse he had heaped on Bhutto during our meeting.

Through Khar, I met the two Bhutto sons, Shahnawaz and Murtaza, who were living in a Gloucester Road flat. Shahnawaz, the younger brother, was still a boy, but Murtaza was a sober young man. They were both well educated and committed to saving the life of their father by organising an international campaign. Khar was helping them but it was Murtaza who was in charge. He had established contact with various British MPs as well as Shiekh Zayed bin Sultan Al-Nahyan of the UAE, Colonel Gaddafi of Libya and Hafez al-Asaad of Syria. He had already made several trips to the UAE, Libya and Syria. In his first meeting with the Libyan leader, he had been given a cheque for $75,000 as a contribution to the Save Bhutto Campaign. Although he did not tell me, there was little doubt that he had also received money from Syria for the same purpose. There was no shortage of Bhutto's admirers in England. He had gone to Christ Church College, Oxford, where he had studied under Professor Hugh Trevor-Roper. Another of his sympathisers was Conor Cruise O'Brien, editor-in-chief of *The Observer*. He knew all the important British journalists personally and many members of parliament were among his friends. The group working to save Bhutto was led by MP Jonathan Aitken who was joined by David Watkins, C.B. Fowler, Julian Amery, Nigel

Fisher, Ronald Bell, William Craig, Dennis Walters and Julian Critchley.

In February 1978, a Committee for Press Freedom and Democratic Government was formed in London by Claude Morris with an office in Regency Street, SW1. I held several meetings with him and once accompanied him to the House of Commons to meet a number of MPs. I never asked him but I think it was Murtaza who was backing the committee financially. Claude Morris and Jonathan Aitken also arranged a lunch once at the palace of Westminster on the banks of the Thames a few days after Bhutto was sentenced to death by hanging by Maulvi Mushtaq Hussain. Speakers at the lunch made impassioned appeals for clemency for the former prime minister. Fifty MPs, including Mrs Margaret Thatcher and Neil Kinnock, signed an appeal asking for Bhutto's life to be spared. A full-page advertisement appeared in *The Times* asking for clemency for the Pakistani leader and the restoration of democracy in the country. This advertisement also bore the signatures of various writers and journalists.

Three large protest marches took place in different British cities as part of the campaign to save Bhutto's life. The largest was in London's Hyde Park on 18 March 1978 in which at least 50,000 people took part. *Millat* played a leading role in publicising this march, which led Zia's people in London to spread the rumour that *Millat* had received a lot of money from the PPP. The truth was that we were not even paid for the scores of advertisements we carried to publicise the marches. Later, our board filed a case against Khar, who had placed the advertisements, and even obtained a court decree in its favour. One rumour was that I had met Jam Sadiq Ali, who was now in London, at Heathrow to receive a briefcase full of money. I knew of Jam of course but I had never met him. *Millat* did not even have a picture of him in its files. I was not even sure what he looked like, so I simply ignored such rumours. Besides *Millat*, the other Urdu daily in London was *Jang,* which supported the military regime. We both had sizeable circulations but I think ours was larger because we reflected the people's sympathies for Bhutto and their contempt for Pakistan's military rulers.

During this period, Khar asked me to accompany him to Birmingham where a public meeting was being held in support of Bhutto. A couple of London journalists also came along on the train with us. Facing me in the carriage was A.R. Bangash, editor of the weekly *Mashriq*, and a man with a close-cropped beard. Fifteen minutes into the journey, Bashir Riaz, a steadfast Bhutto supporter, brought us all tea in plastic cups. Khar was sitting to my right, absorbed in conversation with the bearded man. Suddenly Bangash said to me, 'This is really strange. You have taken all that money from Jam Sadiq Ali and you don't even recognise him.' 'Come again,' I said. Bangash pointed to the bearded man sitting next to him and said, 'Meet Jam Sadiq Ali, former minister in the government of Sindh.' While Bangash was going on and on about the big briefcase of money *Millat* had received, I felt two hands gripping my ankles; it was Jam Sadiq Ali. He stood up dramatically, joined both hands in mock supplication and said, 'All I want is a tiny bit of money from the big briefcase I gave you at Heathrow. My financial situation is, well, unspeakable these days. I will sing your praises for the rest of my life if you oblige me.' Everyone burst out laughing.

I saw a lot of Jam Sadiq Ali after that first meeting. He was the most prosperous of the PPP exiles with a house in Swiss Cottage priced at around £300,000. He had rebuilt some of the rooms and when you entered the place, you knew that here lived a landlord, which he was back in Pakistan. One day, he invited me for dinner and while we sat chatting, in walked a Sindhi doctor. After an exchange of greetings, Jam said to him, 'Dinner is ready; eat whenever you want.' After a short while, the man went to the dining table, where food was served to him. He ate by himself and left. This happened at least four more times, as visitors would drop in, eat and leave. I was puzzled. 'I thought it was I who had been invited to dinner,' I finally asked. 'So you are indeed,' Jam said, 'but among us Sindhis, the custom is that no one who visits us at home can leave without eating our food.

You and I will have our dinner at 11 o'clock.' When it was time for me to leave, he presented me with a large painting in a lovely frame as a parting gift.

One day, Jam walked into my office carrying a handful of newspaper clippings and asked me to base a story on them for *Millat* because it would do a lot of good to a lot of people. The clippings related to a Punjabi woman who had established a *ghee* (clarified butter) mill near Birmingham which produced the popular brand Khanum Ghee. She had fallen in love with a young engineer and they had married. The husband had talked her into transferring 51 per cent of the company shares to his name. Before long, the two had separated. The husband had then filed a suit claiming ownership of the company. There had been a good deal of litigation with the verdict going partly in her favour and partly in that of the husband. The story was interesting but I was curious. 'Why are you interested?' I asked. 'Sain,' he replied, 'it is a matter of the heart. If you do what I ask, it would be the answer to my prayers.' It turned out that while the case was in court, this woman used to visit London often. Her house was next to Jam's and the two had met. Things had developed from that point on. I published the story and learnt some time later that Jam and the woman were married. However, the marriage did not last long. I never asked him why.

Another report about *Millat* then being circulated by the regime's friends was that we had received a lot of money from Husna Sheikh, who was reported to be Bhutto's undeclared wife. Her husband, an East Pakistani businessman, had gone missing in 1971. She had gone to Karachi and there were rumours in 1972 that Bhutto and she were secretly married. No evidence of that had ever surfaced so I was not sure if that was indeed a fact. The story being circulated was that Husna Sheikh had been sent to London with a lot of money, some of which had been passed on to *Millat*. Certain Pakistani publications, such as the pro-Zia *Urdu Digest*, Lahore, carried these baseless stories and Pakistan being Pakistan, many believed them. I had never met Husna but was curious to do so. One day, I asked Ghulam Mustafa Khar if he could arrange a meeting. The very next day he had her invite us to dinner.

As he and I were driving towards Bayswater where she lived, I asked him if she was indeed Bhutto's wife. He replied that she was. He also told me that before he had left for London, Bhutto had instructed him to help Husna if she needed it. I told him that if what he had told me was true, it was Bhutto's personal business and I had no interest in it. However, *Millat* was getting a bad name because of these false allegations of being funded by Husna Sheikh. Khar's reply was that if I had taken on the ruling regime, then such allegations should not worry me. My response was that I was not a member of the PPP, nor was *Millat* a party paper. We were opposed to military rule and we wanted the restoration of democracy in Pakistan. He agreed with me and suggested that when I met the lady, I should tell her what was on my mind.

Husna Sheikh was around thirty-five, tall, graceful, and elegantly dressed. Jam Sadiq Ali was already there when we arrived. She complained that for the last week she had not received her copy of *Millat*. She said it was Jam who had taken out a subscription for her but it was mailed to her in another name, not her own. She asked me to kindly renew her subscription, if it had run out. I noted down her mailing address in my diary. I asked her straight out when Bhutto and she had been married. I had hardly finished asking my question when Jam said, 'Sain, it is better that such questions are not asked. It is something personal and it should remain that way.' Husna Sheikh, however, replied, 'I am married to Bhutto. What more can I say?' Khar spoke at this point, saying that I was asking this question because reports were being circulated that *Millat* had received a lot of money from Husna Sheikh so that a pro-Bhutto movement could be launched. She said, 'If I had money, I would not hesitate to spend it for that purpose. But maybe I will win the football pools.' It was quite clear to me that Husna Sheikh was not living in any great style. I never met her again. During dinner, she gave me a piece of paper on which she had written

the names of three books on the Watergate scandal. The books
were American publications. She asked me to get them from
somewhere and pass them on to Jam Sadiq Ali who would see
to it that they reached Bhutto in jail. She had asked Jam to buy
them but he had replied that book buying was not his thing. I
did manage to buy those books with my own money and sent
them to Jam, hoping that they would reach Bhutto.

Though Mir Murtaza, Bhutto's eldest son, lived in the
Kensington area in a nice mews flat, he worked from a leather
factory in Aldgate East where a tiny room with a table and a
typewriter had been set aside for him. That was where he and
his younger brother Shahnawaz went regularly to do their paper
work. The factory belonged to a PPP supporter by the name of
Bashir. One day, as we were talking about the future, Murtaza
told me that he was planning to go to Afghanistan where he
would set up a radio station to beam programmes into Pakistan.
Since he knew that I had worked at the BBC, he asked me if I
would come to Kabul to help him if he succeeded in setting up
the radio station. I told him that the work could be accomplished
in London by recording material and shipping it to Kabul.
Nothing ever came of it; it remained an idea, like so many other
ideas at the time.

It was during this time that I got to know the London barrister,
John Matthews QC, who had a reputation as a brilliant criminal
lawyer. Murtaza hired him to defend his father and sent him to
Lahore when the Bhutto case was being heard at the Lahore High
Court. I met him in his chambers after Bhutto's sentencing. He
was full of praise for the people of Lahore. He told me that when
he tried to leave a tip for a hotel waiter, he would say, 'I cannot
take this; you have come all the way to save Bhutto's life.' Taxi
drivers were the same. 'Everyone I met inside or outside the
court considered it an honour to shake hands with me,' he
recalled. I asked him what his opinion was about the case and
the verdict. He laughed. 'Had I been a judge, I would have
thrown the case file through the nearest window at the first
hearing.' I asked him if he was a close personal friend of Bhutto.

'I have never met him, nor am I aware of his politics. I was engaged by the family to go to Lahore to see in what way the prime minister could be helped and to judge if the trial was proceeding in accordance with law and the requirements of justice.' I asked him what he had found. He replied that the prosecution witnesses were unreliable and the way the court had accepted their testimony had created grave doubts. He said the Lahore High Court was a creation of martial law. That was something he had observed and that was what everyone he had spoken to believed. The acting chief justice, Maulvi Mushtaq Hussain, was known for his enmity to Bhutto and it seemed that with or without trial, the regime wanted to get rid of Bhutto.

I asked him why he thought Maulvi Mushtaq was prejudiced against Bhutto. 'That was not hard to determine,' he replied. 'To begin with, the court refused to let me appear, saying that I was not a member of the Pakistan Bar Council. I pointed out that another British lawyer, Sir Dingle Foot, had been allowed to appear for Sheikh Mujibur Rahman in Dhaka, but was unable to sway the court. Perhaps the military government of the time had permitted Sir Dingle Foot to appear for political reasons. I was present when Mr Bhutto objected that the court was not competent to try him because the former chief justice had refused to take an oath of allegiance to the military government and had been removed. The present acting chief justice was still the chief election commissioner. He could not hold two offices. Mr Bhutto's second objection was that the chief justice was on record as having said that the 1977 elections were rigged and he had held Bhutto responsible for the rigging.' Matthews said no judge in the world could continue to hear a case after such grave charges had been made against him by the defence. He told me that Maulvi Mushtaq's behaviour underwent an improvement the day he found him in his court, but his attitude towards defence lawyers in general was unacceptable. Even the record of the proceedings was unreliable, having been doctored. A good deal of the cross examination of prosecution witnesses was not recorded. Some of the arguments by the defence were similarly left out. It was clear that this tainted record would determine the outcome of the appeal in the Supreme Court. He was doubtful that Bhutto would win in the Supreme Court either. Time proved him right.

Meanwhile, Murtaza and Shahnawaz had moved from Gloucester Road to Lowndes Square, next door to the Pakistan embassy. One night, Shahnawaz phoned the police emergency number saying that there was a bomb in 10 Downing Street which would explode in an hour. He hung up quickly but he did not know that calls to emergency numbers are logged along with the name and address of the caller. The call is also recorded on tape. In about fifteen minutes, the police came to the Lowndes Square flat and arrested both brothers. They were taken to the station and Shahnawaz's voice was identified. He phoned his solicitor, Morris Nadeem, who organised his release on bail. He was tried in the Horseferry Court and fined £5000. Shortly after this incident, the two brothers left England for Kabul where they set up Al Zulfikar, a terrorist group.

The PPP leaders and workers in exile whom I came to know included the party's senior vice president, Sheikh Mohammad Rashid, Rana Shamim Ahmed Khan, cricketer Aftab Gul, Dr Naseer A. Sheikh, Colonel Shamim and Brigadier Usman Khalid. The last two addressed a press conference in their Pakistan army uniforms to announce their resignations. Colonel Shamim worked as a caretaker in a school in Derby for over ten years. He returned to Pakistan when Benazir Bhutto came to power, was arrested and released. He became managing director of the Karachi Steel Mill. Brigadier Usman Khalid settled in London and went into business. He later became sympathetic to the Muslim League led by Muhammad Khan Junejo. Another noted personality who also paid visits to London at the time was Begum Nasim Wali Khan, wife of the NAP leader Khan Abdul Wali Khan. I had never met her but I always admired the contribution made by her husband and her father-in-law, Khan Abdul Ghaffar Khan, to the freedom movement though I may not have been in agreement with their politics.

Once when Begum Nasim Wali Khan came to London, her husband was in Europe. I am not sure if she had her own place or if she was staying with friends. I do know that the couple had relatives in Birmingham. Also in London at the same time was Sardar Sherbaz Mazari. One day, she went to Oxford Street for a McDonald's hamburger but first walked into the famous store, Marks & Spencer, where she stole some undergarments and stuffed them in her shoulder bag. She was caught by one of the store's security cameras and as she was leaving the store, she was stopped. When the security officer asked her if she had paid for what she had taken, she replied that she had bought nothing. She was taken to the manager's office and searched. All the stolen goods were recovered from her bag. The police were sent for and took her to the station, from where she phoned Mazari who arrived with a solicitor and had her released on bail. Eventually, the case went to court. Not long before, an Arab princess had been caught stealing goods worth no more than a few pounds. Much diplomatic pressure had been exerted on her behalf but in vain. She had been fined £10,000. When she was caught, she had thousands of pounds in her purse in cash. This story was displayed prominently in the press but Begum Wali Khan's arrest did not make the papers.

While an ordinary person caught shoplifting is not news, a public figure is. I came to know of the Begum Nasim Wali Khan incident two days later. When I called her people, I was informed that no such incident had taken place. I called the police who told me everything. *Millat* carried the Begum Nasim Wali Khan story under a big banner headline. We called Marks & Spencer the next day to obtain a list of the goods she had stolen. Their total worth was under ten pounds. That was our banner headline the next day. The reaction was immediate, with people calling *Millat* and expressing their shock and condemnation that Pakistan should have been so disgraced by one of its well-known public figures. Some callers said that she should have indulged her kleptomania in Pakistan rather than abroad. General F.A. Chishti was in London and Begum Wali Khan met him at the

Pakistan embassy, asking him to help stop the 'indecent' propaganda against her by *Millat* which, she said, was a pro-Bhutto and pro-PPP newspaper. She even asked that steps should be taken to close down *Millat*. General Chishti spoke to the ambassador who told him that there was nothing the embassy could do. If what the newspaper was printing was libellous, then a suit should be filed against its editor and publisher. She walked out of the embassy in a state of fury. The entire story of what had transpired at the embassy, which we got from one of our sources, was printed in *Millat* the following day.

Sardar Sherbaz Mazari had, in the meantime, returned to Pakistan where he and NAP leaders tried a whitewash job by alleging that Begum Wali Khan had fallen victim to an 'international conspiracy' hatched by *Millat* at the insistence of the PPP, to give the Zia regime a bad name. Mazari, who had the reputation of being a seasoned politician and a man of dignity, issued a rather strange statement from Karachi. He said that it was all an attempt by Bhutto and his people to malign Begum Wali Khan. He asked why she should have felt the need to steal undergarments when she did not wear any. 'How does he know?' people asked as they snickered. When the case was heard, her lawyers produced several international magazines in which her husband and his party had been featured. It was said that she was the wife of one of Pakistan's most respected politicians and her mistake should be condoned. She was fined £500 and ordered to pay costs. She left for Pakistan soon after. Throughout the sixteen days that the story was alive, it ran on the front page in *Millat* every single day. Though her husband came to Britain several times after that incident, she never returned.

20 Benazir Bhutto and I

On the second day of December 1988, Benazir Bhutto was sworn in as the first woman prime minister of Pakistan. I was by then working as the London correspondent of *The Pakistan Times* and three other National Press Trust (NPT) newspapers, *Imroze, Mashriq* and *Morning News*. A new age of democracy had dawned in Pakistan.

My association with the NPT newspapers began in September 1988 after a meeting with Maqbul Sharif, chief editor of *The Pakistan Times*, who was returning to Pakistan via London after attending a conference in Vienna. I had first met him in 1960 when he was secretary of the First Wage Board Award. He knew my views about military dictatorships. I should add that he had been quite close to General Ziaul Haq and considered him a great man. He was sad that the general had died in an air crash at a time when he was laying the foundations of a new polity in Pakistan. He was sure that, had Zia succeeded, no politicians would then have been able to practise their 'antics'. Although he was the chief editor, he had no hire and fire power. When he asked me to work for the newspaper group, he also told me that my appointment would be confirmed after it was cleared with Ziaul Islam Ansari, chairman of the NPT, whom I had known since 1955. I told him that as I had known Ansari for so long, he was not likely to oppose my appointment. He suggested that we should phone him. We got him in Lahore, having failed to find him in Islamabad. I asked him if he would have any objection were my proposal to be sent to him by Maqbul Sharif. He assured me that he would sign it the moment it arrived. He told me that he did not have to be told what my professional abilities were; he had always believed me to be a journalist of great professional competence. I handed the phone to Maqbul Sharif and the matter was settled.

Maqbul Sharif was still in London when the Lahore High Court announced that General Ziaul Haq's dismissal of the Junejo government was illegal and unconstitutional. Members of the National Assembly had thereafter demanded that the Assembly should be summoned immediately to deal with the new situation. Maqbul Sharif was greatly agitated by the High Court decision and told me that he would only know about the attitude of the interim government, which had been set up since Zia's disappearance from the scene, once he arrived in Pakistan. He also asked me to visit Pakistan as soon as I received my letter of appointment. He wanted me to meet members of the newsroom as those were the people I would be dealing with, not him.

On 19 October, I received a letter from the general manager of Progressive Papers Ltd, appointing me London correspondent of all NPT newspapers. I was to be paid in Pakistani rupees plus an out-of-pocket allowance of fifty pounds in London. I had no objection to those conditions; I was keen to return to the profession as I had been out of it for quite some time due to health problems. The interim government in the meanwhile went to appeal in the Supreme Court, which, I have always maintained, acts as a handmaiden of the military government when it is in power, but as soon as it is out, the Court begins to take bold decisions. One Zia decision that the Court overturned was his ban on party-based elections. It also confirmed the High Court judgment that the dismissal of the Junejo government had been unconstitutional. However, it did not revive the National Assembly, which had been dissolved after Zia's dismissal of the Junejo government. The Court said that since the interim government had declared 16 November 1988 as the date for new elections, there was no need to revive the old assembly.

The Pakistan of Ziaul Haq was gone, as was the judge who had threatened me. I decided to return to the country, first to straighten out my arrangement with NPT newspapers, and secondly, to witness how the election campaign was shaping up. I landed in Karachi and stayed there for a few days. I decided to meet Benazir Bhutto who was busy with her campaign. I had met her a number of times in London in 1986. My first meeting had not gone well because when I referred to her father as Mr Bhutto, she asked me to call him 'Shaheed Baba', forgetting that I was a journalist, not a member of her party. Several times she faulted me for having met Ziaul Haq. Her secretary at the time was Safdar Hamdani. Bashir Riaz, who became her spokesman when she was prime minister, was nowhere in evidence. In one of my meetings she told me to give Bashir Riaz a job next time I brought out a newspaper. Because there were so many people I had to meet in Karachi after more than eleven years of absence from the city, I did not manage to meet Benazir. I left for Lahore to straighten things out with the newspaper whose London correspondent I had become.

Maqbul Sharif met me with great warmth and introduced me to everyone in the newsroom. He had continued to remain a Zia loyalist and the paper remained anti-PPP as far as possible. After a few days in Lahore, I came to the conclusion that it was not Maqbul Sharif but Z.A. Suleri, adviser to the ministry of information, who had influence over the newspaper's policy. Suleri, who was a Zia appointee, was also an adviser to President Ghulam Ishaq Khan. One day, as I was sitting in Maqbul Sharif's office, he received a call from the federal information secretary who wanted to know under whose authority a certain front-page analysis had appeared. Maqbul Sharif had not read it but he looked it up as he spoke to the official and told him that it had nothing to do with him; as the author was none other than Suleri, he was the right person to ask. He told the secretary that Suleri had sweeping powers and he could do what he liked, not only to the news columns but the editorial page as well. The secretary told Maqbul Sharif that he had President Ishaq on the other line and would, Maqbul Sharif, like him to tell the president what he had just told him. 'Go right ahead,' Maqbul Sharif replied.

Maqbul Sharif then looked at the article that had prompted the agitated call from Islamabad. Suleri had written that it seemed the world press wanted to build up Benazir Bhutto like Corazon Aquino of the Philippines and to bring her back. Maqbul

Sharif phoned the secretary and confirmed that the article was indeed written by Suleri. The secretary told him that the president was in a rage, saying that he was not there to smooth Benazir Bhutto's path to power. In fact, if it was in his power, he would prevent her attaining the high office being sought for her. On 16 November 1988, nationwide elections were held and the next day, it was clear that although it did not have a clear majority, the party with the largest number of votes was the PPP. It was also evident that after some political give and take, it would be the PPP that would emerge as the ruling party.

The day provincial assembly elections were held, I was on my way back to London. Despite his reservations, President Ishaq could not block Benazir Bhutto and on 2 December 1988, she was sworn in as prime minister. One of her first announcements was that she would order the dissolution of the National Press Trust, a relic of the Ayub years, and lift all restrictions on the press. She also vowed to abolish the 'press advice' system. Javed Jabbar, who had joined the party during the election campaign, was appointed minister of state information and broadcasting. These were inspiring announcements and I felt that authoritarianism would end in Pakistan once and for all.

On 29 December, I ran into Nasim Ahmed, *Dawn*'s former chief overseas correspondent, in London, who had been to Paris to accept an award given to Benazir Bhutto as one of the best dressed women in the world. He told me that on 10 January 1989, she was going to Saudi Arabia to perform Umra and meet King Fahd and other Saudi leaders. He had learnt of this in Paris. He had also come to know that Benazir Bhutto was among the heads of state and government being invited to the next Bastille Day for her contribution to the promotion of human rights. That morning, I had heard a programme on BBC radio that, following a survey, declared Benazir Bhutto to be one of the three women who had most influenced international events. (The other two were Mrs Margaret Thatcher and Edwina Curry, who had resigned from the British cabinet after a dispute over her findings concerning a health hazard associated with eggs.) I filed all these stories to *The Pakistan Times* which carried them in its Islamabad edition on 30 December. I viewed the stories more in the nature of good public relations which would enhance Benazir's image. However, the story about her Saudi visit created a storm.

The Saudi ambassador in Pakistan had been told of the prime minister's desire to visit the kingdom and call on King Fahd. The Saudi embassy had completed the necessary protocol arrangements but no formal confirmation had yet been received from Riyadh. Meanwhile, the opposition group, Islamic Jamhoori Itehad (IJI) was lobbying the Saudis not to have Benazir Bhutto received by the king if she went to Riyadh. Azad Kashmir president, Sardar Abdul Qayyum, had been flown to the kingdom to persuade the Saudis that the prime minister's visit should be treated as a private one and, further, that she should not be received by King Fahd. When my story was published, the Saudi ambassador called on the prime minister to complain that her visit had not yet been formally approved by Riyadh yet the story was already in the press, and, what was more, in an 'official' newspaper like *The Pakistan Times*. I am told that Benazir Bhutto was so angry over the publication of the story that she summoned Javed Jabbar and asked him to inquire how the story had got out. She told him that the announcement should have come from the Saudi government.

Next day, the Foreign Office contradicted the story. There was no NPT chairman as Ziaul Islam Ansari had resigned when the government had changed. An additional secretary of the ministry of information was looking after the NPT in the interim. As soon as he got to know what had happened, he went on leave, appointing the general manager of the NPT acting chairman in his place. This man immediately issued orders that Inam Aziz, the London correspondent, should be sacked. At *The Pakistan Times* there was much upheaval. Maqbul Sharif was removed and in his place, Mohammad Idris, a senior assistant editor of the newspaper, was appointed. Unfortunately, he died of a sudden heart attack a couple of days later and his place was taken by I.A. Rehman. He took up his post on the 1st or 2nd of

January 1989. In London, the filing authority, or the ITU card, that *The Pakistan Times* had issued in my name had expired on 31 December. I had been working on a story about Pakistan's return to the Commonwealth and spoken to sources in the British government, the Pakistan embassy and the Indian high commission in London because India was likely to block Pakistan's re-entry. I only learnt that I had been sacked when I phoned the general manager of the Trust in Islamabad asking for my ITU card's renewal.

My summary removal was significant in view of the changed situation in Pakistan. After all, the new government had declared that there would be complete press freedom in Pakistan and the press advice system had been abolished. There had also been promises of respecting the rights of working journalists and doing everything to protect their freedom and dignity. There had also been an announcement that journalists who had suffered under Zia's authoritarian rule would be compensated. I could not forget what Benazir Bhutto had said in her address to the nation on 2 December:

> Individual freedom is the basis of a democratic system. Our long struggle will, *Insha Allah*, succeed. We will revoke all laws and rules which are against the freedom of press in order that the press in Pakistan is free. We will dissolve the National Press Trust. We will give autonomy to television and radio so that they may fully serve the masses. The Pakistan People's Party will ensure restoration of the credibility of the media in order to gain the confidence of the masses and freely bring to them correct information and provide healthy entertainment. The practice of press advice will be discontinued. We are resolved to safeguard the rights, honour and dignity of working journalists and to better the conditions of their work and of the laws in respect of their wages. We will rehabilitate in a dignified manner those who had to undergo sufferings during the struggle for restoration of democracy, and adequate compensation will be paid to them. We will build monuments to commemorate the martyrs of democracy and light eternal flames to perpetuate the memories of those martyrs of democracy who paid the supreme sacrifice of their lives in order that the nation's conscience may live.

The amusing part is that my story turned out to be accurate and Benazir Bhutto left for Saudi Arabia on 10 January 1989 where she performed Umra and met King Fahd. I had been punished for filing a truthful report. I contacted the new chief editor, I.A. Rehman, as did my friend in Vienna, Khalid Hasan, who protested about the treatment I had received. Rehman responded by writing both to Khalid and to the information minister, Javed Jabbar. To Khalid he wrote,

I have been trying to sort out the case of Mr Inam Aziz who also spoke to me on the telephone and later on sent a telex message. The whole thing happened before I came here. Investigations reveal that the prime minister had taken strong exception to a news item filed by Mr Inam Aziz and the NPT was so frightened that it ordered immediate termination of his services. The situation here is that there is no chairman of the NPT and an additional secretary of information was asked to take charge but he too had proceeded on leave. The general manager of NPT is acting chairman and about his ability to deal with important letters I had better not write. I took up the matter with Senator and Minister Javed Jabbar and he promised to look into it. Now I have written a personal appeal to him because the NPT will not be moved until it receives instructions from the PM. You might ask as to what the hell I am doing here. I don't know myself because I was rushed out of *Viewpoint* to come to *The Pakistan Times* and will take charge after sunset and I am still looking into the affairs of the paper so as to be able to determine what needs to be done and what kind of powers I should have. Please rest assured that all the debts to friends—as all those who stood up against the hated regime are our friends—will be duly redeemed.

I.A. Rehman's letter to Javed Jabbar on 22 January said,

This is in continuation of my reference to the case of Mr Inam Aziz, briefly the NPT correspondent in London, to which I had drawn your attention when we met in Islamabad last. Mr Inam Aziz rang me up from London to protest against the abrupt manner in which his services have been terminated. Mr Khalid Hasan, our valued friend, whom perhaps you know well, telephoned from Vienna to draw

attention to the injustice done to Mr Inam Aziz—who has suffered
a great deal during the past decade for his support of the people's
struggle for democracy. The facts of the case are that Mr Inam Aziz
was appointed correspondent in London some months ago by the
then chief editor Mr Maqbul Sharif. About three weeks ago, he filed
a story regarding Mohtarma Benazir Bhutto's projected visit to
Saudi Arabia. The report was not incorrect but the prime minister
did not want protocol arrangements for her in Saudi Arabia to be
leaked in advance and by sources other than the Saudis. She was
naturally upset and legitimately annoyed. Learning of her
displeasure, the NPT overreacted and sacked Mr Inam Aziz. I will
be in a position to vouch for Mr Aziz's suitability or otherwise for
the London post only after some time, though I have great respect
for his steadfastness in the years of adversity. However, I cannot
uphold dismissals of staff members in the manner evident in this
case.

I.A. Rehman's letters to Khalid Hasan and to Javed Jabbar
held out the promise that the period now beginning would not
bring disappointment to journalists, especially those who had
continued to struggle for democracy and had stood up against
authoritarian rule. Unfortunately, however, Pakistan slipped back
into the darkness out of which some of us had believed it had
finally emerged. Benazir surrounded herself with an army of
advisers, each one of whom was busy feathering his own nest.

When I realised that I.A. Rehman's letters had had no effect,
I spoke to Dr Nasir A. Sheikh, who had been appointed Benazir's
adviser for overseas and scientific affairs. He came to London at
the beginning of March 1989 on an official trip. When he had
been living here in exile, he used to meet me with the greatest
humility and friendliness, but when I spoke to him this time, I
felt that I was standing on the ground looking up and he was
somewhere up high looking down on me. When I told him what
had happened, he promised to have it all sorted out on his return
but he did nothing of the kind. Later in the same month, I had
to go to Pakistan on personal business where I met Javed Jabbar
twice and his ministry's adviser, Irshad Rao. Both agreed that

what had happened to me was unfair and they would have it undone. However, they did nothing.

In July 1989, Javed Jabbar was in London for an interparliamentary conference. I met him at a reception held by the English Speaking Union. He had forgotten about our two meetings in Islamabad. When I said to him that he and his principals should at least stop declaring to the world that there was press freedom in Pakistan and that journalists could work without restrictions, he asked me to give him a note and he would do the necessary on his return to Pakistan. I gave him the note he had asked for on 11 August, along with related documents. When he returned to Pakistan, he became involved in a fracas with Irshad Rao, whom he sacked. Not long after, Javed Jabbar himself was eased out of his ministry and put in charge of scientific affairs. Nothing came of his promises, nor was I reinstated. All I can say is that those who used to shout themselves hoarse about freedom of the press slunk into their holes like rats on tasting power.

Such is life.

F/KIN

FRANCIS CLOSE HALL LEARNING CENTRE

CHELTENHAM
&
GLOUCESTER
College of Higher Education

Francis Close Hall
Swindon Road, Cheltenham
Gloucestershire GL50 2QF
Telephone: 01242 532918 714600

TEACHING RESOURCES

FIND THE WHITE HORSE

DICK KING-SMITH

—FIND THE—
WHITE HORSE

Illustrated by Larry Wilkes

VIKING

VIKING

Published by the Penguin Group
Penguin Books Ltd, 27 Wrights Lane, London W8 5TZ, England
Penguin Books USA Inc., 375 Hudson Street, New York,
New York 10014, USA
Penguin Books Australia Ltd, Ringwood, Victoria, Australia
Penguin Books Canada Ltd, 2801 John Street, Markham, Ontario,
Canada L3R 1B4
Penguin Books (NZ) Ltd, 182–190 Wairau Road, Auckland 10, New
Zealand

Penguin Books Ltd, Registered Offices: Harmondsworth, Middlesex,
England

First published 1991
1 3 5 7 9 10 8 6 4 2

Filmset in Century Schoolbook
Printed in England by Clays Ltd, St Ives plc

A CIP catalogue record for this book is available from the British
Library

ISBN 0–670–83296–0

Contents

Chapter ONE   In the Nick of Time   7

Chapter TWO   Out Through the Door   15

Chapter THREE   'A Girt Explosion'   25

Chapter FOUR   The Barbecue   33

Chapter FIVE   Horseview Cottage   41

Chapter SIX   To Find a Motorway   48

Chapter SEVEN   Deserted   58

Chapter EIGHT   Down the M1   66

Chapter NINE   Long Odds   76

Chapter TEN   A Battering-ram   80

Chapter ELEVEN   A Nice Bright Red Coat   87

Chapter TWELVE   Dreams   96

Chapter THIRTEEN   Backed Like a Weasel   99

Chapter FOURTEEN   Snap!   108

Chapter FIFTEEN   Nearly Home   113

Chapter SIXTEEN   'He's Brought
Some Friends'   122

Chapter SEVENTEEN   Happy Ending   127

Chapter One

IN THE NICK
OF TIME

They say that people often look very like the animals that they keep. That would have been difficult for the Manager of the Dogs' Home, for in it, at any one time, were always lots of very different-looking dogs, so that he could not possibly have resembled them all.

In fact, the Manager had a rather sharp face with a pointed chin, and a whiskery little moustache and small neat ears, so that he looked much more like a cat than a dog. Which was odd, because he hated cats.

In particular he hated the one and only cat that lived at the Dogs' Home. It was a Siamese tom, belonging to the Manager's wife.

She had bought it as a kitten, and had made a great fuss of it for a while, and then – for she was that sort of a person – had grown bored with it and paid it no attention.

The only attention it got was from the Manager, in the shape of a sly kick aimed at it whenever they met. The Manager nursed a secret hope that the cat would find its way

into the kennel of a large fierce dog.

In the central part of the Dogs' Home was the kennel-block, a row of a dozen wired enclosures facing a similar row, with a corridor in between. Every morning the cat came down the corridor on a tour of inspection of whatever stray or lost or unwanted dogs chanced to be in the Home at that time.

He came chiefly out of a sense of mischief. It was fun to rub himself against the wire of the kennel doors and listen to the furious growls and barks and yaps and snarls of the inmates, inches away, as they told him in no uncertain terms just what they would do with him if only they could get at him.

Not all of them did this – some were too

dispirited to take notice of him – but certainly no dog had ever said a kind word to him. Until one day he made a friend.

There was a new arrival that morning, a large and hairy mongrel whose collar carried a metal disc that said simply LUBBER. His ears were floppy, his tail was long and bushy, and in colour he was white with brown patches. The Siamese was on his rounds at the time, and he waited until the kennelmaid had shut the dog in and gone away. Then he rubbed himself against the wire and waited for the outburst. None came. Instead the big mongrel looked down at the cat and wagged his tail, with a kind of grin on his hairy face.

'Hello,' he said. 'I'm Lubber. What do they call you?'

'Squintum,' said the Siamese.

Slender and elegant, with a short glossy coat and eyes of a brilliant blue, he was a very well-bred cat, but with a fault. Siamese should actually not be the least bit cross-eyed. Squintum was.

'Well, it's jolly nice to meet you!' said Lubber in his deep voice. 'And I shall look forward to having a good old chinwag later. But just now, I'm tired out. Do forgive me, I simply can't keep my eyes open,' and he lay down upon the bench at the back of the kennel, and fell fast asleep.

Cats are nothing if not curious, and in the days that followed, Squintum spent a good

9

deal of time outside Lubber's kennel. There was not much in the way of conversation between them for it was plain that Lubber, as well as being large and clumsy-looking, was the laziest of dogs, and each morning he would excuse himself after a few words and go back to sleep. But those few words were always kindly and friendly ones, and Squintum had never before been treated in such a way by a dog.

Accordingly, as time passed, he grew worried for his new friend, because he knew the rules of the Dogs' Home. Every morning, round about eleven o'clock, any dog that had not been claimed or placed after two weeks in

the Home was taken from its kennel to the vet's surgery along the corridor. There it was painlessly destroyed.

On the thirteenth morning of Lubber's confinement, when the clock on the wall of the kennel-block said five minutes to eleven, a kennelmaid came in. She opened the door of one of the kennels and took away a small, jolly-looking black-and-white terrier, not much more than a pup.

'Where are they going?' asked Lubber.

'For a little walk,' said Squintum shortly.

That night he made his way out into the streets of the town, and sat on a wall in the moonlight, and looked back at the shadowy outline of the Dogs' Home, and thought about freedom.

I can go where I please, he thought, and

11

some, a few, of those dogs in there may come out of that prison, but for Lubber, tomorrow, it will be too late. Unless I can help. Worth a try, surely?

And so, next morning, Squintum sat waiting and watching, his long thin tail curled neatly round him, as the kennelmaid opened Lubber's door. Lubber, of course, was asleep. Five minutes more, thought Squintum, and you will sleep for ever.

'Come on, old chap!' said the kennelmaid brightly. 'We're going for a little walk,' and as the big dog got to his feet, yawning, she fastened a lead on to his collar.

'What a shame!' she said, stroking the hairy head. 'Can't think why someone hasn't claimed you. Or why someone didn't want you for a pet. Must have been because you're such a lazy old

thing, I think. Every time anybody came to choose a dog, you were asleep. They probably thought you were ill. Ah well! Come along then, Lubber. At least you won't feel anything.'

She led Lubber out and along the corridor. Squintum followed. It was three minutes to eleven.

In the surgery, the vet was loading a syringe. He turned as the door opened and the kennelmaid and the dog came in. Unobserved, Squintum slipped through behind them.

The vet looked consideringly at Lubber.

'He's a big one,' he said, laying down the syringe. 'Don't try to lift him up on to the table by yourself, you'll slip a disc. I'll give you a hand. Does he need muzzling?'

'No,' said the kennelmaid. 'He wouldn't bite anyone. It'd be too much effort. He's ever such a lazy old thing.'

Together they lifted Lubber up on to the table, where he stood patiently, wagging his tail, slowly, so as not to tire himself, and gave them a smily look from under his bushy eyebrows.

The vet picked up a pair of scissors.

'Just going to take a little of this hair off your foreleg, old fellow,' he said, and he snipped away, making a small, close-cropped patch. Then he felt for a vein.

'Right,' said the vet, 'that'll do,' and to the kennelmaid he said, 'Just grip the leg tight, here,' and he picked up the syringe. With his

13

other hand he patted Lubber, who wagged a trifle faster.

'Now,' said the vet, 'this won't hurt.'

Through the surgery window came the sound of a distant church clock, striking the first stroke of eleven.

Siamese have particularly harsh voices, unpleasant to many people's ears, and just as the vet was about to slip the needle into the vein, Squintum let out a sudden ear-splitting yowl.

To the two startled humans the noise, of course, meant nothing. It was just a nuisance and a distraction, making the vet put down his syringe and the kennelmaid release her hold on the dog's leg.

But to Lubber, wondering why he was being made to stand on a table and feeling he would be much more comfortable lying down and perhaps taking a nap, it was clear what the Siamese was saying.

'Run for it!' squalled Squintum at the top of his awful voice. 'Follow me! Or else they'll kill you!'

Chapter Two

OUT THROUGH
THE DOOR

Lubber was not the most quick-witted of dogs, and the full meaning of Squintum's final words hadn't really dawned upon him. But he had been trained, from a puppy, to respond to simple commands, and now he had received two – to run for it and to follow the cat – and he obeyed. With one mighty leap, he was off the table and out of the surgery door. Behind him, the vet and the kennelmaid stood open-mouthed. On the floor, knocked off by a passing blow from Lubber's shaven foreleg, lay the syringe.

Along the corridor raced Squintum, and into the kennel-block. Unlike the inmates of the Dogs' Home, who knew only their prison cells, Squintum knew every inch of the place.

Now, like all their kind, the dogs in the kennel-block grew wildly excited as Squintum sped down the central passage between their cages, followed, at his best speed, by the lumbering Lubber. Here was a scene to relieve the monotony of their days! How each and

every one of them longed to be in Lubber's place, doing what all right-minded dogs should do – chase a cat!

'Go get him, Lubber boy!' they shouted. 'Knock his block off! Beat the living daylights out of him! Tear 'im and eat 'im!'

On ran the Siamese, the bloodthirsty cries dying away behind him, through the office, through the Manager's sitting-room, through the kitchen, making for the back door. Behind him Lubber galloped wildly, swerving round corners, sliding on polished floors, skidding on rugs, knocking over little tables bearing little ornaments that broke into little pieces, intent only on following the cat as he had been told.

Squintum was the most quick-witted of cats, but on this occasion not quick enough. Intent only on saving the dog's life, he had momentarily forgotten the difference in their sizes.

The back door of the Dogs' Home was a

glass-panelled one, with a metal cat-flap set in the bottom of it, through which went Squin-tum with the ease of long practice and the speed of light. Passers-by in the street outside saw a lean cream-coloured cat with a dark face and legs and tail come shooting out of a cat-flap, and then they jumped in startled surprise.

With a shattering crash, the glass-panelled back door of the Dogs' Home exploded into a thousand shards and splinters, as through it, as easily as if it had been a paper hoop in a circus ring, burst a large hairy dog. Away he went in pursuit of the distant cat, and then there was nothing to be heard but a tiny tink-ling as a last fragment of glass fell on to the pavement.

Squintum was making for the park, by a short cut, through quiet back streets. Lubber, it was plain, was accident-prone, and the Siamese saw little point in saving a life only to have it extinguished beneath the wheels of a passing car or lorry. Also, he wanted to confuse possible pursuers, so he doubled and twisted through a maze of narrow alleys and passageways until he came to the park gates.

Over the grass he ran, past the ornamental gardens and the adventure playground, till he came to the bandstand, in the centre of the park. Up its steps he went, and stopped in the middle of its circular interior, and sat and waited.

In a minute or two Lubber arrived, puffing and blowing like a grampus, and flumped down upon the ground, exhausted. Squintum waited for the big dog to get his breath back.

He speculated upon Lubber's probable first words. After all, he thought, I've just saved his life.

'Oh, how can I ever thank you enough?'

That's what he'll probably say.

But then he heard a snore.

'Lubber!' said Squintum sharply. 'I hope you realize that I've just saved your life?'

Lubber sat up. It is not possible to say that he looked shamefaced, for his face was so hairy as to be expressionless. But he scratched himself in an embarrassed way, and seemed unwilling to meet the slightly in-turned gaze of the Siamese's blue eyes.

'I don't understand,' he muttered. 'You said those humans were going to kill me. But humans aren't like that, Squintum. I've never seen that man in the white coat before, but that girl – she was kind to me while I was in that place. And my own people at home – where I've always lived, before I got lost, that is – they've always been ever so good to me. Humans don't kill dogs, surely?'

'Sometimes they do,' said Squintum, and he explained everything about the Dogs' Home and places like it, and why, because people are either thoughtless or cruel, there are so many stray dogs abandoned by their owners.

'Too many to cope with,' he finished, 'so they just put them to sleep.'

'But I don't mind going to sleep,' said Lubber. 'In fact, I love it.'

'It's an expression,' said Squintum. 'They kill them. They were about to kill you. I saved you.'

'Oh,' said Lubber slowly. 'Oh, how can I ever thank you enough?'

'That remains to be seen,' said Squintum drily. 'In the meantime, are you hurt?'

'Hurt?'

'In case you didn't notice, you ran straight through a glass door.'

'Oh,' said Lubber.

He stood up and shook himself. Small pieces of glass flew out of his coat. 'No,' he said. 'I don't think so.'

'It's that thick hair of yours,' said Squintum.

And that thick head, he thought.

'They'll be angry, won't they?' said Lubber. 'The people at the Dogs' Home?'

'They will,' said Squintum, 'And not only with you. I think I'd better steer clear of the place for a while.'

'But don't you belong to someone?' asked Lubber. 'I do.'

Squintum chose not to answer the dog's question. Instead he said, 'Just now you mentioned your people at home. Whereabouts is your home?'

Lubber hung his head.

'I don't know,' he said.

The Siamese cat leaped nimbly up on to the balustrade that surrounded the covered bandstand. From this vantage point, he could see all around the park. He settled himself comfortably.

'Tell me, Lubber,' he said. 'How exactly did you come to be lost?'

Lubber sighed.

'I expect you think I'm a bit thick in the head,' he said.

'Oh, what an idea!' said Squintum. 'Why do you say such a thing?'

'Well, you must think it funny that I don't know where my home is. But you see, Squintum, it's nowhere near here. In fact, it must be hundreds of miles from this town.'

'You've walked hundreds of miles?'

'No. I rode.'

'In a car?'

'No. In a furniture van.'

'Start at the beginning,' said Squintum.

'Well,' said Lubber, 'I belong to two old ladies, sisters they are, and we live in a thatched cottage in a little village under a big hill. Ever so nice to me, they are – were – and I was as happy as could be. Mind you, their legs weren't too strong, even though they each had three of them.'

'Three legs each!' said Squintum.

Lubber's eyes twinkled under his bushy brows.

'Yes,' he said. 'Two ordinary ones and a wooden one. They both walked with a stick, you see. I was pulling *your* leg. Anyway, we never had to walk very far, which was a mercy.

I'm not too fond of exercise. What's more, I like to take a nap every now and then.'

He yawned.

'All that running's tired me out,' he said. 'Can't I tell you the rest later?'

'No,' said Squintum sharply. 'Go on.'

'One day,' said Lubber, 'the family in the house next door to our cottage were moving, you see, and this big furniture van came and parked outside. My old ladies had gone down to the shop at the other end of the village – I kept out of the way, it's a good quarter of a mile – and then it came on to rain and I couldn't get into the cottage. So I climbed into this furniture van. The removal men were inside the house – they'd finished loading everything and I expect they were having a cup of tea – so I thought I'd just shelter for a bit. Now one of the things in the van was a very comfy-looking sofa, and I suddenly felt like having forty winks. I dare say you can guess the rest.'

'They shut the doors and drove off,' said Squintum.

'That's right. Next thing I knew we were moving. I couldn't see out and I didn't know where we were going. I just hoped it wouldn't be too far, and then perhaps I could walk home.'

'That would have been very tiring, surely?' said Squintum.

'I suppose so,' said Lubber. 'But as it was, we went on and on for ages before at last they

stopped and opened the doors and I jumped out and ran off. Like I said, I must be hundreds of miles from home. I wandered round the town for a bit, sleeping rough, you know, eating out of dustbins, that sort of thing, until a man in uniform caught me . . .'

'. . . the Dog Warden,' said Squintum.

'. . . and put me in that place where you live.'

'And where you nearly died.'

'Grrrrr!' said Lubber, shaking himself. 'Whatever am I to do, Squintum?'

The Siamese stood up on the balustrade of the bandstand and looked all around the park for possible danger. Seeing none, he stretched himself luxuriously, unsheathing his claws and dragging each forefoot in turn along the wooden rail with a rasping sound.

'Talk about needles in haystacks!' he said. 'A thatched cottage in a little village under a big hill. Gordon Bennett! There must be thousands of such cottages.'

'Ah, but wait!' said Lubber. 'I've just remembered. There's a White Horse on the hill. We can see it from our garden.'

'There must be thousands of white horses,' said Squintum. 'Anyway, the horse might have been moved to another place or sold or anything.'

'No, no! Not a live horse. A great picture of one, cut into the turf of the hillside.'

Squintum's tail-tip twitched.

'That's interesting,' he said. 'They don't

23

have such things in these northern parts. Must be chalk country. Looks as if we should head south.'

Lubber, who had lain down, exhausted by so much talking, sprang to his feet.

'"We"?' he said. 'D'you mean . . .?'

'Thought I might accompany you,' said Squintum. 'I can't say I'm very happy here, and I'm still young, and I've a good few lives left. Mind if I come along?'

'Mind?' barked Lubber. 'I should say not! Why, with you to help me, I might stand a better chance of finding my way home. And my old ladies would love you!'

What a nice sort of animal you are, he thought.

'But,' Lubber went on, 'I don't know why you should do this for me. I don't know why you saved my life this morning. Have you done that before, for other dogs?'

'No,' said Squintum.

'Why me?' said Lubber.

I don't really know, thought the Siamese. I just rather like you.

'Ask me no questions and I'll tell you no lies,' he said. 'And now get some sleep. I'll keep watch. As soon as darkness falls, we must be off.'

Chapter Three

'A GIRT EXPLOSION'

No one came near the bandstand that afternoon, and Lubber slept like a log. Squintum catnapped.

Darkness fell and the moon rose.

'On your feet!' said Squintum sharply.

'What. . .? why. . .? where. . .?' began Lubber as he obeyed.

'To answer your questions in order,' said Squintum. 'One, we're off. Two, because that's what you want. And three, to the thatched cottage in the little village under the big hill with the White Horse on it.'

He ran down the steps of the bandstand and set off for the park gates.

'But wait,' said Lubber, ranging alongside the padding Siamese. 'How do you know which way to go? How shall we know which way is south?'

Briefly Squintum raised his blue eyes to the glittering heavens, and stared at one especially brilliant point of light.

'We follow the Pole Star,' he said.

25

'I don't understand,' said Lubber.

'You wouldn't,' said Squintum. 'You're a dog, and dogs are daytime beasts. We cats are creatures of the darkness. We can read the night skies.'

Lubber too looked up.

'Is there only one Pole Star then?' he said.

'Two,' said Squintum. 'One for the South Pole, one for the North.'

Lubber considered this.

'But,' he said, 'we could be going in completely the wrong direction.'

Squintum gave one of his sudden harsh yowls. It could have been of surprise, or of amusement, or of annoyance at being asked so many questions, Lubber wasn't sure.

'Look,' said the Siamese. 'If the sun rises on our left tomorrow morning and sets on our right tomorrow evening, we're going the correct way. Just wait and see, eh? And now save your breath, there's a good dog. I want to be well clear of this town and deep in the countryside by dawn.'

And they were.

By first light, which was very early, for it was near to the longest day of the year, they had travelled perhaps a dozen miles from their starting-point. Squintum disdained such things as roads and struck straight across country, following his star, and then, when this had paled and vanished, trusting to some instinctive compass in his brain. Then the sun rose, on their left.

'You were right!' barked Lubber. 'We're going south! We're going home!' His bushy tail wagged wildly.

'Keep your hair on,' said Squintum. 'We've a long way to go yet. Let's have a rest.'

'Oh, let's!' cried Lubber.

They found an old deserted field-shed in the middle of nowhere, and Lubber flumped down anyhow on its floor of dusty straw. Squintum climbed into a manger half filled with frowsty hay, and curled himself comfortably.

A distant cow lowed, a late cuckoo called, and swallows flew in and out of the doorway, fetching insects to feed their young in their mud-nests under the roof. Dog and cat slept.

It was food, or rather the sound of food, that woke Squintum. The field-shed was full of mice, and the cat's keen ears caught the rustle of their movements. He slipped down from the manger.

In quite a short while, he caught and ate three, and lastly he found a nest of fat pink naked babies behind an old straw bale, and

polished them off for afters. Then he fell to licking his paws and cleaning his face and combing his whiskers.

His grooming completed, he sat and looked at the untidy heap that was Lubber. I can feed myself, thought Squintum, but what about him? He's going to be ravenous when he wakes up.

Lubber stirred, got to his feet, stretched, and shook himself.

'I'm ravenous!' he said.

'I could catch you a mouse,' Squintum said.

'A mouse! I could eat a horse!'

At that moment they heard, not far off, the bang of a gun.

'We'd better be on our way,' said Squintum. 'I've no wish to be mistaken for a rabbit by some trigger-happy farmer.'

But before they could make a move there was a sudden whirr of wings, and in through the door of the field-shed flew a large bird; it landed clumsily on the top rail of the manger and perched there unsteadily, its beak wide open with shock and fear.

To Lubber it was just a bird, but the worldly-wise Squintum could see that it was a pigeon, and not an ordinary pigeon either. This was no wild bird nor a stray from a town square, but a racing pigeon, with long, slaty-blue, tapering wings, and on one pink leg a blue ring stamped with its number. This, though Squintum did not actually know it, was to identify the bird should it become lost

in its efforts to reach home. And this pigeon certainly appeared to be lost. It looked about it in a dazed way, and seemed unaware of any possible danger from cat or dog.

'What is it?' said Lubber.

'It's a racing pigeon, a homer,' said Squintum. 'The owners take them a long, long way away and then let them go, and each bird knows instinctively exactly where its home is. They race, you see, and the first one back into its loft is the winner. This one isn't going to win anything by the look of it.'

The look of the pigeon was just plain appetizing to the hungry Lubber, but Squintum's reaction, perhaps because he was full fed, was one of simple curiosity.

'What's the matter, stranger?' he said. 'You look scared out of your wits.'

For a moment the pigeon did not answer, but sat and panted, beak agape. Then it gasped, 'Man . . . gun . . . 'E nearly shot me!'

'Outside, quickly, Lubber!' hissed Squintum. 'See what you can see. If he catches us in here, we could all be dead ducks.'

'Ducks?' said Lubber. 'I don't see how . . .' he began, but the Siamese spat angrily at him, so he hurried outside. He was soon back.

'There is a man with a gun in the distance,' he said, 'but he's walking away from us.'

'I'm glad to hear that,' said the pigeon. 'That I am.'

It seemed to have recovered a little, and even began to preen its feathers. Out of them it picked a number of tiny round black objects.

'What are those?' said Lubber softly to Squintum.

'Shot,' said the cat. 'Pellets. He's had a narrow escape,' and to the bird he said, 'Are you wounded?'

The pigeon stretched one wing, slowly, to its full extent, and then the other.

'I don't reckon,' it said, 'but my head's buzzin' like a bees' nest. I thought I were a goner, I did. There I was, swingin' along nice and easy, only about a hundred mile to go to my loft, and next thing I know there's a girt explosion, right in my ear-'ole. That didn't half give me a shock, I'll tell you!'

'Squintum!' said Lubber in an excited voice, as the pigeon fell to hunting for more shot in

its plumage.

'What?'

'You hear the way that bird talks? Its accent, I mean?'

'Yes. Very rural. A clodhopper, I should say.'

'Well, they talk like that in my part of the world! Where I come from! That bird might live quite close, maybe even in my village!'

'A hundred miles away,' said Squintum drily. 'And that's as the pigeon flies.'

'Yes, but if it knows exactly where its home is, like you said, maybe it could guide us.'

'Quite how we should keep up with a racing pigeon, I have no clear idea,' said Squintum. 'But there may be the germ of an interesting possibility there. It may be worth our while to befriend the creature rather than to eat it.'

'You must allow us to introduce ourselves,' he said to the pigeon in the politest of tones. 'I am called Squintum, and this is my friend Lubber.'

'How do?' said the pigeon.

'May we have the pleasure of knowing your name?'

The pigeon raised the leg with the blue ring on it, and scratched the side of its face.

'It's more of a number,' it said.

'Oh?'

'Ar. Eighty-two stroke seven o eight stroke KT, that's me.'

'82/708/KT?' said Squintum. 'Charming, charming! It does not however tell us to which

31

sex you belong.'

'I be a hen,' said the pigeon.

'A hen?' said Lubber. 'I don't see how . . .?'

'A female pigeon,' said Squintum. 'And a very beautiful one, if I may say so.'

The pigeon gave a bubbling trill.

'I bet you do say that to all the girls,' she cooed.

'But,' said Squintum, 'your name is quite a . . . mouthful. Perhaps you would allow us to shorten it? May we just use the final letters, KT?'

'Don't make no odds to me,' said the pigeon.

'Katie it is then,' said Squintum. 'Now then, Katie, am I correct in thinking you to be a homing pigeon?'

'You're right.'

'And you are returning home, travelling south?'

'I was.'

'You were? You mean you've changed your mind?'

'I haven't changed it,' said Katie. 'That girt explosion changed it.'

'I don't follow,' said Lubber. 'Surely you can remember instinctively exactly where your home is?'

'I could,' said Katie. 'Trouble is, I been and gone and lost my memory.'

Chapter Four

THE BARBECUE

'That,' said Squintum, 'is too bad.'

He caught Lubber's eye.

'Please excuse us for a moment,' he said to the pigeon. 'We must just make sure that the coast is still clear.'

Outside, and out of the bird's hearing, Squintum spoke briefly and to the point. 'She's disoriented,' he said.

'Sorry?'

'Lost her sense of direction. No use to us. Might as well eat her.'

'Oh no!' said Lubber.

'Why not? Thought you were hungry.'

'I am, I am. But I couldn't kill her. The way she talks reminds me so much of home. And, anyway, the poor thing's only just escaped death.'

'Lubber,' said Squintum, 'when I first met you, I thought you were a bit soft in the head. I don't think that now – not so much anyway – but soft-hearted you certainly are. Come along now. We must get a move on.'

'But what about Katie?' said Lubber.

'What about Katie?'

'Well, shouldn't we at least say goodbye to her?'

Before the cat could answer, the pigeon came waddling out of the field-shed and walked trustingly up to them. Automatically, Squintum extended his claws, his tail-tip twitching, but Lubber stepped in front of him and said in a kindly voice, 'Well, Katie, it's been so nice meeting you and I hope you'll soon be better, but we must be off now. Goodbye.'

'Which way are you goin', Mr Lubber?' said Katie.

'South.'

'You gennulmen got any objections if I come along?'

'None at all!' said Lubber heartily.

Squintum sighed and sheathed his claws.

'Are you proposing to walk?' he said acidly.

Katie gave a bubbling trill of laughter.

'Oh, Mr Squintum!' she said. 'You and your little jokes! You'll be the death of me!'

Squintum passed his tongue over his lips.

'Walk indeed!' said Katie. 'I hope not! But I'd best make sure everything's workin',' and she took off and flew, a trifle unsteadily at first, and then more strongly. They watched as she gained height and began to fly around them in circles, each larger than the one before.

'What's she doing?' said Lubber.

'Trying to pick up her bearings,' said Squin-

34

tum. 'If the shock wears off and her homing instinct returns, that'll be the last we shall see of her.'

But at that moment the pigeon broke off her circling and, with lifted wings, volplaned down to land beside them.

'Bit stiff at first, bruised, I expect,' said Katie, 'but I don't reckon I suffered much damage. Only to my head, it seems. Lost my sense of direction, I 'ave. Anyway, that shooter's gone, there's no sign of him.'

A look-out, thought Squintum. A scout. This bird could still be useful to us. To fly ahead and spy out the lie of the land and keep an eye out for possible danger.

'I am so glad, Katie,' he said in his silkiest tones, 'that you should wish to honour us with your company.'

Beneath all its hair, Lubber's face wore a look of astonishment.

As for Katie, she made a little bob.

'Oh, the honour's mine, Mr Squintum, sir,' she said.

'You see,' said Squintum, 'the three of us are, you might say, in the same boat.'

'In a boat?' said Lubber. 'I don't see how . . .?'

'That is to say,' continued Squintum, 'we are all heading south and we are all lost.'

'Lost?' said Katie. 'A clever gennulman like you?'

Squintum could not restrain a small purr of pleasure.

'Let me put it this way,' he said. 'Lubber –

Mr Lubber, that is – was taken from the bosom of his family by an unfortunate mischance.'

Katie looked puzzled.

'Sounds terrible,' she said.

'And I have volunteered to assist him in rediscovering his place of abode.'

'His place of a what?' said Katie.

'He's going to help me find my home,' said Lubber.

'But,' said Squintum, 'there are difficulties in our path. For example, we want to avoid contact with humans, who might wish to detain us out of the kindness of their hearts, or – for a great many humans are not kindhearted – to harm us. Secondly, we need to find sources of food, to sustain us. And, thirdly, it would be most useful to know what obstacles or hazards lie ahead – to know where a river might be crossed or a town avoided. In all these matters, my dear Katie, you could be of paramount assistance.'

'You reckon?' said Katie dazedly.

She looked at Lubber for help in interpreting this speech.

Lubber extracted from it what was, for him, the most important thing.

'Food,' he said. 'I need food. D'you think you could fly around and have a look? Red meat, that's what I want.'

Katie gave another of her little bobs.

'I'll find you something, Mr Lubber,' she said. 'Never you worry,' and off she flew. She

circled once and then skimmed low over them.

'You gennulmen make a start, if you please,' she called down. 'I shall find you, sure enough.'

'Red meat!' sniffed Squintum as they set out. 'She'll likely bring you a worm.'

But, in fact, Fortune positively beamed upon them.

It was a beautiful summer's day, a Sunday, though none of them knew this, and everywhere people were relaxing in the sunshine. Just over the next hill beyond the field-shed, Katie found a village and looked down on house and cottage and bungalow. Everyone seemed to be out in their gardens, and in one, a very large garden belonging to a very large house, there was a swimming-pool. Some humans, large and small, were swimming in it, Katie could see, and some were lying beside it. Not far from the pool was a summer-house, in front of which stood a large, odd-looking contrivance on wheeled legs. Katie swooped down to investigate.

She had never in her life seen a barbecue and had no idea what it was, but there was no mistaking the array of meat, laid out ready for cooking when the bathers should feel like lunch.

There were thick steaks and fat chops and juicy kidneys for the grown-ups, and sausages and beefburgers for the children, enough to feed an army. Katie wheeled and was off at

37

racing speed.

Twenty minutes later, Lubber and Squintum lay concealed behind a hedge. On the other side of it was the summer-house, on whose roof Katie was perched. Wonderful smells wafted to the sensitive noses of cat and dog.

Squintum had masterminded the plan of the robbery.

'You,' he said to Lubber, 'must eat everything you can, as quick as you can.'

'I will, I will!' said Lubber.

'Dogs are like that, I know – they bolt their food in the coarsest way and digest it later. Coming as I do from a more cultivated race, I cannot do that. I shall simply carry away the largest piece I can manage. And you, Lubber, when you have eaten all you can hold, must do the same. Take away with you the biggest bit you can grip in your jaws. As for you,

Katie, you must keep up the diversion for as long as you can, if possible until you hear the signal.'

'I'll fool 'em, never you fear, Mr Squintum,' said Katie. 'You just give the word.'

This Squintum now did.

He yowled softly, too softly to be heard by the laughing, splashing humans, and at the sound Katie took off from the summer-house roof and flew up over the swimming-pool.

Though she was an almost pure-bred racer, one of her ancestors had been a tumbler, a variety of aerobatic pigeon, and she now put on a dramatic show. From high above the pool she suddenly dropped, twisting and turning and somersaulting and spinning like a falling leaf.

'Oh look!' cried the bathers. 'Look at that bird!'

'It can't fly properly!'

'It's been hurt!'

'It's been shot!'

'Look out, it's going to land in the water!'

But with a few feet to spare, Katie righted herself to make what looked like a forced landing on the pool side. Here she stumbled about, dragging one wing, the very picture of a sorely injured pigeon.

The English are reputed to be a nation of animal lovers, but, as Squintum had foreseen, the bathers reacted in very different ways.

'Poor thing!'

'Oh, it's only an old pigeon.'

'We must help it!'

'Knock it on the head, I should.'

'Put it out of its misery.'

'Don't be so horrible!'

'Be nice under a pie-crust with a bit of bacon.'

'Can I have it for a pet, Mummy?'

'Can I have a shot at it with your air-rifle, Daddy?'

'We must take it to the vet. Catch it, someone.'

But somehow every time someone was just about to catch the pigeon, it managed to struggle a little further off. Until suddenly, from the direction of the summer-house, there came a loud bark, and at this signal the pigeon jumped lightly into the air and flew easily away.

Like Old Mother Hubbard's cupboard, the barbecue was bare.

Chapter Five

HORSEVIEW COTTAGE

In a thatched cottage in a little village under a big hill with a White Horse on it, Miss Bun and Miss Bee sat drinking cocoa. Miss Bun was eating one of her favourite biscuits, Custard Creams, and Miss Bee one of hers, Garibaldis.

Long ago, eighty and seventy-eight years respectively, to be precise, the two sisters had been christened Margaret and Beatrice, but their parents had usually called them Bunty and Beatie. Gradually these names became shortened to Bun and Bee, and everybody in the village (where everything is known about

everyone else) always referred to them as 'Miss Bun and Miss Bee'.

'Oh, Bee,' said Miss Bun sadly, 'how I wish we knew where he was.'

'Oh, Bun,' replied Miss Bee, 'how I hope that he is still somewhere.'

Both sisters looked up at a framed photograph that hung on the kitchen wall. It was an enlarged snapshot of Lubber as a puppy, lying on the lawn, asleep of course.

'Even if he is alive,' said Miss Bun, 'we shall never see him again, shall we?'

'Not after all this time,' said Miss Bee. 'He's been gone weeks.'

Miss Bun drained her cocoa.

'Ah well,' she said. 'Time for our game.'

Like many elderly folk, Miss Bun and Miss Bee were great creatures of habit, and their days followed an exact pattern. Each of these days, of course, ended with bedtime, and lately this had presented the sisters with a problem. What with rheumatism and arthritis and suchlike things, neither was too steady on her pins. And the stairs at Horseview Cottage were very steep.

On the flat Miss Bun and Miss Bee, short, sturdy, tubby people both, did pretty well. They walked arm in arm as they had done since childhood, but now each had a walking-stick in her outer hand. Miss Bun (whose left leg was the stronger) walked on the right, Miss Bee (whose right leg was the stronger) on the left. It was thus that the villagers

always saw them, like a pair of six-legged Siamese twins.

Now a gentle walk to the village or a stroll in the garden was one thing, but climbing the staircase was quite a different matter, and getting to bed at night became a very difficult business, where neither sister could help the other.

Miss Bun and Miss Bee consulted their friends, one of whom told them that there was a device on the market called a chair-lift. This could be installed at the side of the staircase, and would carry them, one at a time, up or down.

'All you have to do,' said the friend, 'is to sit on a comfy little seat and press a switch, and this thing will carry one of you up to the top of the stairs without you moving a muscle.

Then out you get and press another switch to send the seat down again for the other one.'

So Miss Bun and Miss Bee had this wonderful machine fitted and it worked a treat, and what fun it was, such fun that at first they spent hours riding up and down on it, sending their electricity bill sky-high. But it still left them with a problem at the day's end. Who should go to bed first? This, after all, would be a great advantage, giving one or other of them first go at the bathroom and the certainty of being the first to be snuggled down in bed, while the unlucky one was left with the chores of locking up and putting out lights.

All through their long lives together, Miss Bun had never taken advantage of the fact that she was the elder, nor would Miss Bee have allowed her to do so, and simply taking turns to ride upstairs first would, they thought, be boring. So they decided to play for it.

Each evening, after their cocoa and biscuits, Miss Bun and Miss Bee would sit opposite one another at the kitchen table and solemnly play a game, one of the games that they had played together seventy years before.

Sometimes it was Snap, sometimes Beggar My Neighbour or Happy Families, but always it was conducted with the greatest seriousness, until at last one or other would give a little cry of triumph. Then she would hobble to the foot of the stairs, sit on the seat, press the switch and, smiling broadly both at the victory and the sensation, glide happily aloft. On this particular night, Miss Bun was the lucky one.

'Mrs Dose the Doctor's wife, if you please, Bee,' she said, 'and' (with special relish) 'Miss Bun the Baker's daughter, and I'm the winner!'

It was a warm night, a night of the full moon, and Miss Bun did not get into bed when she was ready, but stood by the window in her flannelette nightgown (pink with white roses), her silver hair in a long braid, looking out to the big hill that rose above the little

45

village. She waited till her sister, in her flannelette nightgown (blue with yellow daisies), her hair in two neat pigtails, came to stand beside her, and they leaned comfortably on one another, to ease the weight on their bad legs.

Together they stared at the shape of the great White Horse opposite them.

'It's funny,' said Miss Bun, 'but I sometimes think he's up there.'

'On the Horse?' said Miss Bee.

'Yes. You could see him tonight if he was there, the moon's so bright.'

'I sometimes think that too. But it's hard to imagine him walking that far.'

'And uphill too.'

'Lazy old thing.'

'But so sweet-natured, wasn't he?'

'Wasn't he! Shall we ever have another dog, d'you think, Bun?'

'I shouldn't like to, Bee.'

'Just in case he should come back one day, you mean?'

'Yes, and find someone else in his place.'

For a moment longer, the sisters stared at the huge moonlit form of the White Horse.

'Magical, isn't it?' said Miss Bee.

'And magic makes miracles,' said Miss Bun.

'And miracles do happen,' they said with one voice.

Then they turned and smiled at each other, rather ruefully, and sighed, and climbed into their beds.

Chapter 6

TO FIND A
MOTORWAY

Flying at about a hundred feet, for her recent experience of gunfire had made her wary of low altitudes, Katie could see the thieves running away, southward of course. The cat bounded neatly over the short sun-dried summer grass, his head held high against the weight of something carried in his mouth. The big dog galloped awkwardly, tripping now and again over what looked to the pigeon like some sort of rope, one end of which he had in his jaws.

They crossed a couple of large fields and disappeared from sight into a small copse. Katie circled, watching, but they did not emerge on the other side, so, after one more circuit to make sure there was no danger, she dropped quickly down in among the trees.

She pitched upon a low branch, beneath which Lubber and Squintum lay side by side. Squintum had taken as his spoils a large juicy piece of fillet steak, and this he now ate, delicately, without hurry, biting off a bit at a

time and licking it luxuriously with his rasping tongue, before getting to work with his needle-sharp white teeth. He was relishing every mouthful.

Lubber, Katie could see despite his hairiness, looked a good deal fatter and small wonder. In the short time that Katie's diversionary tactics had taken, he had polished off the meat set out to feed a party of a dozen adults and as many children. Now he lay sprawled, groaning a little at the pressure of the food inside him. Beside him lay what had looked from high above like a rope. It was, Katie could now see, a long pink string of sausages.

For a while no one spoke. Then Squintum, swallowing a final mouthful, said simply, 'Excellent!'

Lubber belched loudly. 'Have a sausage,' he said.

'Decent of you,' said Squintum, 'but I'm F.T.B.'

'F.T.B.?'

'Full to the brim.'

'Me, too,' said Lubber happily, and he stretched out and went to sleep.

Squintum sat, licking his paws and cleaning his face, and when he had finished, he turned his blue eyes up to the pigeon sitting above him.

'My dear Katie,' he said, 'how can we ever thank you?'

Katie bobbed on the branch.

'Oh, don't mention it, Mr Squintum, sir,' she said.

'But,' said Squintum, 'here we are, replete, and you have not eaten. I don't imagine you could fancy a sausage?'

'Oh no, thank you kindly,' said Katie, 'but I could do with summat to eat, no doubt about it.'

'Such as?' said Squintum.

'Corn,' said the pigeon. 'A good cropful of wheat, now that's the stuff to put feathers on your chest.'

'Is there any near?'

'Oh ah, Mr Squintum, there's wheatfields all about this time of year, comin' ripe for harvest. I shan't go short nohow. What d'you

know, talkin' about it's made me even more hungry! Will you two gennulmen excuse me if I pop out for a quick snack and a drink?'

'Watch out for farmers with guns,' said Squintum.

'I will, never you mind! And I'll have a good look round, make sure no one's comin' after us, see what lies ahead,' said Katie. 'So long!' and up she flew.

Squintum lay beside the sleeping dog and thought.

So far, so good, he said to himself. We've put a few miles behind us, we've picked up a useful ally, and we're well fed; better, I suspect, than we shall be again for many a day. But there is without doubt a very long way to go, even supposing we are lucky enough in the end to find the thatched cottage in the little village under the big hill with the White Horse on it. And let's face it, I am the only one who is going to give the matter any thought. Unless the bird recovers her homing instinct, she is useless in that respect, and Lubber here is much too happy-go-lucky a chap to worry his hairy head about the outcome. He simply trusts me to perform a miracle and take him home. If only we could travel south as fast as he travelled north in that furniture van.

Squintum sat up sharply.

That's it, he thought. We'll get a lift! But how? Stand by the southbound side of a main road and put my paw in the air? No telling

where we'd finish up, probably back in a home for strays. No, there's no way we could hitch-hike, but maybe we could be stowaways, just as Lubber was. It'd have to be in something like a heavy lorry, where we could get aboard without the driver's knowledge. But all the heavy lorries use the motorways, where they're not allowed to stop.

'But wait!' said Squintum out loud. 'They do!'

The squally voice woke Lubber, who opened an eye and said, 'Who do?'

'Go back to sleep,' said Squintum, and when Lubber had promptly obeyed, he continued his train of thought. The big lorries *do* stop, at the motorway service stations. I remember seeing that when I was sold as a kitten and my breeder was driving me down to the Dogs' Home. The drivers stop there to fill their lorries with fuel, and themselves with tea and butties in the service station restaurant. That would be the time! Worth a try, surely? All we need is to find a motorway, and that's something Katie ought to be able to do. She should be back soon.

Even as Squintum thought this, there was a noise of flapping wings and then a crackle of twigs, as not one, but two pigeons, landed in the tree above.

'Hello, Katie,' called the Siamese. 'Found a friend, have you?'

There was a moment's silence, and then a voice said, 'By gum, did you hear that, lad?'

'Ay, I did,' said another voice. 'But don't fret thyself. It's only an old cat.'

Squintum was no expert on regional accents, but he could clearly hear a difference between these broad Yorkshire voices and Katie's Wiltshire dialect. He squinted up and saw that the speakers were a pair of fat wood-pigeons.

Katie he had spared, for a reason, but these birds deserved no such mercy, and he leaped across the slumbering Lubber and shot up the tree-trunk towards them.

'Watch tha step!' shouted one. 'T'old moggy's after us. Stir thy stumps, lad!' and with a great clatter of wings, they burst up through the canopy and flew away.

The noise woke Lubber. He looked around

and could see no sign of the cat.

'Squintum!' he barked loudly. 'Where are you?'

'Up here!' spat Squintum, angry at missing. 'And keep your voice down, do!'

He ran down the trunk and began to stalk away, lashing his tail.

'Where are you going?' asked Lubber.

'To look for that Katie.'

Lubber hesitated. On the one hand, he did not want to be left behind, so dependent was he on the cat. On the other hand, he did not want to leave the string of sausages which, now that he had had time to digest the rest of the meat, was looking most attractive.

'Shall I come?' he said.

'No,' said Squintum.

'You won't be long?'

'No,' said Squintum.

'Shall I keep you a sausage?'

'No,' said Squintum.

So Lubber took the end sausage of the string in his mouth and began to chew. And, curiously enough, the next sausage seemed anxious to follow its neighbour, and the next, and the next, until, quite soon, there was only one sausage left.

I suppose I really ought to keep it for him, thought Lubber, in case he changes his mind, but while he was thinking this, somehow the last sausage disappeared too.

Squintum sat at the edge of the copse, watching the skies. They were cloudless and,

high above him, a number of inland gulls were rising effortlessly on a thermal, their white wings spread. Swallows and martins flew busily in pursuit of insects, and a long way above them, higher even than the circling gulls, coal-black swifts cut through the clear summer air on their sickle-shaped wings.

How pleasant to be a bird, thought Squintum. If Lubber and I could only fly, how quickly we could complete our journey.

Then he saw Katie coming, racing towards him at a fine rate. Catching sight of the waiting cat, she dropped down and landed beside him. Squintum could see that her crop was bulging.

'Aah! That's better, Mr Squintum, sir!' she said. 'That ought to keep me goin' for a while. I feel quite my old self again.'

'D'you mean to say that you've got your sense of direction back?' said Squintum.

'Wish I had,' said Katie, 'but that shooter never done me no good. It's comin' back a bit – I think I know which direction home is. But I couldn't fly straight to it, not to save my life.'

Despite himself, Squintum passed his tongue across his lips at these last words, so strong a thing is instinct. He controlled his thoughts.

'Tell me, Katie,' he said, 'do you know what I mean by a motorway?'

'That I do, Mr Squintum,' said Katie. 'Hugeous girt roads, full of cars and coaches and lorries. Hear the noise of the traffic from ever so high up, I can. They run right across

the country, for hundreds and hundreds of miles. We pigeons use 'em for aids to navigation. Supposin' I get blown a bit off course by a strong wind, or just lose my bearings for a minute, I say to myself, "Where've you got to, 82/708/KT?" and then I look down and see a girt motorway, and that tells me I'm too far this way or that. Matter of fact, there's a motorway not too far from where I do live. Runs due east and west, it does.'

'But some run north and south, don't they?' said Squintum. 'It's south we want to go.'

'Oh ar,' said Katie. 'There's two girt long 'uns that run north and south, one each side of the country.'

'Anywhere near here?'

'I dunno, I'm sure.'

'But you could find out, you could find a motorway for us, could you, Katie?'

'I reckon. Might take a bit of flyin', unless there's one handy. Which there might be, you never know. Why, Mr Squintum? What d'you want a motorway for? Surely you're not going to walk down one of them?'

'No, no,' said Squintum, and he explained to the pigeon the idea that he had in mind.

'Think how fast we could get south!' he finished.

'Oh ar,' said Katie. 'They do travel, even the big lorries do. I reckon to do sixty mile an hour with a following wind, but I can't keep up with they.'

'You wouldn't need to,' said Squintum. 'You

could ride too.'

'It's an idea and no mistake,' said Katie.

'Worth a try, surely?' said Squintum.

'Give us a bit of time to digest this cropful of wheat,' said Katie, 'and I'll go and have a look. Visibility's good today; I should be able to see a long way.'

'A bird's-eye view,' said Squintum thoughtfully.

'Ar,' said Katie. 'It's surprisin' what you can see from a height.'

'Have you ever seen a white horse?'

The pigeon gave a bubbling trill of amusement.

'A white horse?' she said. 'Why, bless you, I've seen white 'uns, black 'uns, brown 'uns, spotted 'uns, all sorts!'

'No, I don't mean a live horse. I mean a picture of one, a huge picture, cut into the turf so that the chalk shows up white.'

'Oh there's several of those about. There's one not so far from where I do live.'

'On a big hill?' said the Siamese.

'Ar.'

'Is there a little village under the hill?'

'Ar.'

'Is there a thatched cottage in the village?'

'More'n likely. I dunno for sure. I've never looked.'

'But you could do it, couldn't you, Katie?' said Squintum. 'Once we get near enough?'

'Do what, Mr Squintum?'

'Find the White Horse.'

Chapter Seven

DESERTED

'Once we gets into chalk country, I'll find you a white horse all right, Mr Squintum,' said Katie confidently. 'Might take time.'

'We have plenty of that. You use some of it now – to digest your food. And talking of food, I fancy a sausage,' said Squintum, and he turned and disappeared into the copse.

His first impulse, on finding that Lubber had scoffed the lot, was to wake the greedy beast and bawl him out. But that won't bring the sausages back, said Squintum to himself. And we can't move on until Katie reports about motorways. So I might as well take it easy. And he curled himself against the big dog's hairy stomach and closed his blue eyes.

An hour passed, while Squintum dozed and Lubber snored, and then came the sound of wings and a crackle of twigs overhead. Squintum was instantly alert to the chance of bagging another Yorkshire woodpigeon, but it was Katie.

'We're in luck,' she said. `

'You've found one?' said Squintum.

Lubber opened an eye.

'Found what?' he said.

'A motorway,' said Katie.

'A motorway?' said Lubber. 'I don't see how . . .?'

'I'll explain in a minute,' said Squintum. 'How far, Katie?'

'No more than five or six mile away as the pigeon flies. Due west, cross country. What do you think of that then?'

'Brilliant!'

'And that's not all.'

'Don't tell me you've found us a horse as well?'

'A horse?' said Lubber. 'I don't see how . . .?'

'No, no,' said Katie. 'I found what you was talkin' about, Mr Squintum. You musta had your sixth sense workin' overtime!'

'A service station!' cried Squintum.

'I reckon. Buildings and petrol pumps and that by the side of the motorway, and folk pullin' off in their cars and gettin' out of 'em, and as for girt heavy lorries, why, there were dozens of them.'

'82/708/KT,' said Squintum. 'You're a duck!'

'A duck?' said Lubber. 'I don't see how . . .?'

'Save your breath,' said Squintum. 'We're off!'

As cross-country travellers, the trio were not well matched. Squintum, for example, could

creep through small holes in thick hedges or through the mesh of sheep-wire, where Lubber could not.

Lubber could leap obstacles or push his way through standing corn or thick undergrowth where Squintum was at a disadvantage.

Katie, airborne and free of all obstacles, could travel at ten times the speed of the other two.

But they soon settled into a routine.

The pigeon would fly ahead, watched by cat and dog, and then perch, on a tall tree or other vantage point, until they caught up with her. Sometimes these hops of hers were barely a hundred yards in length, but where the going was easy and the countryside open, she would often fly on a quarter of a mile or more.

Before long, they came upon a country lane at a point where it joined a main road. Katie had flown forward a little way, and Lubber and Squintum lay concealed in some long grass, waiting to cross when the traffic should allow. Above their heads, a signpost spread its four arms.

Had either animal been able to read, they would have found that the northern-pointing arm (the direction from which they had come) said WOODSETTS, the southern arm THORPE SALVIN & HARTHILL, the eastern WORKSOP and the western SHEFFIELD & M1 MOTORWAY.

For a moment there was a pause in the

60

stream of passing vehicles.

'Come on!' said Squintum, and they dashed across the A57 and into open fields once more.

Now, as Katie led them due west, the going became easier, and after a couple more miles they could actually hear the distant roar of the motorway traffic. A mile more, and they could see the motorway itself, and, almost directly ahead of them, the buildings of the service station.

As they drew nearer, they could see the pigeon sitting on the roof of the restaurant. They could also see that the entire compound was surrounded by a high wire fence, its mesh far too small to admit the slenderest of Siamese cats, let alone a large hairy mongrel dog.

'It's all fenced round,' said Lubber.

Squintum spat angrily. I should have known, he thought, that anything to do with motorways would have to be guarded against straying animals. At that moment, Katie flew down to join them.

'What are you goin' to do now, Mr Squintum?' she asked. ''Tis all fenced round.'

Squintum spat again, his tail lashing. What were they to do?

But then Lubber, whose sight was keener than the cross-eyed cat's, said, 'I can see a gate in the wire.'

They moved cautiously forward to the edge of a concrete approach-road, and there, sure enough, was a large double gate, bearing a

notice that read:

> **M1 WOODALL SERVICES**
> **EMERGENCY ENTRANCE**
> **FOR POLICE USE ONLY**

It was firmly shut.

'It's shut,' said Lubber.

'You have a talent,' said Squintum acidly, 'for stating the obvious.'

For once, good-natured Lubber reacted angrily to the cat's patronizing tone. 'You have a talent,' he growled, 'for making catty remarks. And I'm not as stupid as I look. Sooner or later someone will open it. That's the thing about gates, you see – humans put them there to get in and out by. All we have to do is wait,' and he lay down, put his head on his paws, and went to sleep.

'What do you know?' said Katie. 'Mr Lubber's right,' and she settled herself comfortably in a nearby bush.

Squintum sat and waited, with the infinite patience of his kind. Lubber is right, he told himself, once his frustration had died down. We must just wait, no matter how long it takes.

In fact, it took a long time.

Not till dusk had fallen and the motorway was ablaze with headlights did anything come near their hiding-place. Then suddenly a car drove past them and stopped, its lights shining full on the gate.

'Quick! Wake up!' hissed Squintum to the

sleepers, and he watched intently as a man in a blue uniform, wearing a peaked cap, got out and unlocked and opened the gate.

'Now!' said Squintum softly, and as the policeman got back into the driving-seat, all three animals slipped in past the near side of the patrol car. They hid in the shadows until it had driven past and away, and then looked round to get their bearings. They were, it seemed, on the edge of the service station's public car-park. This was brightly lit, but it was now too dark for Katie to find where the lorry-park might be.

'Pop up on that roof where you were before,' Squintum told her, 'and join us again at first light.'

'I can smell food,' said Lubber when the pigeon had gone, 'over there,' and he pointed with lifted muzzle.

'That'll be the restaurant,' said Squintum. 'You going to walk in there and sit up and beg?'

'No,' said Lubber, 'but there'll be dustbins outside. Humans are ever so wasteful of food.'

'Dustbins have lids.'

'Lids come off easy – no problem.'

'Worth a try, surely?' said Squintum.

Side by side, they began to slink along the inside of the perimeter fence, when suddenly a car drove in from the motorway. Instead of stopping near the restaurant, as most had done, it went quickly to the furthest part of the car-park and stopped there. In it, Lubber and Squintum could see, were a man and a

woman, and as the animals watched, the man got out. He looked about him, furtively it seemed, saw no one, took from his pocket a length of stout twine and opened a rear door. A dog leaped down and jumped up against the man's legs, licking at his hand and wagging its tail joyfully. Hastily the man fastened the twine to its collar, led it to the fence, and there tied the other end of the cord to an iron stanchion. Then he turned and hastened, ran, indeed, back to the car.

The dog had followed him trustingly to the fence, and even now, for a few seconds, it stood and wagged, watching its owner. But then it began to whine anxiously as the car's engine was restarted, and then to bark, frantically, as the man drove fast, out of the car-park and away to rejoin the motorway. And as the car disappeared from sight, there came, above the ceaseless roar of the passing traffic, a dreadful, doleful, heartbroken howling.

'Wait for me!' cried the tethered dog, straining and pulling madly at the end of the length of twine. 'Don't leave me! Come back! Oh, wait for me!'

Left to himself, Squintum would probably have passed by on the other side, but the terrible wailing was more than the soft-hearted Lubber could bear and he galloped to the rescue.

At his approach, the howling changed to a frightened yap.

Lubber slid to a halt and stood waving his

64

bushy tail and giving a smily look from under his hairy eyebrows.

'Everything's going to be all right,' he said comfortingly. 'Don't be scared, old chap.'

'I'm not a chap,' said the other in a voice that trembled. 'And everything's not going to be all right. Everything's terribly wrong. My owners – they just left me here. Why? Why have they deserted me?'

Lubber looked down at the dog, who, he could now see, appeared very young, not much more, in fact, than a puppy.

'Oh, they'll come back for you,' he said. 'They just forgot, I expect. When they realize, they'll turn back.'

'Forget it,' said a voice, and Squintum appeared. 'The motorway's like life,' he said. 'There's no turning back.'

Chapter Eight

DOWN THE M1

The moon was now fully up and by its light Lubber and Squintum could clearly see the abandoned dog. Youthful she might be, and gangling in build, but she was tall, almost as tall as Lubber. Like Lubber, her ears were droopy and her tail long and plumy, but here the resemblance ended. It was not simply a difference of her coat – silky and wavy, and her colour – a rich red. It was an air about her, of elegance, of distinction, of breeding.

To the blue-blooded Squintum, this was instantly obvious.

To Lubber, she was simply a dog in distress, and his first thought was to release her from the tether against which she still strained, whining and staring at the spot where the car had disappeared.

'We'll soon have you free!' he growled, and was about to chop through the twine when Squintum hissed at him, 'No, Lubber, no!'

'Why not?'

'Let her free now and she's a dead dog.

66

She'll run straight on to the motorway, trying to follow her owners. Wait a little, and let's see if we can calm her down a bit. Ask her some questions, to distract her. Ask her what breed she is. Politely, mind.'

Lubber cleared his throat.

'I say!' he said in a jolly voice. 'I hope you won't mind if I ask – I mean, I ought to know but I've never actually seen anyone quite like you before – most attractive, that silky coat, and such a lovely colour – what I mean to say is, what kind of dog are you?'

'I'm a Red Setter.'

'Oh,' said Lubber. 'Er . . . pedigree, eh?'

'Of course.'

Squintum purred.

'What kind of dog are you?' said the Red Setter bitch.

'Well, I'm not really sure,' said Lubber. 'My mother was a cow-dog, there are lots of cows where I come from.'

'And your father?'

'Well, I'm not really sure.'

'What's your name?'

'Lubber. Oh, and this is my friend Squintum. What's yours?'

'I haven't got one.'

'But surely . . . those people who left you here, they must have called you something?'

'They never decided. They couldn't agree. They hadn't had me very long, you see.'

'How long?'

'A week.'

'But why . . .?' began Lubber, when Squintum interrupted.

'Look,' he said, 'there's plenty of time, we've the whole night before us. Why don't we ask our friend here just to lie down quietly and tell us all about herself, and then we'll see what we can do to help her? Worth a try, surely?'

'OK,' said Lubber. 'If you feel like it, that is . . . er . . . oh, it's awkward, you not having a name.'

The young Setter bitch, who had by now stopped pulling and whining, lay down as Squintum had suggested and looked at the large hairy mongrel dog, sighed deeply, and said, 'Why don't you give me one?'

'Oh gosh!' said Lubber. 'I'm no good at that sort of thing. Squintum here's the brainy one. He'd be better at it.'

'Well now,' said Squintum smoothly, 'let's think. Something to do with your breed, perhaps? A Red Setter, you said?'

'Yes. Irish Setters, some people call us.'

'Really! An Irish colleen!'

'That's nice!' said Lubber. '"Colleen"! I like it, do you?'

A little wag of the long red tail signified assent, so Squintum said quickly, 'Go on then, Colleen. Tell us about yourself.'

The story was easily told. The bitch had at first been kept on by her breeder who had intended to show her, but he'd later changed his mind and sold her as a pet.

'To those people who dumped you here?'

68

asked Lubber.

'Yes,' said Colleen.

'After only a week? Why? Why didn't they like you? My old ladies loved me. What did you do wrong?'

'I don't really know,' said Colleen. 'I did howl at night a bit, because I was homesick. And I did nip their little boy once – he kept pulling my tail and it hurt.'

'Is that all?'

'Well . . . I did have a couple of accidents.'

'Accidents?'

'On the carpet. But really, I did want to please them. They were my owners. I didn't mean to be bad.'

'Bad?' growled Lubber. 'It's not you who are bad. To desert you and just drive off! I wouldn't have believed there were humans as wicked as that!'

'I would,' said Squintum.

'Listen, Colleen,' he said. 'Listen to a cat who is certainly older and possibly wiser than you. There are people who are fit to keep dogs and there are people who are not. You – whatever happens to you in the future – have had a lucky escape. Just now you are unhappy because you think that you have been a disappointment to your owners, and that it is your duty to go back to them and try to do better. If Lubber here were to chew through that twine, you might still want to follow them. First of all, you wouldn't have a cat in hell's chance of ever finding them. Second, you'd be

a fool to try. And third, if you do try, you'll be run over and killed before you've gone half a mile. Have you understood what I'm saying to you?'

'Yes,' said Colleen, quietly now. 'But what am I to do? I'm homeless.'

'So are we!' said Lubber. 'But we're going to find a home – mine! Come with us! My old ladies would love you!' and he grabbed the twine in his teeth and bit through it. 'Come on!' he said. 'We're going to the dustbins to find some grub,' and he walked off, Squintum following.

For a moment, the Red Setter hesitated uncertainly. Then she ran after them.

Lubber's dustbin technique was simple but effective. First, he nosed off the lid. Then he stood against the rim and tipped the bin over. Humans, it seemed, were even more wasteful in motorway restaurants and cafeterias than in their own homes, and the pickings were good.

Lubber would happily have stayed snuffling about among the rubbish all night, but Squintum was fearful of discovery.

'Come away now,' he said to the two dogs, 'before someone finds us. We'll lie up till morning.'

They found a secluded corner at the back of a storage building, on to the roof of which Squintum climbed.

*

Flying out at first light, Katie soon spotted the cat and landed beside him. 'Morning, Mr Squintum, sir,' she said. 'Where be Mr Lubber?'

Squintum stretched and yawned.

'Below,' he said.

Katie peered over the edge of the roof.

'Well I never!' she said. 'Who's that with him then?'

'She's called Colleen,' said Squintum. 'She's coming with us.'

Katie gave her bubbling trill of amusement.

'He's a fast worker, Mr Lubber is!' she said. 'Fancy pickin' up a nice-lookin' girlfriend in a motorway service station! How'd she get here?'

'It's a long story,' said Squintum, looking up at the lightening sky, 'and there's no time for it now. Go and find the lorry-park, quick as you can.'

Ten minutes later, the four of them were assembled under the body of a giant lorry, one of a number whose drivers had stopped for an early breakfast.

'You three stop here,' said Squintum, 'while I have a look round,' and off he slunk.

At first it looked as though his plan would come to nothing. Each lorry that he investigated had its rear doors firmly closed, and even had they been open, the tailboards were too high. He might have scrambled up, the bird could have flown in, but the dogs could

never have made such a leap. In fact, it was almost midday before Squintum found what he wanted.

A big articulated lorry pulled in, the load on its trailer covered with a huge tarpaulin sheet under which they could crawl; and, as luck would have it, it parked next to a loading-platform that was level with the lorry bed; all they had to do was to climb the steps of the platform and walk aboard. He went to fetch the others.

Had they been able to read, they would have learned two interesting things about this particular articulated lorry. First, they would have seen, in large letters on the door of the tug:

J. DAVIDSON
NIGHTLY TRUNK
LEEDS–LONDON

Second, once they were safely under the tarpaulin, among dozens of cardboard boxes arranged on pallets, they would have known that each box contained

50 TINS 'BONZO' TOP-QUALITY DOG
MEAT.

As it was, they lay in innocence both of the contents of the boxes and of their destination,

and then they heard the engine start up and felt the artic move out, and then pick up speed on the motorway.

'This is the life!' said Squintum. 'Every hour that passes, we'll be sixty miles further south.'

'Without liftin' a wing!' said Katie.

Colleen lay shivering, appalled by the noise and the swaying motion. 'I'm scared,' she said.

Lubber licked her nose. 'I'll look after you,' he said. 'Just try and relax.'

'Look at that,' said Katie softly. 'Don't they make a lovely pair!'

Two hours passed.

Squintum was watchful, Colleen dozed uneasily, Katie fell into a light sleep and Lubber into a heavy one.

Then the engine note changed, the motion lessened, and the trailer swayed as the artic driver pulled off the motorway, parked and switched off. They heard the door of the tug

slam, and then the sound of footsteps walking away.

'He's stopped for a cuppa,' said Squintum. 'Wake up, everyone. Katie, can you try to find out where we are?'

Katie slipped out from beneath the tarpaulin to find herself in the lorry-park of just such a service station as the one they had left a couple of hours earlier. The only difference, had she been able to read the sign, was its name.

M1 TODDINGTON SERVICES

Katie flew up above the motorway and immediately she felt that there was something wrong. Maybe it was the position of the sun or the direction of the prevailing wind, or maybe, she thought, my homin' instinct's comin' back a bit, but we're goin' wrong, I feel sure. We're too far east or my name's not 82/708/KT.

The higher she flew, the surer she felt that they must get out of here, that if they stayed in the artic they would be carried further and further away from their hoped-for destination.

At that moment, she saw a flight of homing pigeons racing along, following the exact line of the M1 and she put on speed to intercept them.

As they swept up to her, she flew alongside

them.

'Which way be us going, ladies and gennulmen, can you tell me?' she cried.

'Cor lumme luvaduck!' they called to one another.

'Proper old mangel-wurzel, ain't she, mate?'

'Talk about a country bumpkin!'

'We're goin' to the Smoke, me old china, that's where we're goin'.'

'The Smoke?' said Katie. 'Whatever do you mean?'

'London Town!' cried the racers. 'Down the old M1 to London Town!'

'To Lunnon!' cried Katie in horror. 'Oh, my heavens, we don't want to go there!' and she wheeled and went racing back.

Chapter Nine

LONG ODDS

Racing was what Miss Bun and Miss Bee were watching, at that moment, on the TV in Horseview Cottage.

For a long time, they had resisted having the television. They suspected (rightly) that much of it was taken up with panel games (which they would not understand), with situation comedies (which they would not find funny), and with the News (which they were sure would be all about war and famine and disasters).

'The only thing we should enjoy,' they said to one another, 'would be the weather forecast.'

'And, anyway,' they said, 'one of those ugly aerials would quite spoil the look of our roof.'

But then quite recently a friend, the one who had suggested the chair-lift, persuaded them that it really would be worth their while to have a set, if only to see the wonderful natural history programmes, since both were so fond of animals.

'And make sure you get a remote control,' the friend said, 'so that you can change channels or switch on and off without having to get up out of your chairs.'

The friend was right – Miss Bun and Miss Bee loved the animal programmes. And the sisters were right – they didn't at all like the panel games or the situation comedies or the grim news, but they did very much enjoy using the remote control to switch them off. 'Zapping', they called it, and whichever sister had the thing in her hand would point it at the set, and narrow her eyes like a gunfighter, and press the off switch with a cry of 'ZAP!' Then they would look at one another and giggle like young girls.

But the biggest bonus of all for Miss Bun and Miss Bee concerned one animal – the horse.

By chance, they had their television set installed at the start of the flat-racing season, and soon their greatest pleasure was to sit in front of the screen and watch every race of a televised meeting.

Partly this was because they happened to live in an area where horse-racing was almost a religion. Just on the other side of the hill across which the White Horse strode were some famous racing-stables, and the talk in the village pub (where the sisters did not go) or the shop (where they did) or between locals meeting in the street was always of form and racing certainties and red-hot tips and long-priced outsiders.

Partly they watched because Miss Bun and Miss Bee turned their race-viewing into a competition. They made their selections for each race and kept a careful score of points – 10 for a winner, 5 for a second place, 2 for a third. They took no notice of the tipsters' forecasts in the newspaper, nor of anything they might have heard in the village, but picked their horses for what they considered the most sensible reasons – liking the look of a particular animal, or its name, or the colours of its jockey's silks. No money was involved, but whichever sister scored the highest was allowed the sole use of the remote control for the rest of the day's viewing.

And the third reason for their pleasure in watching racing lay in the beauty of the animals themselves. To see a well-bred, per-

fectly turned-out racehorse parading around the paddock, or cantering to the start, or galloping at full stretch down the course, was sheer delight to Miss Bun and Miss Bee.

On this particular afternoon they were watching a meeting at Windsor, and by the end of the sixth and last race they had each had a very successful day at the races. Miss Bun had had three winners and three also-rans, but Miss Bee, though she had selected only two winners, had had two seconds and a third and only one horse out of the frame. She had therefore scored a total of 32 to Miss Bun's 30.

'Well done, Bee,' said Miss Bun. 'It's you to zap for the rest of the day.'

'You know, Bun,' said Miss Bee, 'I sometimes wish we were actually betting. That nag that I picked for the 3.30 – you know, the one with the pretty pink and green quartered colours – came in at 40 to 1. I'd have made a packet.'

'You'd soon have lost it all,' said Miss Bun. 'Betting's a mug's game.'

'I bet Lubber would have enjoyed watching racing,' Miss Bee said.

'We shall never know,' said Miss Bun.

'Never?'

'Well, it must be very long odds against his ever coming home again.'

'How long?'

'1,000 to 1 against, I should think.'

Chapter Ten

A BATTERING-RAM

As Katie approached Toddington Service Station, she saw the artic pulling out on to the motorway again. She dived and turned and flew alongside, to see three faces peering out from under the edge of the tarpaulin.

'You're goin' the wrong way!' she cried, but the roar of the engine drowned her voice.

As the artic picked up speed, the driver prepared to pass an old car that was doddering along in the slow lane. He glanced in his side-mirror and then began to pull out. As the tug angled a little to the trailer, he saw to his amazement that in addition to a load of meat for dogs, he was carrying two of them and a cat as well, while a racing pigeon flew alongside, its beak open for all the world as though it was talking to the other animals.

For a second or two he gazed spellbound, his eye off the road ahead, and veered over towards the fast lane. There was a furious hooting from a speeding car; the artic driver yanked back his steering-wheel, the tail of the trailer began to swing, and with a scream

of tortured tyres, J. Davidson's Nightly
Trunk, Leeds to London, jack-knifed.

As the trailer swung, so it began to tip, and
as it struck the guard-rails of the central reser-
vation, the guy-ropes holding down the tarpaulin parted, the tarpaulin lifted like a
flapping sail, and twenty cardboard boxes were
catapulted over on to the other carriageway.
Each box burst on impact, and in an instant the
air was thick with the screech of brakes, the
blaring of horns, and the cursing of drivers, as
a thousand tins of Bonzo Top-Quality Dog Meat
went rolling madly across the northbound M1.

So occupied were all the drivers in dodging
the tins and each other that they hardly
noticed two dogs and a cat go dashing across
to the safety of the western verge, a pigeon
flying above them.

Miraculously, no blood was spilt, and
though the ensuing chaos resulted in much
loss of time and temper and much damage to

vehicles, the only other thing that was really hurt were the artic driver's feelings.

'Never 'ad an accident before,' he said to the police, when a patrol car arrived on the scene. 'Never in all me years of drivin'.'

The patrolmen looked at the jack-knifed artic and the small army of cars and vans and lorries, stationary now amidst a sea of tin cans.

'Well,' said one of them, 'you certainly made up for it today. Road's dry enough. You fall asleep or something?'

'Nah, guv,' said the driver. 'I just come out of Toddington Services.'

'Had a drink there, did you?'

'Tea, guv, just a cuppa, that's all.'

'How did it happen then?'

'Well,' said the driver, 'it was like this. I looks in me mirror, and there's a pigeon flying alongside and a Siamese cat and a brown-and-white dog and a red dog lookin' out over the edge of the trailer!'

'Fancy!' said the patrolman. 'And where was the pink elephant? Here, blow in this bag.'

The animals meanwhile had made themselves scarce. There was no getting through the motorway fence to open country beyond, but a quick recce by Katie had established that there was, not far away, a road-bridge that crossed the M1, so they hurried along the verge towards this.

Squintum was counting on the chance that there might be some way out for them at such a junction, only to be disappointed when they reached it. Then he noticed something, partly because he was the most observant, partly because he was the most observant, partly because he was lowest to the ground. An open concrete drain had been laid to run under the fence, whose wire netting had been extended to cover the area of the culvert and prevent wild animals like badgers or foxes from using it as an access to the motorway.

The drain was bone dry now, but many wet winters, Squintum could see, had rusted the wire that blocked it. He scratched at it and flakes fell from the metal.

'See this bit of wire here, Lubber?' he said.

Lubber looked at it. 'It's rusty,' he said.

'Exactly,' said Squintum, 'and therefore weakened. How do you fancy yourself as a ram?'

'A ram?' said Lubber. 'I don't see how . . .?'

'A battering-ram,' said Squintum. 'Charge at it. Bust your way through it. Worth a try, surely? You made a pretty good job of that door at the Dogs' Home, remember?'

'That was glass,' said Lubber.

'Oh well,' said Squintum off-handedly, turning away, 'if you're afraid of hurting yourself . . . pity, it's our only chance of going on . . . still, if you're going to be a scaredy-cat . . .'

'Scaredy-cat, my paw!' shouted Lubber. 'Mind out of my way!' and he took a run and dived headfirst into the wire. Showers of rust fell off it, but it held firm, and Lubber was thrown backwards with a howl of pain and a bloody nose.

'Oh, poor Mr Lubber!' cooed Katie, perched on the rail of the bridge. ''Tis too strong for 'un, Mr Squintum.'

Squintum said nothing, but Colleen came forward and licked tenderly at Lubber's bleeding muzzle.

'It's not too strong for you, is it, Lubber?' she said softly. 'Not for you!'

Lubber's bushy tail, which had been clamped between his legs, began slowly to wave again, and he shook his hairy head to clear it and stood well back a second time.

'Once more unto the breach, dear friends!' he cried. 'Once more!' and with all his might he hurled himself recklessly forward and this time burst his way through.

'Faint heart,' said Squintum musingly, as he followed Colleen through the gap, 'ne'er won fair lady. Fly on then, Katie. Westward ho!'

Now they fell once again into the pattern of progress as before, Katie flying some way

ahead, and then waiting for the others to catch up.

Now she seemed much more confident of her direction. 'What do you think, Miss Colleen and gennulmen,' she said. 'I reckon it's comin' back to me,' and away she went again.

'What's coming back to her?' asked the Red Setter.

'Her sense of direction,' said Lubber. 'She lost it when a man nearly shot her. We're hoping that if she can find her home, she may find mine too.'

'In the thatched cottage, you mean?' said Colleen, for by now she had heard something of Lubber's story.

'In the little village,' said Squintum.

'Under the big hill,' said Lubber.

'With a White Horse on it!' they all chorused.

They pressed on through the fields bordering the road which had crossed the motorway. On the other side of the hedge Katie was waiting for them, sitting on top of a signpost, the better to be seen. The signpost pointed to a side road that ran up over the shoulder of a great sweep of downland. It said:

WHIPSNADE PARK ZOO

As they came near, the pigeon suddenly flew up high, and then commenced to treat them to a display of the aerobatic skills inherited from her distant tumbler ancestor, rolling and looping and diving and soaring and fluttering

madly about the sky.

'Whatever's the matter with her?' said Colleen. 'Is she in trouble?'

'No,' said Squintum, 'it's high spirits. She's just doing it for a lark.'

'For a lark?' said Lubber. 'I don't see how . . .?'

'For fun,' said Squintum. 'She's as happy as a . . . Oh, forget it.'

Katie recovered herself at the last possible moment from a long twisting fall that seemed likely to be the death of her, and came to hover over them.

'Proper chalk country this be!' she cried down to them. 'You never know, we might be lucky soon!'

The others lay down in the grass, to have a rest and to see where Katie's next staging-point should be.

Suddenly they saw her swerve violently in flight, the kind of evasive action a pigeon might take if shot at or attacked by a bird of prey. But there was no sound of a gun or sight of a hawk, and almost immediately she turned and raced back to them, landing so fast beside them that she tipped over, beak first, as clumsily as if it had been her maiden flight.

'I saw it, I saw it!' she gabbled wildly. 'A girt big one!'

'A girt . . . I mean, a great big what?' said Squintum.

'A White Horse!'

Chapter Eleven

A NICE BRIGHT
RED COAT

'A White Horse?' barked Lubber. 'My White Horse?'

'More'n likely, Mr Lubber,' said Katie. 'It's on a big hill all right, on the side of the downs opposite, a hugeous girt thing it is. If you get high enough, you'll be able to see it too. Go on up that slope ahead.'

'Come on, Colleen!' shouted Lubber, and the two dogs raced off. One was still not much more than a puppy and the other was a great big puppy at heart, and they gambolled wildly, barking with excitement and chasing one another as they ran up the rising ground.

Squintum followed at his own pace. A White Horse there might be, but he remembered Katie's words as they had talked together at the fringe of that copse, many miles to the north.

'Oh, there's several of them about,' she had said.

We must hope, he thought as he padded up the rise behind the dogs, that it is not only a

87

White Horse but the right horse, for to find his home means everything to Lubber. As for me, it does not signify. I shall be glad for his sake if we succeed, very glad, and I feel sure that Colleen will be welcomed too, but for myself, I shall wait and see. Lubber's old ladies may not be cat-loving people, and I am none too sure that I am a people-loving cat. If we do not suit, it will not be the end of the world.

At the top of the rise he caught up with the rest of the party. Lubber and Colleen sat with their backs to a post-and-rail fence on which Katie perched, and all three stared south-ward, where, from this added height, they could now clearly see the enormous shape on the shoulder of the downs opposite them.

'There 'tis,' said Katie with satisfaction. 'Funny-lookin' old horse, but there 'tis.'

'That's not my White Horse,' said Lubber dolefully. 'It doesn't look anything like it.'

'It doesn't look much like a horse at all to me,' said Colleen.

The Siamese looked and gave a yowl of amusement. For him, there was no mistaking the identity of that huge figure cut in the chalk, with its massive maned head and power-ful body and long tufted tail. It was a picture of the noblest of his family, the King of Beasts.

'It's not a horse!' he said. 'It's a lion!'

'Oh dear!' said Katie in a melancholy voice. 'Oh, I'm sorry, Mr Lubber, raisin' your hopes like that.'

Lubber sighed. 'That's all right, Katie,' he said.

'Katie will find you a white horse sooner or later, I'm sure,' said Colleen comfortingly. 'Won't you, Katie?'

'I hope so, miss,' said Katie. 'I'll try my best, I will.'

'Well spoken, Katie,' said Squintum. 'You can't say fairer than that.'

Morale among the troops was at a low ebb, he saw, and he set himself to distract them. He knew, like another, more famous little general before him, that an army marches on its stomach, and he felt sure that a good feed and a rest would work wonders.

'Time we all had some grub,' he said. 'We'll meet back here later. No problem for you, is it, Katie?'

'Oh no, Mr Squintum, sir,' said Katie. 'Not at harvest-time. The combines is out workin', I did see, but there's corn a-plenty about,' and off she flew.

'Right,' said Squintum, 'I fancy a few field-mice for starters,' and he made to move off.

'Hey, wait a minute!' called Lubber. 'What about us? What are we supposed to do for food?'

'Use your eyes,' said Squintum over his shoulder. 'Look at that big meadow just below you,' and away he went.

'Look at a meadow?' said Lubber. 'What does he expect us to do – eat grass like a cow?'

89

Colleen did not answer. She stood, alert and tense, plumy red tail outstretched, her muzzle pointing down the slope beyond, the picture of vigilance.

'What is it?' said Lubber, and then he saw what she was looking at.

At the far end of the field were a score or more rabbits, grazing, hopping about in the sunshine, chasing one another in play or aggression, or sitting up and grooming.

An experienced dog like a lurcher would have slipped down the outside of the hedge, keeping out of sight, till he was near enough. But Lubber and Colleen were beginners both in the art of rabbit-catching, and they simply took off and charged down the meadow. By the time they reached the far end, there wasn't a rabbit to be seen.

'Little devils!' said Lubber. 'They were too quick for us,' but as the two dogs made their way back up the hill, they almost trod on an outlying rabbit that had remained squatting in a tussock of grass.

Colleen was fast, much faster than Lubber, but the rabbit would have been too quick for her on her own. Indeed, it had almost reached the safety of the hedge when Lubber, galloping madly, cut it off, and it jinked and met Colleen and jinked again and met its death.

When they had eaten it, they began to search the neighbouring fields, and as they hunted together, so their technique improved. There were no more blind charges, but instead they worked stealthily, to come between the rabbits and their hedgerow burrows and force them out into the open. Here, the speedy Colleen would course them, and Lubber, running wide on her flank, would hope to turn them.

The rabbits, they soon found, hadn't the brains to learn from their escapes, and as the two dogs made their rounds, they found that those who had been chased not half an hour before had forgotten all about it and had popped out again. Most escaped, of course, but by evening they had killed three more, plump young ones at that, and their bellies were full.

Indeed, as the party pressed on, rabbits were the staple food of the dogs, expert enough now to provide the odd one for Squintum too as a change from mice and voles. Water was no problem, for if they did not come upon a stream, there were always cattle-troughs to drink from, and the regular foot-slogging, day in, day out, in the fine summer weather, kept them as fit as fleas.

Lubber, Squintum saw, had lost all his tubbiness, and though he liked his night's sleep he had no chance to laze by day, for Squintum kept them on the march.

Sometimes, when the going was easy, they covered ten miles in a day, but it might be no more than three or four where there were towns to be avoided or railway tracks to be crossed or other such hazards. And always the route hugged the northern edge of the great escarpment of chalk that runs from Bedfordshire to Buckinghamshire to Berkshire and so to the Wiltshire downs.

'So long as I do stick close to the chalk,' said Katie. 'We can't go wrong. Whether 'tis pictures of horses or lions or whatever, they're all made of the chalk.'

So the weeks passed, quickly it seemed to the travellers, so happy were they in one another's company, and harvest was over (though there was still plenty of food for the pigeon in the stubbles), and the leaves began to change colour as September drew on.

Now they found themselves on the edges of a great valley, perhaps ten miles wide and as many as twenty or more miles long. They did not of course know its name, though it might have gladdened their hearts if they had, for this was the Vale of the White Horse.

They woke one autumn morning in a little wood at the southern side of this valley, and were about to set out on the day's march,

when an unusual sound came to their ears. A sharp clear sound it was, all the more so in the quiet of a day that had dawned crisp and still. It was the rooty-toot of a huntsman's horn.

Three of them had never heard such a thing before, but Lubber had, once, as a puppy, when the local hunt had met in his village and, moving off to draw, had passed right by the gate of Horseview Cottage.

Instantly he remembered the sound, and the sight of the man who had carried the horn, a big red-faced, scarlet-coated man on a big black horse. How he had whined and struggled in the arms of Miss Bun and Miss Bee to be allowed to join the pack as hounds swung up the lane, huntsman and whippers-in following the Master, and behind, the field of riders, some in scarlet coats, some in black, some in rat-catcher; men, women and children, mounted on horses of every colour, that varied in size from great rawboned hunters to roly-poly ponies.

Now the horn sounded again, nearer.

'What is it?' asked Squintum.

'It's the foxhounds,' said Lubber, 'out cubbing.'

'Cubbing?' said Colleen.

'Cub-hunting,' said Lubber, proud of his knowledge for once. 'They don't begin proper hunting till October, but once the harvest is off, cubbing starts. It's partly to cut down the number of this season's fox-cubs, and partly

to enter young hounds that have never hunted before. They learn from the older ones, you see, and they get a taste of blood.'

'Hm,' said Squintum. 'These hounds . . . they only kill foxes, eh?'

'Oh yes,' said Lubber confidently. 'That's why they're called foxhounds.'

At that minute, they heard a man's voice, quite close, it seemed.

'Leu in! Leu in!' said the voice, and then they heard a crackle of sticks and the whimper of a hound, nearer still.

'Beggin' your pardon, Miss Colleen, gennulmen,' said Katie, 'but I'd be happier aloft,' and she flew up into the crown of a great chestnut tree.

'Me, too,' said Squintum, and he ran up its trunk and settled himself on a branch.

'You're confident,' he called down to Lubber, 'that they only kill foxes? You're sure about that, I hope?'

Whatever answer Lubber made was drowned in a sudden great crash of noise as the pack picked up the scent, and twenty couple gave tongue with one mighty voice. Such was the volume of sound among the trees that it was hard to tell exactly what direction it came from, but one thing was sure. It was very close.

Next moment there was a rustle in the bushes, and out came a fox. This was no cub but an old grey-muzzled dog fox, and he swerved at the sight of Lubber and Colleen,

and snarled at them as he sped past.

'There's a nice bright red coat your girl-friend's got!' he said to Lubber out of the corner of his mouth. 'Mind she doesn't get mistaken for something else!'

Chapter Twelve

DREAMS

At that precise moment, Miss Bun and Miss Bee's old tin alarm clock went off. It stood, as always, on the table between their beds, and it went off, as always, at precisely 6.45 a.m.

The sisters' morning routine always reversed the previous night's privilege: that is to say, whichever sister had lost the evening game and thus come to bed last was allowed to remain in comfort, while the other went down to make tea and bring it up on a tray. In fact, neither minded doing this, as it meant two extra rides on the chair-lift.

It was Miss Bun who had triumphed at last night's Beggar My Neighbour, so it was she who got out of bed, picked up her walking-stick, and, leaning on it, drew back the curtains.

As always happened – whichever sister it was – the first comment referred to the great animal that strode for ever across the slope opposite, yet never made a yard of progress. They liked to imagine that the White Horse

was affected by each day's weather. If it was bad – wet or cold – they fancied that he hung his head a little, sad and downcast at being left up on the down to face alone the worst of the elements. But if the weather was good, he seemed jaunty, they thought, his step brisker, his ears cocked a fraction more. And on the kind of morning that promised a perfectly beautiful day, Miss Bun and Miss Bee were almost certain that there was a twinkle in the single eye of the White Horse.

'How does he look, Bun?' asked Miss Bee.

'Pretty good,' said Miss Bun. 'It's going to be quite nice, I should say. I'll go and make the tea.'

She had come back, riding happily up on the chair-lift with a tray balanced on her knees (Earl Grey for herself, Lapsang Souchong for Miss Bee), and they were sitting up in bed, cup and saucer in hand, when Miss Bee said, 'Do you know, Bun, I was so glad when the alarm went off.'

'Glad? Why?'

'Because I was having a horrid dream.'

'What was it about?'

'I don't really know. It was in a wood, and suddenly there was a terrible noise and the wood was full of dogs, dozens of big dogs. And something awful was going to happen, I felt sure.'

'How odd, Bee,' said Miss Bun. 'I had a dream about a dog too. Not a nightmare like yours though. I just dreamt that I rode

downstairs to make the tea and there was Lubber asleep in his basket under the kitchen table. It was so real that just now I half expected to see him there.'

Miss Bee took a sip of her Lapsang.

'That basket must never be put away, don't you agree, Bun?' she said.

'Never,' said Miss Bun, finishing off her Earl Grey. 'Not if I live to be a hundred.'

'I'd rather you said a hundred and two,' said Miss Bee.

'Why?'

'Because then I should have got to a hundred as well.'

'Fat chance we've got!' said Miss Bun.

'You never know your luck,' said Miss Bee.

Chapter Thirteen

BACKED LIKE
A WEASEL

Luck was running out fast for the second fox to appear. No sooner had the old greymuzzle vanished from sight than the cub came dashing madly along, the pack driving through the trees behind it. The leading hounds were not a dozen yards behind its brush as it ran beneath the chestnut tree, in whose branches Katie and Squintum were perched.

The cub suddenly caught sight of Lubber and Colleen still standing irresolute, and it checked, hesitated, swerved off to one side, and was buried in a growling, snarling, wrenching tide.

'Tear 'im and eat 'im!' yelled the huntsman, thundering up, and Colleen fled in horror.

Just as he had done once before, 'Run for it!' squawled Squintum to Lubber at the top of his awful voice. 'Follow her! Or else they'll kill you!'

Had all the pack been busy at the worry, the two dogs might have made their escape without trouble; but now, while Lubber still

99

dithered, half a dozen young hounds appeared, running wide and pursued by an angry whipper-in. Carried away by the thrill of this their first hunt, they had been chasing anything they could see.

''Ware rabbit!' yelled the whipper-in, and 'Get away back to 'im!' but before he could catch up with them, they caught sight of a fleeing red shape and away they went after Colleen.

From his grandstand seat, Squintum had a perfect view of what followed. He saw Colleen come suddenly upon another horseman who shouted at her, so that, confused and panicky now, she changed direction, almost towards her pursuers.

He saw the six young hounds closing in on her.

He saw the whipper-in dodging among the trees, whip cracking.

And finally he saw Lubber, galloping to the rescue.

'I'm coming, Colleen!' he roared, and he ran blindly at the foxhounds.

Wild with excitement, they had tumbled the Red Setter over and the foremost of them was going for her throat, when a hairy brown-and-white thunderbolt hit him squarely in the ribs and knocked him flying.

For a moment the rioting hounds hesitated, but their blood was up and they were six to one, and now they flung themselves on Lubber.

Bravely he fought them, Squintum saw, fastening his teeth in a foreleg here and a pad there, and roaring his defiance, but it might have gone hard with him had not help arrived in time.

'Garn leave it!' cried the whipper-in. 'Gaaaarn leave it, willya!' and the lash of his whip flicked here and there like a striking snake, till the three couple of hounds ran, yelping like the puppies they had but recently been, back to rejoin the pack. Two of them, Squintum saw, were limping badly.

'Damned dogs!' swore the whipper-in, as he pulled his horse round to follow.

He looked angrily at the trembling Colleen and the panting, dishevelled Lubber, and his whip cracked above their heads like a pistol shot.

'Damned people walking their damned dogs in the countryside!' he said. 'They've got no right!' and away he went.

'Oh, Lubber!' said Colleen. 'You saved my life!'

She licked at one of his ears which was badly ripped.

'My hero!' she said.

'Oh, I say, Colleen!' said Lubber in an embarrassed voice, but he felt a glow of pleasure that more than outweighed the pain of the bites he had received.

They waited until their ears and noses told them that the hunt had moved on to draw another wood, and then they made their way back to the chestnut tree.

Katie, who had seen nothing from her perch in the crown, came fluttering down. 'What a racket they make, they fox-dogs,' she said. 'I don't want to come across them no more if that's what they doos.'

Squintum, who had seen everything, came down the trunk. 'Be good enough to see which way they've gone, would you, Katie?' he said, and when the pigeon had flown away, he said, 'What damage?'

'I'm all right,' said Colleen. 'They knocked me over, but Lubber came up before they could hurt me. He saved my life!'

'A hero,' said Squintum gravely.

'Oh, I say, Squintum!' said Lubber.

'Are you hurt?'

'Not really,' said Lubber. 'It's useful, having

a lot of hair. Just a scratch on one ear, that's all.'

Squintum inspected it. 'A scratch?' he said. 'It's nearly torn in half. You'll carry the mark of that to your dying day.'

Colleen shivered. 'Oh don't, Squintum!' she said. 'Let's get out of this horrible place, can't we?'

As if in answer, they heard Katie's voice above.

'All clear!' she called. 'They're huntin' another fox, goin' east, away from us.'

They made ten miles that day, travelling as fast as the slowest member of the party, Squintum, could manage, anxious to put red coats and thundering horses and the fearful music of hounds far behind them.

As night fell, the Siamese and the two dogs came to the end of their final stage to see Katie sitting, as she often did, on top of a roadside signpost. It was a finger-post really, with just one arm that said:

```
KINGSTON LISLE
```

They spent that night in the shelter of a great sandy bank that ran beneath a long row of beech trees. Katie went to roost in one of these, and the others, tired out by travel and the drama of the day, curled up under the bank and slept like logs. Even Squintum, creature of the night, slept deeply, though later in

the small hours he was conscious of hearing some strange noises, gruntings and chatterings, and of smelling an unfamiliar smell.

At dawn, he discovered the origin of both sound and scent.

Poking out of a large hole, not far away in the bank, was a broad grey head marked with two narrow black stripes and, between them, a wide white stripe.

'Wake up!' hissed Squintum to the dogs.

'What is it?' said Colleen nervously. 'Is it dangerous?'

'I don't know,' said Squintum. He hissed angrily at Lubber, still in the land of dreams.

'Wake up!' he said again.

'Eh? What's the matter?' said Lubber, yawning hugely. He got to his feet and stretched.

'Ouch!' he said. 'I'm sore all over.'

'You'll be sorer in a minute if you don't answer my question,' said Squintum. 'What is that animal?'

Lubber peered from under his bushy eyebrows at the head in the hole. 'Oh, I saw one of those once,' he said. 'Got run over, just outside our cottage. My old ladies were ever so upset about it, you should have heard them.'

'Well, what is it?' said Colleen.

'It's a badger.'

At the sound of its name, the animal came further out, so that they all could now clearly see its low broad body and powerful, strong-clawed feet and stumpy tail. It turned its

striped head and called down the hole. 'Remain within, my dear, I prithee,' said the boar badger, 'and I beg you will not allow the children out. I will send these intruders about their business.'

The badger's tones were deep and cultured, and at the sound of his voice, with its curiously old-fashioned delivery, Squintum perceived immediately that here was no country bumpkin, but a gentleman of breeding, like himself. 'I do assure you, sir,' he said silkily, 'that we have no wish to intrude and must apologize for so doing.'

'What do ye here?' grunted the badger.

'We are merely passing through. We are travellers.'

'Whence come ye?'

'Well, in strict point of fact,' said Squintum, 'I come from Siam and my young friend here from Ireland.'

The badger pointed his snout at Lubber.

'And thou?' he said. 'Where is thy home?'

Lubber hesitated, for this was what he did not truly know, but Squintum cut in quickly.

'My hairy friend,' he said, 'is temporarily lost, and we are trying to return him to his owners. We should be most grateful if you could assist us with your local knowledge. Have you lived long in these parts?'

The boar badger seemed mollified by Squintum's civil manner, and he answered in a voice that was less curt and gruff.

'Verily,' he said, 'I have dwelt here all my

life, cub and boar, and my father before me likewise, and his father, and his father, and so back through the centuries. Always there have been badgers here in this set, even unto the times when ancient men cut the shape of the great beast in the hillside behind us.'

'The ... shape ... of ... the ... great ... beast?' said Squintum slowly. 'What beast?'

'Why, the White Horse,' said the boar. 'Dost thou not know that thou art in the Vale of the White Horse?'

'D'you hear that?' barked Lubber excitedly. 'Colleen, Squintum, d'you hear that? Katie, where are you, come along, we're there, we've found it, we're nearly home!' and he dashed off over the top of the bank with Colleen following, and Katie flying after.

'I must apologize for my friend's exuberance, sir,' said Squintum, 'but a white horse

is the key that we seek. He lives opposite it. Many thanks for your help,' and off he went after the others.

'Good fortune attend thee,' called the boar badger after him, 'but take heed, this Horse is like none other that I ever saw. Methinks it is like a weasel. It is backed like a weasel.'

Oh no, thought Squintum as he ran, not another disappointment for poor Lubber, but when he caught up with the rest he could see straightaway how dejected the big dog looked. He hung his head, while Colleen licked at his ripped ear.

Squintum looked across at the distant downs, and there was another chalk figure, a figure of the strangest shape. It was long, almost four hundred feet in length, and thin. One hindleg and one foreleg were detached from the snake-like body, and at the end of the curved neck was a head with a curious beaked muzzle. To the ancient men who had designed it, it was their idea of a horse, but to Squintum it looked like nothing so much as the skinniest of alley-cats slinking away over the crest of the hill. He could think of nothing to say, but Katie summed it up.

'Backed the wrong horse again, haven't we?' she said.

Chapter Fourteen

SNAP!

'Ah well, third time lucky,' said Squintum drily. 'Come on, let's find something to eat, we'll feel better then.'

In fact, as though to make up for the disappointment, they had a couple of bits of good fortune.

First of all, the dogs found a leveret, or young hare, that was lying so still and scentless in its form in the middle of a pasture that Lubber almost trod on it, and Colleen grabbed it before it could get into its stride.

Then, passing through a spinney, they came upon a fine cock pheasant, a runner, one wing having been broken by a sportsman's shot, and run though he did, they ran faster.

On the following day, they came to another motorway that ran east and west.

'It's the one I was tellin' you about, Mr Squintum,' said Katie when she came back to report it. 'We're on the right track, that's for sure.'

'The right track for your home maybe,' said

Lubber heavily, 'but what about mine?'

'We'll find yours,' said Colleen. 'We've only got to find the right White Horse and we're there. Katie's got to find her loft, that's much harder.'

'It is now,' said Katie. 'Time was when you could have thrown me up anywhere in England and I'd have gone for home straight as a die. Used to come down from Lunnon, following this very motorway and then turn off . . . somewhere . . . only now I can't remember where. I know we're goin' roughly right, but I'm not exactly sure of the way. From here on 'tis a matter of luck, I reckon. I'll tell you somethin' though – I don't care all that much whether I find my loft or no. I just like bein' with you gennulmen and Miss Colleen! I don't think I want to go racin' any more – I'm not so young as I was. What do you think, Mr Lubber, do you think your old ladies might like a pigeon for a pet?'

'I'm sure they would, Katie,' said Lubber. 'I'm sure they'll welcome all of us. If only we can find them.'

'We're not going to find them by sitting here chattering,' said Squintum sharply. 'Have a look for a road-bridge across the motorway, Katie. We'll have to cross in the dark.'

That evening the pigeon led them close to the M4 and they lay up with the roar of the traffic in their ears. They crossed in the small hours, over a bridge signposted:

and seeing the loom of a nearby town, said farewell to the Vale of the White Horse and struck up on to the downs.

They slept through the morning, but for none of them, not even for Lubber, was it a deep sleep. Thus far the weather had been perfect for their odyssey, but summer was long past now and the wind had gone round into the east, blowing cold and strong across the high downlands.

Squintum in particular thought longingly of a cosy fireside. His pads were sore from travelling, and he was more than usually sharp-tongued.

At midday they sought shelter in a beech-hanger and rested awhile. Then they split up to find the day's food.

Katie flew off to find stubbles as yet unploughed, the dogs went rabbiting and Squintum set out on mouse patrol.

He was out of temper, with the weather, with his sore feet, with the whole business that he had let himself in for. How much longer must they keep on, day in, day out, with winter coming and no guarantee that they would ever find this thatched cottage in this little village under this big hill with this confounded White Horse on it. Yet there was no going back, they could only keep on.

'Damnation upon all white horses!' spat Squintum, as he padded hastily and angrily

along a tunnel-like runway in the under-growth.

Suddenly there was a sharp metallic 'snap', and Squintum felt an agonizing pain in one hindfoot, a pain so sudden and searing and shocking that he gave a loud shrill scream.

Maybe if he had been less angry, he would have seen or smelt the gin-trap set in the centre of the runway under a scatter of leaves. But then again, if his ill-temper had not made him stride out in haste, he might have put a foot squarely on the pan of the trap and been caught now, firmly and finally, by the toothed steel jaws.

As it was, he had almost cleared it, by chance leaping over it and only springing it at the last instant with a trailing hindfoot, two of whose toes were held now in a vice-like grip.

Gone in a flash was all Squintum's self-possession, all his worldly-wisdom, all his powers of leadership and decision. He was nothing but a terrified wild beast, and he scrabbled madly with his three good feet to get free of the dreadful thing that had him in its power.

But the gin-trap was fixed with a strong strand of wire to a stout peg driven well into the ground, precisely to prevent the escape of whatever creature its jaws might hold, for trappers do not discriminate when they set their vile, unlawful machines.

Squintum was a prisoner, destined first for suffering and then for death. Lubber and

Colleen came rushing at the sound of his first piercing yowls, arriving to find him lying stretched upon his side, gasping for breath. The gaze in his blue eyes seemed to cross even more than usual as he looked dully up at them, and he could only mew 'Help me! Help me!' in the voice of a hurt kitten.

All was plain to the two dogs. They saw the peg that held the wire that held the gin that held the crushed and bleeding toes. All this they saw, but not what they could possibly do to save the Siamese.

Then they heard a sound, not far off. It was a crackling in the bushes, and then they caught the scent of the man who, walking his trap-line, had heard the screams and was coming to investigate.

Squintum scented him too and knew, through his pain, that if he could not get free, this was the end, however many lives he might have in credit.

A man who set illegal gins, for rabbit or hare, for weasel or stoat, for fox or badger, a man who cared not what was caught, would have only one response to a trapped cat. He would smash in its skull with a stick.

With all the strength that fear lent him, Squintum made one final effort. He drew back a little, and then he hurled himself desperately forward.

When the trapper arrived at the spot a couple of minutes later, all that remained in the bloodstained jaws of the gin were two dark brown, sharp-clawed toes.

Chapter Fifteen

NEARLY HOME

Ever since Squintum had screeched that first order at him, in the vet's surgery in the Dogs' Home, Lubber had been accustomed to obeying the Siamese cat. Squintum was the leader, and it was the duty of the rest of them to abide by his decisions.

How different things were now.

Lubber, bringing up the rear, watched his friend anxiously as the three of them hurried through the beech-hanger as fast as they could; as fast, that is, as Squintum could limp. A little trail of blood-drops marked his progress.

They had gone perhaps half a mile when Squintum suddenly stopped and lay down. He was panting, with exertion, with pain and with shock.

Lubber looked back. There was no sign of the man following them yet, but he might, and the further they went from this place of traps, the better.

'Come on, Squintum, old chap,' he said. 'We must get on.'

'Can't!' whined Squintum, still in a kitten's voice. 'My foot hurts!'

'What shall we do?' said Colleen, but she said it not to the Siamese, as always before, but to Lubber. 'Lubber, what shall we do?'

Suddenly, for the first time in his life, Lubber felt masterful.

'I'll tell you what we'll do,' he said.

He looked ahead to the crest of a high hill that rose in front of them.

'Colleen,' he said, 'you make for the top of that hill and wait for us there. Keep an eye out for Katie, she'll probably spot you anyway, and if you can pick up a rabbit on the way, so much the better. Go on, off you go.'

'Yes, Lubber,' said Colleen obediently, and away she went.

'And as for you,' said Lubber to Squintum, 'on your feet, or three of them anyway, and get moving!'

He forced himself to speak in a brutal way, fearing that the cat was giving up, and when the only reply was another 'Can't!', he said, 'Yes, you can and you will. Just thank your lucky stars you've got plenty of lives left yet, and get up and go, or I'll bite you, d'you hear me?'

When at last they reached the distant hill-top, Colleen was waiting with a rabbit in her jaws. Katie was perched on a nearby bush. She hopped down when she saw the limping cat and waddled over to him.

'Oh my heavens, Mr Squintum, sir!' she cried. 'Whatever's happened? Why, there's only two toes left on that foot!'

Squintum made no answer but only lay and licked at his wounds. The bleeding had stopped, Lubber could see, but he saw also that the patient would need rest, and good feeding, and time for healing, and protection against other possible enemies.

Lubber drew the Setter and the racing pigeon to one side.

'Listen to me,' he said. 'We're staying put for as long as it takes him to recover, understand? From up here we can see anyone coming, and by the look of things, there's no shortage of rabbits around. That's your job, Colleen, on your own now, because I'm staying here on guard. You'll have to provide for the three of us. Can you manage?'

'Oh yes,' said Colleen confidently. She too seemed to have drawn strength from Squintum's weakness. 'There are quite a few young ones still about,' she said, 'without as much sense or speed as the adults. I'll keep you supplied, don't worry.'

'Right,' said Lubber. 'Now, Katie, this delay gives you the perfect chance to make a really detailed survey of the area. We're on the highest point for miles around, and if you fly out on a straight course in a slightly different direction each day, you'll have every chance of finding the White Horse.'

'Yes, Mr Lubber, sir,' said Katie respectfully.

'I'll find it, see if I don't.'

In fact, once Squintum was properly rested and the shock of his experience had faded, his recovery was swift. Fit and hard, with the natural resilience of his kind, and well fed now by Colleen who had hunted tirelessly and successfully, he was soon something like his old self again. To be sure, the loss of his toes was to leave him with a permanent slight limp, but the wound healed swiftly and well, and before a week was up he told Lubber he was fit to travel.

As an added bonus the weather, which had threatened to be wintry, changed completely, and it seemed now, in mid-October, that they were to be favoured with that lovely late fine spell that humans call St Luke's Little Summer.

Only Katie, methodically flying out on a different radius each day, had as yet nothing to report. But Lubber was anxious to move on.

Added to his new-found authority was a strong feeling, which he had never had before, that the end of their quest was not so very far away; and one morning before dawn he led Squintum and Colleen south, on a line of his own choosing.

On their right or western side ran a main road, and, moving parallel to this over the downs, they came shortly upon the strangest of places.

Long before they reached them they could see the standing stones, huge slabs of rock,

116

maybe thirty of them in all, set upright in the turf in two concentric circles.

'Whatever are those?' asked Colleen as they approached.

'Stones,' said Lubber laconically.

'But why? . . . How did they get to be like that? . . . Who put them there?' she said. 'Squintum, do you know?'

Squintum prowled among the standing stones, making an odd singsong yarring in his throat. He did not know the reason for these great strange objects, or for the many long barrows that they had passed, or for the enormous bee-hive-shaped hump that he could now see not far ahead of them. But he felt instinctively that these were mystical magical places, places of long-dead folk.

'I don't know what they are,' he said, 'but there is something in me that fears them.'

'Afraid of a stone?' said Lubber. 'What rubbish!'

'I don't know *why* they are there, either,' said Squintum.

'I do,' said Lubber, and he walked up to the largest one and cocked his leg on it.

At that moment they saw Katie coming in fast from the west. She did not make her customary circuit before landing, but dropped straight down and pitched on top of the newly christened standing stone. She bobbed backwards and forwards, not in her usual respectful manner, but out of excitement. Yet she did not speak.

117

Then they saw why. She had something in
her beak – a white object about the size of a
sugar lump – and now she dropped it in front
of them and said in a triumphant voice, 'What
do you think of that then?'

'It's a lump of chalk,' said Lubber, sniffing
at it.

'You're right,' said Katie. 'But where did I
get it?'

'Where *did* you get it?'

'Off a horse.'

'Off a horse?' said Lubber. 'I don't see how
. . . oh . . . oh yes, I do! You've found it, Katie!
You've found the White Horse! Was it on a
big hill?'

'So it was.'

'Was there a little village under the hill?' asked Colleen.

'So there was.'

'Was there a thatched cottage in the village?' asked Squintum.

'You're right,' said Katie, 'and what's more, I flew down there to have a proper look, and there was two old ladies walkin' in the garden of that cottage, arm in arm they were, and each of 'em had a walkin'-stick in her other hand. What do you think of that then?'

'Well, Lubber,' said Squintum, 'it looks as though you're nearly home.'

'We're nearly home, you mean,' said Lubber. 'How far is it, Katie?'

''Bout four mile.'

'Fly on then. Lead us on.'

Katie led them first over the main road that they had been skirting. There was hardly any traffic and they slipped across unseen. It was the same with a second main road, running east and west this time, and then they found themselves entering a valley whose flat bed was carpeted with long stretches of firm, close turf. Here, though they did not know it, were the gallops of a racing stables, and they were half-way along the valley when they heard a distant rumble of hooves. They watched from cover as the long string of racehorses, their glossy coats gleaming in the early sunshine, went galloping by in single file. Black and brown, chestnut and bay, they thundered past,

the hunched men on their backs seeming hardly larger than monkeys.

'Every colour but the one we want,' said Lubber to Katie when next they caught up with her.

'Not long now, Mr Lubber,' she said. 'See that round clump of trees on the skyline yonder? Meet me up there. It's just beyond.'

Lubber's instinct was to rush madly after her, but he knew too well how much he owed to Squintum, and he forced himself to match his pace to the cat's limp.

The clump was almost silent when they reached it, for it was late in the year for bird-song, and the only sounds as they made their way under the trees were the gentle noise of the wind in their leaves and the contented cooing of 82/708/KT, perched somewhere high above.

Before them, as they emerged on the far side, the northern slope fell steeply away, and staring down it they saw, almost at their feet, the outline of yet another great figure cut in the chalk.

'Is it?' cried Colleen eagerly. 'Is it your horse, Lubber?'

'I don't recognize it,' said Lubber slowly. 'Its legs are sticking up. It seems to be lying on its back.'

Squintum looked down at it and then further down, to the little village that lay under the hill, and saw there, a short way along a lane, the thatched roof of a cottage.

He gave one of his strange yowls, of amusement this time.

'That's because you're standing up above
it,' he said. 'You're looking at it upside
down!'

'Of course!' said Lubber. 'How stupid of me!'
and he ran down the slope, across the body of
the White Horse, and further still, and turned,
and looked back up at it.

There it was, twenty times as large as life,
striding eastwards, ears cocked, one foreleg
raised, docked tail carried gaily, just as he
had always seen it.

He ran back up the slope, up the curve of
the proud white neck, and on to the head,
where a piece of turf the size of a large table-
top had been left uncut.

This was the eye of the White Horse, and
on it Lubber stood and gazed down upon the
cottage a mile below, and barked and barked
and barked for joy.

Chapter Sixteen

'HE'S BROUGHT SOME FRIENDS'

'Trrrrring! Trrrrring! Trrrrring!' went the old tin alarm clock in Horseview Cottage, and the sisters woke as one.

The night before, Miss Bee had been the winner at Rummy, and so she prepared to get up to make the tea. As she was moving towards the window, she fancied she heard a dog barking somewhere in the distance, but thought nothing of it. She drew the curtains.

'Oh, Bun!' she said. 'It looks as though it's going to be the most perfectly beautiful day.'

Miss Bun stretched, savouring her little extra lie-in and the thought of her cup of Earl Grey.

'Saw the old Horse's eye twinkle, did you, Bee?' she said, smiling.

Miss Bee, staring out, did not answer for a moment. Then she said, 'D'you know, I did! I really did! It moved, I'm sure! There's something moving up there, right on the eye, I'm sure there is! Oh Bun, bring the field-glasses!'

In a drawer of the table between their beds

the sisters kept an old pair of binoculars, which occasionally they used to identify birds in the garden. Now Miss Bun, roused by the urgency in her sister's voice, levered herself out of bed and made her way to the window, carrying the glasses. She propped herself against her sister and, raising them to her eyes, aimed them at the distant Horse and began to adjust the focus.

Then she gave a little scream.

Then she handed them to Miss Bee.

Then Miss Bee gave a little scream too.

'It couldn't be, could it, Bun?' she cried.

'It could,' said Miss Bun. 'Quick, let's get dressed.'

'But the tea . . .?'

'Oh, blow the tea! You shall ride down first anyway.'

Twenty minutes later, they stood arm in arm propped on their sticks, at the gate of Horse-view Cottage, and gazed up the lane.

And presently down the lane came a large hairy mongrel, white with brown patches, with a long bushy tail and floppy ears, one of them badly torn.

'Lubber!' cried Miss Bun and Miss Bee with one joyous voice, and they threw wide the gate.

So busy were they with greeting him and patting him and stroking him and calling him every endearment under the sun, that at first they did not notice that he was not alone. Waiting politely in the lane were two other animals, a beautiful young Red Setter bitch and an elegant Siamese cat.

'Oh look, Bun!' said Miss Bee. 'He's brought some friends!'

'We must invite them in,' said Miss Bun, and they both cried, 'Come in! Come in, do!'

The sisters watched spellbound as Lubber, tail gently wagging, walked slowly up the garden path, followed by the others. The cat, they noticed, was lame. Like me, each thought.

Then the three animals stopped as if by mutual agreement and stood in a row on the lawn, and looked up into the clear sky. And out of it there came tumbling a racing pigeon with long, slaty-blue, tapering wings; a pigeon that looped and rolled and twisted above the cottage and finally swooped down to land at the feet of Miss Bun and Miss Bee. It bobbed respectfully at them, and then began to strut about the lawn on its pink legs, on one of which, the sisters could see, was a blue ring stamped with a number.

Miss Bun and Miss Bee looked at Lubber, standing masterfully between the Red Setter and the Siamese cat, while the racing pigeon cooed before them. Then they looked at one another, and shook their heads, and smiled.

'Good job we kept the dog-basket, Bee,' said Miss Bun.

'We shall have to get a second one.'

'And a cat-basket.'

'And a pigeon-cote.'

'Make the tea, Bee,' said Miss Bun. 'It's your turn.'

That evening Lubber and Squintum walked round the garden together. They, and Colleen, had had a delicious meal. Miss Bun was

grooming all the burs and brambles from the Setter's red coat, and Miss Bee was feeding Katie with little bits of Garibaldi biscuit.

'Shall you stay, Squintum?' said Lubber.

'I might,' said Squintum.

'Worth a try, surely?' said Lubber, in an imitation of his friend's nasal voice, and the Siamese purred and rubbed himself against the big dog's hairy legs.

'I'll give it six months,' he said.

Chapter Seventeen

HAPPY ENDING

Six months later, on a lovely morning in mid-April, Miss Bun and Miss Bee sat on a seat by the lawn at Horseview Cottage. Squintum was curled lazily between them, and Katie perched on the back of the seat, bubbling and cooing.

In front of them all, Lubber and Colleen lay

on the grass, resting their chins on the edge of a large wicker dog-basket, inside which lay a great many fat little creatures. Some of them were fast asleep, some twitched and squeaked softly in their dreams. Some of them were red, and some were white with brown patches. Some of them were silky, and some of them were already rather hairy.

But on one thing there was general agreement.

These were the most beautiful puppies ever born.

Everybody watched, happy as could be, in the spring sunshine, under the White Horse.